Film and Domestic Space

Film and Domestic Space
Architectures, Representations, Dispositif

Edited by
Stefano Baschiera and Miriam De Rosa

Edinburgh University Press is one of the leading university presses in the UK. We publish academic books and journals in our selected subject areas across the humanities and social sciences, combining cutting-edge scholarship with high editorial and production values to produce academic works of lasting importance. For more information visit our website: edinburghuniversitypress.com

© editorial matter and organisation Stefano Baschiera and Miriam De Rosa, 2020, 2022
© the chapters their several authors, 2020, 2022

Edinburgh University Press Ltd
The Tun – Holyrood Road
12 (2f) Jackson's Entry
Edinburgh EH8 8PJ

First published in hardback by Edinburgh University Press 2020

Typeset in 11/13pt Times New Roman by
Manila Typesetting Company

A CIP record for this book is available from the British Library

ISBN 978 1 4744 2892 7 (hardback)
ISBN 978 1 4744 2893 4 (paperback)
ISBN 978 1 4744 2894 1 (webready PDF)
ISBN 978 1 4744 2895 8 (epub)

The right of the contributors to be identified as authors of this work has been asserted in accordance with the Copyright, Designs and Patents Act 1988 and the Copyright and Related Rights Regulations 2003 (SI No. 2498).

Contents

List of Figures	vii
Notes on the Contributors	ix
Acknowledgements	xiii

	Introduction *Stefano Baschiera and Miriam De Rosa*	1
1	Architectures of Ubiquity: The Colonial Revival in Film and Television *John David Rhodes*	16
2	*No Down Payment*: Whiteness, Japanese American Masculinity and Architectural Space in the Cinematic Suburbs *Merrill Schleier*	37
3	Resist, Redefine, Appropriate: Negotiating the Domestic Space in Contemporary Female Biopics *Victoria Pastor-González*	56
4	Liminal Spaces, Lesbian Desire and Veering off Course in Todd Haynes's *Carol* *Anna Backman Rogers*	72
5	A Home on the Road in Claire Denis's *Vendredi soir* *Maud Ceuterick*	89
6	Acoustic Ectoplasm and the Loss of Home *Beth Carroll*	106
7	Our House Now: Flat and Reversible Home Spaces in Post-war Film and Television *Adrian Martin*	118
8	From Myth to Reality: Images of Domestic Space in Post-Soviet Baltic Films *Lukas Brašiškis and Nerijus Milerius*	134

9   No | Home | Movie: Essay Film, Architecture as Framing
    and the Non-house   154
    Laura Rascaroli
10 At Home with the *Nouvelle Vague*: Apartment Plots and
    Domestic Urbanism in Godard's *Une femme est une femme*
    and Varda's *Cléo de 5 à 7*   171
    Stefano Baschiera
11 Dwelling the Open: Amos Gitai and the Home of Cinema   188
    Miriam De Rosa
12 What Is Cult When It's At Home? Reframing Cult Cinema
    in Relation to Domestic Space   210
    Iain Robert Smith
13 High-fructose Cinema and the Movie Industrial Complex:
    Radicalising the Technology of Representation in a
    Domestic Kind of Way   226
    Bryan Konefsky

Index   237

Figures

1.1	Oldness-as-newness: the colonial revival as 'spectacle of property' and ideological, spatial container in *Christmas in Connecticut* (1945)	21
1.2	The expansiveness of the colonial revival in *Holiday Inn* (1942)	25
1.3	The ground of national fantasy in *Ozzie and Harriet* (1952)	31
2.1	Iko in store window in *No Down Payment* (1957)	46
2.2	Troy Boone in his garage in *No Down Payment* (1957)	49
2.3	Iko and family departing the church in *No Down Payment* (1957)	53
4.1	Carol (Cate Blanchett) dressed in red in *Carol* (2015)	78
4.2	The car as a liminal space of lesbian desire in *Carol* (2015)	82
5.1, 5.2	*Vendredi soir/Friday Night* (2002): focus on a younger woman's gaze and hands in a cafe	98
5.3	*Vendredi soir/Friday Night* (2002): Laure's and Jean's faces almost become indistinguishable as they kiss	99
5.4	*Vendredi soir/Friday Night* (2002): close-up of the lovers' erotic encounter	100
8.1	Andrius Blaževičius's *The Saint* (2017)	148
8.2	Andrius Blaževičius's *The Saint* (2017)	149
8.3	Andrius Blaževičius's *The Saint* (2017)	150
9.1	Forming again the already hyperformed: hyperframing in Alexander Kluge's and Peter Schamoni's *Brutality in Stone* (*Brutalität in Stein*, 1961)	158
9.2	Inanimate objects assert their existence in Ila Bêka and Louise Lemoine's *Barbicania* (2014)	162

9.3	Fragile order: hyperframing of the family home in Chantal Akerman's *No Home Movie* (2015)	168
10.1	Cléo's apartment in *Cléo de 5 à 7/Cléo from 5 to 7* (1962)	183
11.1	Mole Antonelliana: basement	193
11.2	The Mole Antonelliana during Gitai's *Architectures of Memory* (2011): exterior	193
11.3	The Mole Antonelliana during Gitai's *Architectures of Memory* (2011): interior	195
11.4	*Architectures of Memory* (2011): a site-specific installation	197
11.5	The material quality of the image in *Architectures of Memory* (2011)	199

Notes on the Contributors

Anna Backman Rogers is Reader in Feminist Philosophy and Visual Culture at the University of Gothenburg, Sweden. She is the author of *Sofia Coppola: The Politics of Visual Pleasure* (2019), *American Independent Cinema: Rites of Passage and the Crisis Image* (2015), the co-editor of *Female Agency and Documentary Strategies* and *Female Authorship and Documentary Image* (both 2019), and the co-founder and co-editor-in-chief of the experimental journal *MAI: Feminism and Visual Culture*.

Stefano Baschiera is Senior Lecturer in Film Studies at Queen's University Belfast. His work on European cinema, material culture and film industries has been published in a variety of edited collections and journals including *Film International, Bianco e Nero, New Review of Film and Television Studies* and *NECSUS: European Journal of Media Studies*. With Russ Hunter he is the co-editor of *Italian Horror Cinema* (2016).

Lukas Brašiškis is a PhD candidate at New York University in the Department of Cinema Studies. His academic interests include eco-film (with an emphasis on limits and potentialities of documentation and animation of the non-human), politics and aesthetics of the Global Cinema of the twenty-first century, the history of experimental cinema and intersections between moving image cultures and contemporary art scene. He has taught classes at New York University, Barry R. Feirstein Graduate School of Cinema, CUNY and Vilnius Academy of Arts. His writings have been published in academic and film journals including *The Cine-Files, Senses of Cinema, Screening the Past, NECSUS: European Journal of Media Studies*, among others. He is one of the authors of a collective monograph *Film and Philosophy* (2013) and contributor to a collection *Short Film History* (2013). He has also curated and programmed a number of film events for various institutions in New York and Europe.

Beth Carroll is a lecture in film at the University of Southampton. Her research interests include film phenomenology with a particular interest in sound, space, musicals and video games. She is the author of *Feeling Film: A Spatial Approach* (2016) and the co-editor of *Contemporary Musical Film* (2017). She is also co-editor of the Edinburgh University Press series *Music and the Moving Image*.

Maud Ceuterick is a Marie Skłodowska-Curie fellow in Digital Culture at the University of Bergen, Norway. Her research deals with the relations between gender, space and power on screen, including in digital media. Her book *Affirmative Aesthetics and Wilful Women* (2020) considers filmic aesthetics and women's occupation of space in contemporary cinema. She earned her PhD in film and media studies from the University of Otago in New Zealand, and previously published on the road movie genre, masculinity and domesticity in transnational cinema, and space tourism in film.

Miriam De Rosa is Research Fellow at the Centre for Postdigital Cultures, Coventry University. She researches and publishes on film theories, experimental cinema, artists' moving images and screen media arts. She is the author of *Cinema e Postmedia* (2013), the editor of *Post-what? Post-when? Thinking moving images beyond the postcinema condition* (with Vinzenz Hediger, 2016) and of *Gesture* (2019). De Rosa also works as an independent film and exhibition curator. Her last programme, compiled with Greg de Cuir Jr, is *I am the mace* – the first international full retrospective of Kelly Gallagher's films (London, 2019), while among her recent curated exhibitions is *Desktop Cinema* (Pula, 2017).

Bryan Konefsky is the founder and director of Experiments in Cinema international film festival and the president of Basement Films, one of the few remaining first generation micro cinemas. Konefsky has lectured about alternative cinematic practices in countries such as Argentina, Cuba, Germany, Korea, Morocco, Russia, Scotland, Serbia and the UK. Konefsky's creative work has been presented at festivals and museums internationally and his creative research has been supported by organisations such as The National Endowment for the Arts, The National Endowment for the Humanities, The Trust For Mutual Understanding and the Banff Centre for the Arts.

Adrian Martin is an arts critic and audiovisual essayist based in Vilassar de Mar (Spain). He is Adjunct Professor of Film and Screen Studies at

Monash University (Australia), and has been Distinguished Visiting Professor at Goethe University (Frankfurt). He is the author of *Mysteries of Cinema: Reflections on Film Theory, History and Culture 1982–2016* (2018), *Mise en scène and Film Style: From Classical Hollywood to New Media Art* (2014), *Last Day Every Day and Other Writings on Film and Philosophy* (three separate language editions, 2011–15), *¿Qué es el cine moderno?* (2008), *The Mad Max Movies* (2003), *Once Upon a Time in America* (1998) and *Phantasms* (1994). He has chapters in books on Jean-Luc Godard, Chantal Akerman, Vincente Minnelli, Tracey Moffatt, Fritz Lang, Max Ophüls, American comedy, digital cinema, Philippe Garrel and many others. He has written hundreds of articles since 1979 for magazines including *Sight and Sound, Film Comment, Trafic, Cineaste, Cahiers du Cinéma, Film Quarterly, de Filmkrant, Caiman, Screen,* and a range of international art magazines and catalogues. He has served as editor in the online journals *Rouge, LOLA* and *Screening the Past,* and collaborated on the book *Movie Mutations* (2003). Between 1995 and 2006, he was the regular film critic for *The Age* newspaper in Melbourne and Australian Radio National's programme *The Week in Film.* His ongoing archive website of film reviews, covering over forty years of writing, is at http://www.filmcritic.com.au, and can be supported at www.patreon.com/adrianmartin.

Nerijus Milerius is Associate Professor of Philosophy at Vilnius University, Lithuania. For over a decade he has been teaching courses developed on the basis of his research including classes of film philosophy, religious cinema, everyday world and urban studies, cultural studies and aesthetics. He co-edited *P.S. Landscapes. Becoming Urban* (2008) in Russian, together with Benjamin Cope. He is the editor and one of the authors of a collective monograph *Film and Philosophy* (2013), the author of monographs *Apocalypse in Cinema: The Philosophical Presuppositions* (2013) and *Viewing The Viewer: Cinema and Violence* (2018). Milerius is a co-author of a feature film *Isaac* (director Jurgis Matulevicius), to be released in 2019, and co-director of the documentary *Exemplary Behaviour* (directors Audrius Mickevicius, Nerijus Milerius) to be released in 2019/2020.

Victoria Pastor-González is a Senior Lecturer at the Institute of Languages and Culture at Regent's University London. Her research interests include Spanish and Latin American docudrama, and the work of the directors Krzysztof Kieślowski and Benito Zambrano. She collaborated in a special edition of the journal *Studies in Documentary Film*

(Intellect, 2010) with an article on religious iconography in Spanish docudramas, and she published a chapter on contemporary Spanish docudrama in the edited volume *Docudrama on European Television* (2016). She wrote an entry on Zambrano's film *Solas* for the *Directory of World Cinema: Spain* (2011), and her work on Krzysztof Kieślowski appeared in the book series *New Studies in European Cinema* (2005). Her current research focuses on contemporary female biopics and she recently published a study guide for the Spanish television movie *Clara Campoamor, la mujer olvidada* (2017).

Laura Rascaroli is Professor of Film and Screen Media at University College Cork, Ireland. She is the author and editor of a number of volumes, including *How the Essay Film Thinks* (2017), *The Personal Camera: Subjective Cinema and the Essay Film* (2009), *Crossing New Europe: Postmodern Travel and the European Road Movie* (2006), co-written with Ewa Mazierska, and *Antonioni: Centenary Essays* (2011), co-edited with John David Rhodes. Her work has been translated into several languages. She is the General Editor of *Alphaville: Journal of Film and Screen Media*.

John David Rhodes is the author of *Spectacle of Property: The House in American Film* (2017), *Meshes of the Afternoon* (2011), *Stupendous, Miserable City: Pasolini's Rome* (2007), the editor of several books, including *Taking Place: Location and the Moving Image* (2011), and a founding co-editor of the journal *World Picture*. He teaches at the University of Cambridge, where he is Reader in Film Studies and Visual Culture and a fellow of Corpus Christi College.

Merrill Schleier is professor emeritus of Art and Architectural History and Film Studies, University of the Pacific. She publishes widely on the relationship of gender, race and class to the built environment in cinema. Her full-length books include: *Skyscraper Cinema: Architecture and Gender in American Film* (2009) and the *Skyscraper in American Art* (1990). Her edited anthology *Race and the Suburbs in American Postwar Film* is forthcoming.

Iain Robert Smith is Senior Lecturer in Film Studies at King's College, London. He is the author of *The Hollywood Meme: Transnational Adaptations in Hollywood Cinema* (2017) and co-editor of *Media Across Borders* (2016) and *Transnational Film Remakes* (2017). He is the co-investigator of the AHRC-funded research network Media Across Borders.

Acknowledgements

We would like to thank our fantastic contributors for all of their work and for their patience and support during the editing process. Special thanks are also due to Gillian Leslie and Richard Strachan of Edinburgh University Press for their encouragement, help and understanding. A very big thank you to the participants in the 'cinema and domestic space' workshop at the 2016 SCMS conference in Atlanta, which marked the beginning of this project, and in particular to Pamela Robertson Wojcik.

Finally, special thanks are due to Francesco Di Chiara and Laura Rascaroli for their advice on this and other researches, and John David Rhodes for all the incredibly helpful suggestions he made at the early stages of this work. Thanks also to Enrico Carocci and the colleagues from Roma Tre for having allowed us to present and test some of the ideas we are presenting in the volume. Big gratitude goes also to Alice Cati, Marco Dalla Gassa, Greg de Cuir Jr, Catherine Fowler, Nina Kreuzinger, Christine Sprengler and to all of those spread across Italy and the UK who, in various capacities, have supported us along this project – your generosity and openness is where we dwell.

Introduction
Stefano Baschiera and Miriam De Rosa

In an essay published in 2008, Malte Hagener significantly asked the question 'where is cinema today'? Whilst the main argument in the text inclines more towards concerns that are not entirely centred on spatiality per se, we can see, in retrospect, that this question clearly summarised what would eventually be termed the spatial turn in film studies. Such a turn represents a key move in the consideration of spatial 'contexts' as important to the 'text', as well as the experiences deriving from them.[1] A key contribution in this sense is the volume edited by Elena Gorfinkel and John David Rhodes (2011), which very effectively reminds the reader how film not only documents reality but 'takes place' within it. Stressing the strong link between the site where moving images are consumed and film itself, and somewhat reminded of the earlier seminal work by Barbara Kruger (1994) in relation to home video viewing, the authors put a particular emphasis on spectatorship. Space, then, ceases to be a coordinate solely employed by film to locate the narration, and appears in its fascinating complexity as a dimension that is represented on screen but at the same time that is physical, off-screen, where the film actually unfolds. Giuliana Bruno (1993, 2002, 2007), Catherine Fowler (2008) and Alison Butler (2010), among others, have probably written the most captivating pages about the point of encounter of these two spheres. Each of these authors has analysed specific examples and focused on particular elective objects of study: film journeys coupled with itineraries in art spaces for Bruno; gallery films, their relationship with the museum space, and the impact of such relationship on representability in Fowler; the textual component characterising a number of installation works in Butler. Yet, they have a shared merit, namely to demonstrate very clearly that the job of the viewer may go well beyond her/his participation in the screening: a possibility to practice space pairs the cognitive and interpretive work classically elicited by diegesis.

Experiments from the avant-gardes and in the area of expanded cinema (see, for example, Youngblood's classic text, 1970) had already identified the convergence and interaction of diegetic and extra-diegetic space as an interesting and productive area of inquiry and creativity. However, only with the digitisation of moving images, the differentiation of formats, viewing and exhibition situations the variability of moving image configurations became not an exception but rather a new standard, not erasing but certainly complementing the established ones (see De Rosa and Hediger 2016). This contributed to open up the views of scholarship, favouring an acknowledgment of the relevance of the spatial element in film studies, engaging with a recuperation and extension of, and critical engagement with, film practice, history and theory.

It is in the wake of this renewed attention to spatiality, and in the conviction that much still remains to be further explored, that this volume enters the debate. As our title clearly shows, our approach to spatiality develops from the spatial turn in film studies in order to focus on a specific and fundamental profilmic space: the domestic one.

The relationship between domesticity and cinema is multifaceted, layered and, overall, still significantly understudied. To date, only a handful of book length investigations exist within film studies directly addressing this area of enquiry, often as part of a wider understanding of cinematic spaces or featuring a dedicated focus on American cinema and film genre. This is the case for Elizabeth Bronfen (2004), who looks at the representation of home in a series of key Hollywood films (for instance, *The Wizard of Oz*, Victor Fleming, 1939; *Rebecca*, Alfred Hitchcock, 1940; *The Searchers*, John Ford, 1956) in order to reveal how domesticity works within the production of imaginary geographies, producing a 'crossmapping of the emerging cinematic and psychoanalytic engagement with questions of dislocation, home, and of nostalgia' (Bronfen 2004: 22). The highly influential work of Pamela Robertson Wojcik (2010), instead, contextualises the domestic space within a very specific mode of domesticity — the urban apartment — as represented in American popular culture after the Second World War. In this frame she proposes the notion of the 'apartment plot' that describes a narrative where the apartment has an agency on the story, instead of being a mere backdrop. From this perspective, the domestic space not only 'conveys ideologies of urbanism' (Wojcik 2010: 7) but is a key element for the negotiation of class, race, gender, family, work, community and sexuality. The link between gender and architectural spaces is also addressed by Merrill Schleier (2009), again with a focus on the American urban context and with a diachronic analysis of the representation of skyscrapers in films such as *Safety Last!* (Harold Lloyd, 1923), *Baby Face* (Alfred E. Green, 1933), *The Apartment* (Billy Wilder, 1960), *Wall Street* (Oliver Stone, 1987).

In this brief overview of the studies focusing on the domestic space in American cinema, John David Rhodes's *Spectacle of Property: The House in American Film* (2017) is a noteworthy contribution offering a compelling analysis of the house for its spectacular nature as private property. Looking at different architectural styles ranging from the bungalow to the modernist house, Rhodes employs an original theoretical approach engaging with film spectatorship and materialist theory, in order to grasp the role that the house plays as a medium and, more generally, as an object of spectatorial desire.

Looking beyond a national (and American) context, Hamid Naficy's edited collection *Home, Exile, Homeland: Film, Media, and the Politics of Place* (1999) notably considers the home from a perspective of diaspora and dislocation, while approaching the domestic space and the question of belonging: from the house materiality to the conceptual abstraction of homeland. Eleanor Andrews, Stella Hockenhull and Frances Pheasant-Kelly's edited collection *Spaces of the Cinematic Home* (2016) offers instead a view of cinema and the home through a wide array of case studies engaging with different national contexts and cleverly organised following the house spaces. From the living room to the attic, the book dwells on the role that particular domestic areas play in different kind of cinemas and cinematographies.

Even from a brief mapping of the existing literature it is immediately clear that the same question of how domestic space relates to cinema can produce a very broad series of reflections and leads to a variety of theoretical approaches.

We would argue that from the representational perspective – which characterises the majority of the works on home and cinema – domestic space can be understood within three main areas of investigation, which we situate along an ideal line developing from wide (or public) to narrow (or private).

First of all, domestic space has to be understood in terms of spatial scale, one that is deeply interconnected with the urban space. From Henri Lefevbre's reflections on the urban revolution, and the physical networks of services and supplies linking indissolubly the house to the city streets (1991, 2003), to Yi-Fu Tuan's seminal study on the experience of architecture and the way in which the flow of time creates a path which constitutes the home (1977), domestic space is considered as an extension of the cityscape. As such, the *home* can be approached from an architectural perspective, that is, as a *house*. In this view, it can mirror the political and historical situation it belongs to, typically in terms of architectural style, philosophy and manifestation of power (Hirst 2005; Dovey 2008). Brutalist buildings and estates, as well as high-rises, as opposed to colonial revival buildings or penthouses – all considered throughout the chapters of this book – are a case in point. Also, domestic space can notably be conceived of as it is practised in everyday life (de Certeau 2002) and in the way it is linked to the urban by both the movements of the subject throughout the city texture, and the social constructions connected to that. Questions of gentrification and community building overlap with the key role played by the domestic space as a threshold for intimacy, questioning its 'closeness' and *de facto* considering the domestic space as an opening to the world. The picture serving as the cover for this volume, taken from Bêka and Lemoine's film *Barbicania* (2014), intends to point at this duality between a sense of intimate, private and close versus one of collective, public and open that is variably connected to domestic space.

Secondly, the home can be understood as a site able to encapsulate the representation of family and identity. If the attention towards the urban underlined the reciprocal movements in and out of the house, the domestic space as locus of identity focuses instead on the movements within the 'family walls'. In this case, domestic space is a microcosm mirroring the societal manifestations of power and class, where dynamics of socio-cultural belonging are constantly negotiated. For example, this can be observed when looking at domestic space from the vantage point of anthropology and material culture: from here, it is apparent how aspects of materiality and taste, such as the arrangement of pieces of furniture (Baudrillard 2005) or the presence of spatially determined rules are symptomatic of a certain social model (Sibley 1995; Munro and Madigan 1999).

Developed within the tradition of feminist theories, the works by Elizabeth Grosz (1992 and 1997) and Irene Cieraad (1999), among others, engage with the gendering of the house, offering an interdisciplinary framework on how rules and roles dictated by the patriarchal society become evident in the experience of domestic space, which becomes in turn part of the mechanisms perpetuating hegemonic thought.

Finally, domestic space can be approached as the embodiment of a psychological profile, where memories, nostalgia and feelings – very often associated with a sense of belonging or, vice versa, of eradication – are mediated in spatial forms. Home, in this case, is considered as 'where the heart is': an idealised place of intimacy and cosiness, a fantasy of comfort and ease, a heaven seldom experienced that needs to be longed for and thus becomes either an aspiring future or an idealised past. Issues of dislocations, migration and of simply feeling 'away from home' are also part of this approach that tends to embody domestic space with 'the familiar' broadly conceived – be it understood as homeland, as a group of people with blood bonds or as a community sharing ideals and values. Conceptually linked and partially overlapping with the second level of inquiry discussed above, then, studies on the cultural geography of home have widely engaged with these aspects since the turn of the millennium (Duncan and Lambert 2003; Blunt and Dowling 2006), when humanitarian emergencies and refugee crises have increasingly shifted from episodic, cyclical phenomena to a constant, too often demonised issue. Studies such as *Screening Strangers: Migration and Diaspora in Contemporary European Cinema* (Loshitzky 2010) and *Far-Flung Families in Films* (Berghan 2013) echo this historical and political conjuncture, thereby intertwining the question of home with that of nationality, identity and nostalgia.

While a representational take on domestic space in cinema has been the dominant one so far, we shall contend that, in its double concept of home/house, this plays a rather key role in relation to the cinematic dispositif.[2] Most specifically, we wish to posit that domestic space actually works like a proper dispositif, exactly as cinema itself. We believe we cannot but move in the frame of a model where cinema is not to be intended as a monolithic apparatus any longer, and where it can instead be better grasped in its current multifaceted configurations as an assemblage (see Casetti 2015). Similarly, the numerous ways to see the home, and the aforementioned different approaches variably employed to frame domestic space, show that we are dealing with a concept that has been considered a simple and stable construct while in fact it gathers a number of 'heterogeneous elements (some of which derive from other dispositives, and many of which are permutable), which coalesce based on circumstance' (Casetti 2015: 69). Furthermore, the experience of the home/house, its environmental character as a space, the etiquette conventions and the arrangements ruling it in its materiality and physical nature really allow for a reading of domestic space as a dispositif. Finally, as real life situations where the moving image has entered are commonly turned into a site of viewing and dwelling on the image (De Rosa 2012), so the domestic space elicits an experience of dwelling.

The main original contribution of this volume is to explore the relationship between film and domestic space offering an innovative take. With this in mind we draw our attention towards those sites that are thought of as home, as well as those spaces that lend themselves to be built as such. In other words we look at architectures, alluding to the potentiality of a certain space to be entered, practised, modelled and ultimately constructed as a place to call home.[3] This has allowed us to create a bridge between the representational reading of domestic space that is at the heart of the existing scholarship with that centred on the idea of dispositif. The open window on the cover of this volume hints to the possibility and productiveness of the exchange between these two views. The result is a two-fold approach where *representation* and *dispositif* complement each other in that they can both be thought of as (narrative or physical) *architectures*. We hope that such an approach will reveal the complexity of domestic space, opening up new research avenues which, without any ambition to be comprehensive, we aimed at identifying and offering up for further exploration. We believe that whilst these two ways of looking at domestic space can lead to captivating analysis, it is in their combination and overlapping that a new understanding of the domestic space in cinema can be achieved, thus contributing to the growing area of study of spatiality and cinema. The chapters collected in this book, then, mirror such conviction, and offer some room for reflection starting from a variety of points of view, ranging from genre- to gender-related issues, from questions pertaining to the philosophy of space to issues of material culture and urban studies. Combining attention towards both representation and dispositif, the chapters in this volume offer a set of ways to depict and think the domestic space as an architecture, that is, a place to be practised, inhabited, built by a spectator who will feel and acknowledge her/his empowerment towards spatiality.

The texts by John David Rhodes, Merrill Schleier and Victoria Pastor-González open the volume, offering an exquisitely genre-focused entry point into the issues of film and domesticity. In particular, Rhodes's work looks at the ubiquitous American Colonial Revival architecture, understood for its iconographic facades and its empty, fungible internal spatiality, in order to examine the condition of post-war America's belief in its futurity. Examining a series of films such as *Christmas in Connecticut* (Peter Godfrey, 1945), *All That Heaven Allows* (Douglas Sirk, 1955), and *White Christmas* (Michael Curtiz, 1954), he investigates the colonial revival as an aesthetic of surface, and the spectatorial fantasies associated with the house, revealing the tension between inside and outside, appearance and interiority, and their association with the question of iteration. The repetition is understood here as the 'ongoingness' of the life in the house, of the house itself, and of the fantasies that it attempts to secure. Rhodes argues that the coherence of Colonial

Revival architecture's iconography – its pediments, columns and porticoes – becomes the empty vessel for a performance of iterative domestic and social practices.

Merrill Schleier's contribution also engages with the American context but it moves the spotlight on the suburbs, to reveal how the domestic space articulates questions of race, masculinity and social issues. Through an analysis of the suburban house in *No Down Payment* (Martin Ritt, 1957) and its representation of Japanese Americans, the chapter addresses spatial aspects of the melodrama genre considering how architectural styles and spatial plans embed raced and gendered ideologies. *No Down Payment* is considered as a transitional film in its depiction of Japanese Americans into post-war suburban houses, while at the same time reaffirming the white hegemony in its spatial practices. Schleier argues that the construction, depiction and normalisation of whiteness is manifested in the suburban cinematic domestic space and its materiality.

Remaining in the realm of genre-informed studies, Victoria Pastor-González looks at the ways in which domestic space appears in biographical films, with particular regard to contemporary female biopics. Moving from Dennis Bingham's work in the field (2010), the author pushes further his call to resist instead of insist on the traditional patterns of grief and melodramatic excess, rethinking the performance of the female protagonists in the contexts of domestic space. By way of a comparative analysis of selected case studies including *The Invisible Woman* (Ralph Fiennes, 2013), *To Walk Invisible* (Sally Wainwright, 2016) and *A Quiet Passion* (Terence Davies, 2016), Pastor-González argues that these films demonstrate an uncommon understanding of the hybrid nature of the biopic and its unique possibilities: if on the one hand they ensure a narrative and documentary adherence to factual biographical elements depicting the female characters, on the other hand they work as an arena of performance primed for reinvention and dramatic reconstruction which unveils deeper and essential truths about the protagonists.

The female perspective becomes the central element in Anna Backman Rogers's and Maud Ceuterick's chapters. Backman Rogers's contribution takes its cues from Todd Haynes's *Carol* (2015). The author contends that the sublimation of lesbian desire occurring in the transition from Patricia Highsmith's novel *The Price of Salt* (1952) which inspired the film, and the film itself, is figured on screen not only as a trope of authenticity, but more profoundly as an affective and emotional history that plays out in liminal spaces of 'betwixt and between'. The radical nature of lesbian desire is adumbrated as a force that cannot occupy the stratified and hierarchical space of power structures (the patriarchal family home, the public space, the place of work) that are associated with masculinity in the film. Backman Rogers draws principally from Victor Turner's work on liminal spaces (1995) and Sara Ahmed's philosophy of 'queer phenomenology' and the cultural politics of emotion (2004, 2006, 2010) to posit that *Carol* traces a phenomenology of lesbianism through affective disorientation towards objects and spaces that renders lesbian desire as a powerful, disruptive and ultimately uncontrollable force of the 'in-between'.

By looking at poetic images of the house, Gaston Bachelard (1964) emphasised the power of the poetic image as it moves, which is said to be able to carry the imagination along, bringing the reader to experience its language and enter in contact with the spaces that the poetic image represents. In a way similar to Bachelard, Maud Ceuterick's text discusses the aesthetic choices of Claire Denis in *Vendredi soir* (2002). The author argues that Denis's poetics affect viewers, 'forcing' them to live through the film's cinematic spaces. Following the protagonist, Ceuterick embraces a feminist perspective to explore the notion of 'home' through Laure's habitation of other spaces of dwelling, such as her car and a motel room. The chapter proposes an innovative contribution, in that it discards the standard opposition between domesticity and travel by analysing how the haptic evocation of Laure's micro-relations to space convert the concept of home. From a space embedded in gendered discourses, 'home' becomes a space of affects in continual transformation, which Ceuterick frames in her reading of domestic space as a site that does not necessarily need to be navigated in light of patriarchal logics but can instead be practised in an affirmative fashion, contributing also to affirmatively modify the viewers' spatial imaginaries, and, she argues, their own ways of being in the world.

A deep sense of inhabitation and being in the world is also researched by Beth Carroll, who investigates the aural aspect of domesticity in the horror genre. Her compelling analysis of the house soundscape in this kind of films identifies a number of challenges to the idea of safety, ownership and control of the family home. Considering the recurring narrative trope of the haunted house, this chapter moves beyond considerations of architectural space, in order to investigate the uncanny nature of the 'acoustic ectoplasm': ghostly diegetic and extra-diegetic sounds able to reveal links with the past and memories of the place and to instigate the loss of the home as shelter and, consequently, the loss of the self. An analysis of haunted house films such as *The Shining* (Stanley Kubrick, 1980),

Paranormal Activity (Oren Peli, 2007), and *The Others* (Alejandro Amenábar, 2001) reveal that one of the tropes of the genre is its ability to sonically destabilise the safety of the domestic space.

Albeit looking beyond the limitations of genre, Adrian Martin's contribution moves along the same line as that of Carroll, in terms of questioning the traditional value of the home as a safe place. Perfectly exemplifying how domestic space has been a recurrent cultural figure across genres, historical periods, geographical contexts and modes of moving image representation, he offers a unique and fascinating reflection that takes the study of the relationship between film and the home to a rather experimental level. Adopting a captivating style that he defines as a hybrid between academic, poetic and creative research, Martin discusses the ways in which many filmmakers, in the years since the early 1960s, have traversed and explored various domestic environments depicting them as haunting home spaces. Relying on a constellation of case studies, and on numerous suggestions that crystallise around this specific way of conceiving the home and its spaces, Martin's commentary proceeds by accumulation and serendipitous associations. The text takes advantage of the vivid contributions of a number of poems, as well as of suggestions coming from painting to describe the unfolding of a trajectory that shows how the home as a haven has progressively become a faded icon of that secret and safe place at the heart of many movies, John Ford's *The Searchers* (1956) being a sort of imprint for much cinema that has followed. Martin describes the quest from the macrocosm of the world to the microcosm of domesticity as part of a 'inside-out boomerang effect', observing that the threshold between the two has a dynamic role able to invert the direction of the trajectory – a result achieved by contemporary film and TV, as in the films of Olivier Assayas and in Lynch and Frost's *Twin Peaks: the Return* (2017), where the home becomes a flat facade, the illusion of a haven that in fact can no longer exist.

Lukas Brašiškis's and Nerijus Milerius's chapter deals with domestic space in post-communist Baltic films. In the wake of a number of recent studies from Eastern European scholars who acknowledge the innovative potential of a spatial reading of narrative-centred film analysis (Mazierska 2017), the authors aim to situate this chapter in the light of this new wave of studies that prioritises the spatial constituent in cinematic chronotopes. After a reconstruction of how domestic space in post-communist films has been looked at, they posit that the Soviet past inevitably informs the current conditions of post-Soviet domestic space. Inextricably bound to history and its political, contextual, architectural materialisations, the diptych home/house in the socialist period is then interestingly approached in the nature of its residential built environment, as this is depicted in Baltic films produced after the fall of the Soviet Union. The chapter aims at exploring the role of such spaces to better understand the value and symbolic underpinnings of domesticity in the selected context. To do so the authors cleverly consider both the interior and exterior features of domestic space, and track the similarities and contrasts between their body of works (produced in the 2000s and the early 2010s), and the traditional Baltic cinema dating back to the Soviet era, letting the radical change in the cinematic portrayal of passivity and resistance emerge with clarity. Issues of ideology and control, cultural and political history punctuate the chapter alluding to the role of represented domesticity as an architectural and institutional dispositif, too.

Moving within the threshold between on- and off-screen, representation and dispositif, Laura Rascaroli's and Stefano Baschiera's contributions ideally expand on the architectural suggestions offered by Brašiškis and Milerius to develop a reflection that – albeit focusing on very different film and contexts and putting forth rather different arguments – clearly shows the mutual connections between diegetic space and the wider, physical, constructed and 'real' environment inspiring, informing and at times framing the narrative. Rascaroli engages with the construction of the filmic home as a space of signification by considering the ontological question of 'framing' in both cinema and architecture. Her analysis of Ila Bêka and Louise Lemoine's *Barbicania* (2014) and Chantal Akerman's *No Home Movie* (2015) explores how forms of essayistic nonfiction centred on the home (the architectural essay film, the authorial home movie) reveal the chaos of the outside world and the 'non-home' that the house attempts to fence off. The chapter underlines cinema's contribution to a conceptualisation of architecture, and specifically of the house, in relation primarily to its existential values, and therefore concerning issues of narrative, affect, memory.

Baschiera's contribution considers the role played by domestic space in two key films of the nouvelle vague: Jean Luc Godard's *Une femme est une femme* (1961) and Agnès Varda's *Cléo de 5 à 7* (1962). Baschiera argues that the 'urban' dimension of the nouvelle vague – at the centre of several scholarly investigations – leads to the spatial scale of the apartment understood as the shifting locus of identity of the 1950s Parisian 'youth'. Considering the mode of production of early low-budget nouvelle vague films, the chapter analyses how the camera frames 'real' domestic spaces in order to make them places of performativity and stressing the permeability of its walls with the urban environment.

Whilst the latter chapters hint to the fact that narrative space corresponds in fact to a practicable one, it is with Miriam De Rosa's chapter that the shift towards domesticity as a dimension to be dwelled in by the viewer is taken into account explicitly. Her text focuses on the point of encounter between the representation of domestic space as a site of personal and collective identity, family bonds and memory, and its vocation to work as a dispositif. Framing her study across film-philosophy and the analysis of artists' moving images, she considers the most recent works of Israeli filmmaker Amos Gitai in the transition from the big screen to the gallery space. Drawing mainly from Martin Heidegger's philosophy of space (1971, 1993), De Rosa borrows the concepts of space and place to build a reading of Gitai's installation *Architectures of Memory* (2011) that shows how domesticity is ultimately a site enabling the man to dwell. In particular, the author addresses the question of what happens when the 'dwelling' at stake is not simply the on-screen depiction of one's action on an environment, but rather coincides with those forms of inhabitation involving the subject off-screen, that is, the viewer experiencing the film, especially when this is exhibited in a space which she/he physically shares with the image. By way of a close analysis of the installation, the chapter looks at how cinema and the subject similarly enter a space and 'dwell', ultimately arguing for a conception of the home as a place of the open. De Rosa contends that such openness is comparable to that of contemporary moving images, which – in their multiple configurations – negotiate and renegotiate cinema into assemblages that are always new.

The same territory of the lived experience and the practised space also frames Iain Robert Smith's contribution. Looking at the sites where moving images manifest themselves in the redefinition of the cinematic dispositif, domestic space can also be studied as the place of home viewing. Smith explores these practices in relation to cult cinema. If, within the early attempts to study and theorise cult cinema (Hoberman and Rosenbaum 1983; Corrigan 1991; Telotte 1991), cult reception practices tended to be framed in relation to the public sphere of the cinema theatre, in subsequent years this understanding of cult cinema was complicated by the introduction of cult films into the domestic space through video, DVD, and internet streaming (see Klinger 2006, 2010; Church 2015; Hills 2014, 2017). In his chapter, Smith addresses the increasingly blurred distinction between the public space of the cinema and the domestic space of the home caused by the advent of both home cinemas and alternative screening practices, and offers an overview of the implications of these phenomena for how we theorise and understand cult cinema. Drawing on Barbara Klinger's work on home film cultures and Matt Hills work on cult cinema and technological change, Smith's essay interrogates the fluid and dynamic relationship between cult cinema and the domestic space that a wide range of cult film and TV series – from Jim Sharman's *The Rocky Horror Picture Show* (1975), to Alejandro Jodorowsky's *El Topo* (1970), to *Mystery Science Theatre 3000* – is able to trigger, ultimately raising questions for future scholarship in this area.

The volume ends with a coda by Bryan Konefsky. In continuation with the previous chapters, where domestic space is clearly depicted as a complex architecture, where its symbolic value and dispositif nature feed one into the other, this evocative text is based on a personal recollection that imaginatively serves the author as the spark for a wider discussion of what he terms the Movie Industrial Complex. Embarking on a meditation on light and darkness as a vision that bridges Leonard Cohen's famous 'crack where the light gets in', a domestic projection experience akin to those of *pre*-cinema eventually becoming a *pro*-cinema sign marking the author's entire life trajectory, Konefsky dwells on the value of cinema as a catalyst for change in the age of 'Cineplex-type spaces' as opposed to micro-cinemas which are more similar to a domestic viewing situation. Drawing on the author's long experience with Basement Films, his reflection links the 'domestic inflection' of this art collective from New Mexico to other significant alternative cinematic venues, all to be described as micro-cinema practices.

Notes

1 The development of studies dedicated to cities and cinema is a good example of this 'spatial' shift from background to foreground see for instance the work of Mark Shiel (Shiel and Fitzmaurice 2001; Shiel 2012).
2 Arguably, in some circumstances the term 'home' is applied to cinema to define modes of production that are different from the hegemonic system of production and modes of consumption. The practices connected to home movies are a case in point. Putting forth home cinema as first step towards the relocation of the medium, these challenge the established dispositif in ways that are relevant for the purposes of this collection.
3 Space and place are used here as in Heidegger's essay 'Building, Dwelling, Thinking' (1993), in which the philosopher differentiates the terms emphasising the role of architecture – a move that seems in line with the development of our argument.

Works Cited

Ahmed, Sara (2004), *The Cultural Politics of Emotion*, Edinburgh: Edinburgh University Press.
Ahmed, Sara (2006), *Queer Phenomenology*, Durham, NC: Duke University Press.
Ahmed, Sara (2010), *The Promise of Happiness*, Durham, NC: Duke University Press.
Andrews, Eleanor, Stella Hockenhull and Frances Pheasant-Kelly (eds) (2016), *Spaces of the Cinematic Home: Behind the Door*, New York and London: Routledge.
Bachelard, Gaston (1964), *The Poetics of Space*, New York: Orion Press.
Baudrillard, Jean (2005), *The System of Objects*, London and New York: Verso.
Berghan, Daniela (2013), *Far-Flung Families in Film*, Edinburgh: Edinburgh University Press.
Bingham, Dennis (2010), *Whose Lives Are They Anyway? The Biopic as Contemporary Film Genre*, Piscataway, NJ: Rutgers University Press.
Blunt, Alison (2005), 'Cultural Geography: Cultural Geographies of Home', *Progress in Human Geography*, 29, no. 4, pp. 505–15.
Blunt Alison and Robyn Dowling (2006), *Home*, New York and London: Routledge.
Bronfen, Elizabeth (2004), *Home in Hollywood: The Imaginary Geography of Cinema*, New York: Columbia University Press.
Bruno, Giuliana (1993), *Streetwalking on a Ruined Map*, Princeton, NJ: Princeton University Press.
Bruno, Giuliana (2002), *Atlas of Emotion: Journeys in Art, Architecture, and Film*, New York: Verso.
Bruno, Giuliana (2007), *Public Intimacy: Architecture and the Visual Arts*, Cambridge, MA: MIT Press.
Butler, Alison (2010), 'A Deictic Turn: Space and Location in Contemporary Gallery Film and Video Installation', *Screen*, 51, no. 4, pp. 305–23.
Casetti, Francesco (2015), *The Lumière Galaxy: Seven Key Words for the Cinema to Come*, New York: Columbia University Press.
Church, David (2015), *Grindhouse Nostalgia: Memory, Home Video and Exploitation Film Fandom*, Edinburgh: Edinburgh University Press.
Cieraad, Irene (ed.) (1999), *At Home: An Anthropology of Domestic Space*, New York: Syracuse University Press.
Corrigan, Timothy (1991), 'Film and the Culture of Cult', in J. P. Telotte (ed.), *The Cult Film Experience: Beyond All Reason*, Austin: University of Texas Press, pp. 26–37.
de Certeau, Michel (2002), *The Practice of Everyday Life*, Berkeley, Los Angeles and London: University of California Press.
De Rosa, Miriam (2012), 'Image, Space, and the Contemporary Filmic Experience', *Cinéma et Cie. International Film Studies Journal*, no. 12, Fall, pp. 119–30.

De Rosa, Miriam and Vinzenz Hediger (2016), 'Post-what? Post-when? Thinking Moving Images beyond the Postcinema Condition', *Cinéma et Cie. International Film Studies Journal*, no. 26/27, Spring/Fall.

Dovey, Kim (2008), *Framing Places: Mediating Power in Built Form*, New York and London: Routledge.

Duncan, James S. and David Lambert (2003), 'Landscapes of Home', in James S. Duncan, Nuala C. Johnson and Richard H. Schein (eds), *A Companion to Cultural Geography*, Oxford: Blackwell, pp. 382–403.

Fowler, Catherine (2008), 'Into the Light: Re-Considering Off-Frame and Off-Screen Space in Gallery Films', *New Review of Film and Television Studies*, 6, no. 3, pp. 253–67.

Grosz, Elizabeth (1992), 'Bodies-Cities', in Beatriz Colomina and Jennifer Bloomer (eds), *Sexuality and Space*, New York: Princeton Architectural Press, pp. 241–54.

Grosz, Elizabeth (1997), 'Inscriptions and Body Maps: Representations and the Corporeal', in Linda McDowell and Joanne P. Sharp (eds), *Space, Gender, Knowledge: Feminist Readings*, London: Arnold.

Hagener, Malte (2008), 'Where is Cinema (Today)? The Cinema in the Age of Media Immanence', *Cinéma et Cie.*, no. 11, Fall, pp. 15–22.

Heidegger, Martin (1971), '... Poetically Man Dwells ...', in *Poetry, Language, Thought*, New York: Harper and Row, pp. 221–39.

Heidegger, Martin (1993), 'Building, Dwelling, Thinking', in *Basic Writings*, New York: HarperCollins, pp. 343–63.

Hills, Matt (2014), 'Cult Cinema and the "Mainstreaming" Discourse of Technological Change: Revisiting Subcultural Capital in Liquid Modernity', *New Review of Film and Television Studies*, 13, no. 1, pp. 100–21.

Hills, Matt (2017), 'A "Cult-like" Following: Nordic Noir, Nordicana and Arrow Films' Bridging of Subcultural/Neocultural Capital', in Jonathan Wroot and Andy Willis (eds), *Cult Media: Re-packaged, Re-released and Restored*, London: Palgrave Macmillan, pp. 49–65.

Hirst, Paul (2005), *Space and Power. Politics, War and Architecture*, Cambridge: Polity Press.

Hoberman, J. and Jonathan Rosenbaum (1983/1991), *Midnight Movies*, New York: Da Capo Press.

Klinger, Barbara (2006), *Beyond the Multiplex: Cinema, New Technologies, and the Home*, Berkeley: University of California Press.

Klinger, Barbara (2010), 'Becoming Cult: *The Big Lebowski*, Replay Culture and Male Fans', *Screen*, 51, no. 1, pp. 1–20.

Kruger, Barbara (1994), *Remote Control: Power, Cultures, and the World of Appearances*, Cambridge, MA: MIT Press.

Lefebvre, Henri (1991), *The Production of Space*, Oxford: Wiley-Blackwell.

Lefebvre, Henri (2003), *The Urban Revolution*, Minneapolis: University of Minnesota Press.

Loshitzky, Yosefa (2010), *Screening Strangers: Migration and Diaspora in Contemporary European Cinema*, Bloomington: Indiana University Press.

Mazierska, Eva (2017), 'Squeezing Space, Releasing Space: Spatial Research in the Study of Eastern European Cinema', in S. Bahun and J. Haynes (eds), *Cinema, State Socialism and Society in the Soviet Union and Eastern Europe, 1917–1989*, New York: Routledge, pp. 9–24.

Munro, Moira and Ruth Madigan (1999), 'Negotiating Space in the Family Home', in Irene Cieraad (ed.), *At Home: An Anthropology of Domestic Space*, New York: Syracuse University Press, pp. 107–17.

Naficy, Hamid (1999), *Home, Exile, Homeland: Film, Media, and the Politics of Place*, New York, London: Routledge.

Rhodes, John David (2017), *Spectacle of Property: The House in American Film*, Minneapolis: University of Minnesota Press.

Rhodes, John David and Elena Gorfinkel (eds) (2011), *Taking Place: Location and the moving image*, Minneapolis: University of Minnesota Press.

Rutherford, Jonathan (1990), 'A Place Called Home: Identity and the Cultural Politics of Difference', in J. Rutherford (ed.), *Identity: Community, Culture, Difference*, London: Lawrence and Wishart, pp. 9–27.

Schleier, Merrill (2009), *Skyscraper Cinema: Architecture and Gender in American Film*, Minneapolis: University of Minnesota Press.

Shiel, Mark (2012), *The Real Los Angeles: Hollywood, Cinema, and the City of Angels*, London: Reaktion Books.

Shiel Mark and Tony Fitzmaurice (eds) (2001), *Cinema and the City: Film and Urban Societies in a Global Context*, Oxford: Blackwell.

Sibley, David (1995), 'Families and Domestic Routines', in Steve Pile and Steve Thrift (eds), *Mapping the Subject. Geographies of Cultural Transformation*, London, New York: Routledge, pp. 114–31.

Telotte, J. P. (ed.) (1991), *The Cult Film Experience: Beyond All Reason*, Austin: University of Texas Press.

Tuan, Yi-Fu (1977), *Space and Place*, Minneapolis: University of Minnesota Press.

Turner, Victor (1995), *The Ritual Process*, New York: Aldine de Gruyter.

Wojcik, Pamela Robertson (2010), *The Apartment Plot*, Durham, NC: Duke University Press.

Youngblood, Gene (1970), *Expanded Cinema*, New York: Dutton.

CHAPTER 1

Architectures of Ubiquity: The Colonial Revival in Film and Television
John David Rhodes

The Colonial Revival house is an unavoidable context in cinematic and televisual representation. The ubiquity of Colonial Revival architecture – in the American landscape and in film and television – means that as a signifier it is both too empty and too full; there would appear to be too little and too much to say about this subject. The problem of Colonial Revival architecture itself is that it is an architecture of surfaces, appearances, facades, exteriors: it is a skin, the skin, we might say, of national fantasy. For not only is the term Colonial Revival in architectural history a loose, floating, perhaps even radically empty signifier (empty perhaps – as well – because overfull with too many contents), in actual architectural materiality, the term names the look of a house's exterior but indicates very little about the disposition of its interior spaces.

In a book dedicated to thinking about the house in American cinema, I have argued that when we look at houses on screen we are looking at what I call a 'spectacle of property'. Whatever the nature or style or dimensions of the houses we see on-screen, when we look at a cinematic image of a house, we are in thrall to and enthralled by property, its images and its image-ness (Rhodes 2017). Cinema turns cinemagoers into short-term tenants, whom I call 'spectator tenants' – subjects who (in the traditional context of theatrical moviegoing) *'pay for the right to occupy a space in order to gaze up at a space they can never occupy'* (Rhodes 2017: 13 [italics in original]). This looking is structured slightly differently and receives different inflections according to the style of architecture that is being looked at. In the case of Colonial Revival architecture, an architecture of ubiquity, we seem to be looking at the omnipresent and inescapable nature of the property relation itself, a relation that houses and structures our intimate relationship to capitalism. Moreover, this architecture's emptiness, the lack of connection between its surfaces and its interiors, its malleability, plasticity, nominalism of reference and endless iteration (it is a 'revival' style, after all) mean that its architecture and moving images provide refracted but highly concrete embodiment of the endless fungibility of property relations in twentieth-century capitalism.

An Architectural Style that is Not One

The residual traces of the Colonial Revival are found everywhere across the American landscape and certain of its stylistic features remain nearly constant, if camouflaged or obscured, elements in architectural design across American history. This ubiquity, however, makes talking sensibly about the subject somewhat difficult. Richard Guy Wilson, one of the foremost critics and historians of Colonial Revival architecture, writes that, as 'the United States's most popular and characteristic expression' the Colonial Revival is '[n]either a formal style nor a movement'. Wilson argues, rather: 'Colonial Revival embodies an attitude that looks to the American past for inspiration and selects forms, motifs, and symbols for replication and reuse' (Wilson 2004: 6). Not even a style – itself a fraught, vague and difficult to define term – the Colonial Revival is an 'attitude' that articulates itself through a variety of signifying materials. Wilson asserts that '[s]ome element of Colonial Revival exists in every American town; it is our national architectural idiom' (Wilson 2004: 6). The notion of a 'national idiom' and what that would look or sound like are hard to entertain when the same writer informs us that Colonial Revival architecture 'is broad and includes many styles', among them Dutch Colonial, Creole Colonial Revival and Spanish Colonial in addition to the styles associated with its New England manifestations (Wilson 2004: 6). Kenneth Ames writes that '[u]nder the colonial rubric we can find extraordinary varieties and digressions as well as regional interpretations with startlingly different visual effects, all of which nevertheless embody some notion of the colonial' (Ames 1985: 2). Ames and Wilson both suggest that ubiquity constitutes specificity, and that ubiquity is underwritten by a formal plasticity that sustains itself through a minimalism of reference. We might call to mind Philip Johnson's AT&T tower (now the Sony Tower) in New York City completed in 1984: all it takes is the addition of the scroll pediment to convert an International style skyscraper into an exercise in Americana.

Revivals of the colonial past, especially in architecture, began only a few decades after the conclusion of the period of the colonial itself. Wilson's admittedly rough periodisation of the colonial period itself runs from 1607 (the founding of Jamestown, Virginia, the first permanent English colony in the Americas) to 1783 (the signing of the Treaty of Paris). In his *Notes on the State of Virginia*, Thomas Jefferson expresses contempt for early American architecture. Of Virginia's colonial houses, he writes 'It is impossible to devise things more ugly, uncomfortable, and happily more perishable' (quoted in Wilson 2004: 13). By the 1820s, however, his attitude had shifted; he was at least in favour of preserving the Philadelphia house where he lived while writing the Declaration of Independence. His nascent preservationism suggests architecture's importance in creating a secular religion of the nation and its history: 'Small things [i.e., his former house], may, perhaps, like the relics of saints, help to nourish our devotion to this holy bond of our Union' (quoted in Wilson 2004: 7). Jefferson's change of heart was contemporary with a growing interest in the preservation of the nation's wider architectural heritage. The 1828 restoration and redesign of the tower of Philadelphia's Independence Hall (also known as the Pennsylvania State House), where the Declaration of Independence was signed in 1776, marks one early and significant episode in the growing interest in preserving colonial architecture (Wilson 2004: 15).[1]

The first colonial building to be elevated to the level of secular shrine and pilgrimage destination is surely Mount Vernon, George Washington's plantation house, a rigorously classical country mansion the construction and improvement of which Washington maintained, even while leading the American forces during the Revolutionary War. The house had fallen into some disrepair by the mid-nineteenth century, and there was the chance that the family would be forced to sell it on the open market. To avert this end and to make this private house permanently an object and site of civic pilgrimage, Anna Pamela Cunningham, a resident of Charleston, South Carolina, formed the Mount Vernon Ladies Association, which raised money to purchase and restore the house and open it to the public. It was hoped that the house's preservation might contribute to the effort to avoid the Civil War. Although its power did not extend that far, following the war Mount Vernon quickly became and remains the most visited house in the United States (Wilson 2004: 32–3). Mount Vernon's mass-touristic veneration and its circulation as national icon in mass culture are early indications of the Colonial Revival's imbrication with various forms of (national) spectacle and also links its history to that of the house tour, which I have elsewhere suggested should be seen as the genealogical precursor to the cinematic (un)pleasure in looking at another's property (Rhodes 2017: 23–5).

Other significant episodes or cycles of the Colonial Revival include the International Centennial Exposition, held in Philadelphia in 1876, an event that, according to Vincent Scully, coincided with a revival of interest in the 'colonial revival which has … never entirely subsided'

(Scully 1976: 113–14). Even more important is the obsession with the style across the period of the Great Depression and the presidency of Franklin D. Roosevelt. Obviously the nation's economic precarity put an enormous strain on national feeling, thus colonial architecture offered itself (again) as a trope of national togetherness – a kind of architectural salve.[2] The diffusion of Colonial Revival architecture during this decade can be traced through architectural competitions in popular magazines that promoted colonial architecture for middle-class homeowners to the preservation-cum-invention of Colonial Williamsburg in Williamsburg, Virginia. In order to 'restore' Williamsburg to its colonial glory, 459 modern buildings (constructed in the nineteenth and twentieth centuries) were demolished so that ninety-one 'colonial' buildings could be reconstructed, ex novo (Wilson 2004: 167).

Cinematic Iterations

Classical Hollywood cinema reveals a sympathetic (and symptomatic) reflection of and intervention in the colonial's perennial revival. David Gebhard, writing as an architectural historian, ties a firm knot between Colonial Revival architecture and Hollywood filmmaking:

> The colonial, as *the* American ideal in the thirties, received its ultimate stamp of approval from Hollywood's motion picture industry. The characteristic Beverly Hills house of motion picture stars and directors was a colonial one ... The colonial image provided the backdrop for almost every film that was set in a contemporary American suburban environment. (Gebhard 1987: 116–17)

Though he does not offer hard statistics to back up the 'almost every', Gebhard does quote an article that was published in *Good Housekeeping* on the occasion of the release of *Bringing Up Baby* (Howard Hawks, 1938), part of which was set in a (fictional) Colonial Revival Connecticut farmhouse: 'Hollywood went traditional when it created this refreshing version of an old Connecticut house to serve as a background ...[Y]ou will find in this house numerous good ideas that you will like to use in your own house' (quoted in Gebhard 1987: 116). It is an entertainingly complex chore to consider the spectator's dual labour as she or he (here the article is clearly interpellating an imagined 'she') keeps track of the film's screwballery while simultaneously compiling a list of decorating tips. The comedy of the film is clearly unrealistic, but the decor, the article suggests, is meant to be taken as substantive, realistic and instructive.

Christmas in Connecticut (Peter Godfrey, 1945), a wartime comedy, foregrounds a similar Connecticut Colonial Revival farmhouse as the site of erotic/professional deception and national fantasy. Barbara Stanwyck plays Elizabeth Lane, a food and lifestyle writer for a popular women's magazine. (The magazine goes unnamed in the film, but is clearly meant to be an analogue for the likes of *Good Housekeeping*; '*American Housekeeping*' is named at one point in the film's dialogue as the competitor magazine.) Elizabeth's monthly column about her domestic life as a Connecticut mother and housewife is pure fabrication: she is unmarried, lives in small apartment in New York City and cannot cook (she orders food in from Restaurant Felix downstairs). The owner of her magazine, Yardley (Sydney Greenstreet), ignorant of the fact that Elizabeth is a fraud, concocts a publicity scheme in which Elizabeth will invite a wounded soldier, Jefferson Jones (Dennis Morgan) for Christmas dinner with her and her family in Connecticut. (Mister Yardley proposes his own attendance, too, to keep an eye on things and because his own children have left him out of their holiday plans.) Because Yardley is a 'stickler for the truth', Elizabeth must construct overnight the lineaments of the life she has been narrating in her columns. The house is borrowed from Elizabeth's on-again/off-again boyfriend, John Sloan (Reginald Gardiner), an architect and property developer, who will play-act the part of her husband while (unsuccessfully) exploiting the situation to try to get Elizabeth actually to marry him. Sloan's maid babysits for local women who work in a munitions factory (which is never visualised onscreen), and their babies are employed to 'act' the part of Elizabeth's child – much to the confusion of Elizabeth's guests, given that different babies (of different genders) are dropped off on different days. (Interestingly, the film codes all of these women as recent immigrants from Europe.) Felix (S. Z. Sakall), the proprietor of the restaurant downstairs from Elizabeth's apartment, posing as her uncle, does the cooking.

Although the film's narrative emphasises the solution to the erotic plot (in which Elizabeth and Jefferson fall in love), considerable visual pleasure is derived from the Sloan's farmhouse – its cavernous central hall (or living room) and its collection of antiques. The film's privileging of this farmhouse engages the historically contemporaneous context of Colonial Revival architecture's ongoing popularity, as well as the consumerist discourse on domesticity purveyed by women's magazines like the fictional one whose authenticity is at stake in the film. In an ancillary plot development, Yardley offers Sloan the editorship of a 'build your own home section for postwar planning'. The Colonial Revival house is the medium of a national fantasy in terms of both the film's diegesis and its appeal to its viewers, who are established as analogous to, but perhaps slightly less naively informed than Elizabeth's

Figure 1.1 Oldness-as-newness: the colonial revival as 'spectacle of property' and ideological, spatial container in *Christmas in Connecticut* (1945). Film still.

somewhat apparently gullible readers. Sloan's narcissistic discourse in his conversations with Yardley on the quality of his construction methods reminds viewers that Colonial Revival architecture might be tinged with the kind of (modern) artificiality that lies behind Elizabeth's elaborately staged phoney Christmas gathering. Sloan's attractive, spacious house, however, pleases; its spaces are both intimate and enormous. The large open plan of the house's ground floor clearly owes everything to twentieth-century architectural design and nothing to the sixteenth and seventeenth centuries, but it is crammed full of colonial Americana of every variety (Figure 1.1). The house figures a vertiginous configuration of old and new, which in a sense makes it an interesting figure not for authentic colonial architecture, but for the Colonial Revival itself, which is ontologically and definitionally a mode of oldness-as-newness (and vice versa), as well as a dumping ground (or empty container) for nationalist ideological content. Spectators in the world, like Elizabeth's readers, could fall prey to this spectacle of property and the pursuit of desires that it both animates and houses; however, despite the film's generic conclusion, the discourse on authenticity that it sets in motion undermines the credibility of this house's colonial architecture and places its charm in quotation marks.

Yardley's offer of the special house design section in his magazine to Sloan corresponds to various famous real-life attempts to engage reading publics with the question of contemporary architecture. In 1938, *Life* magazine ran a well-publicised contest in which its readers voted on house designs submitted by leading architects. The contest pitted 'modernists' against 'traditionalists', with the likes of Frank Lloyd Wright representing modernism and Royal Barry Wills, a Boston-based purveyor of Colonial Revival design and frequent champion in contests like this one, tradition. According to Gebhard, 'the two most remembered' houses were the designs submitted by Wright and Wills, but the latter was the readers' choice. Similar sorts of demonstration houses were built across the country in the 1920s and 1930s, often under government patronage (Gebhard 1987: 115–16). The 'Better Homes in America' movement was first begun in 1922 in the pages of the popular women's magazine *The Delineator* under the auspices of its editor Marie Meloney. The movement sought to direct attention to the plight of home ownership in the US and to inculcate good housekeeping values among the nation's citizens. Initially the movement enjoyed merely the endorsement of federal and state officials; by 1924 the federal government had effectively assumed control of its operations. The movement was launched with the construction of the 'National Better Home' which was built on the mall, not far from the White House, in Washington, DC in 1922. The house was, naturally, Colonial Revival in style – in fact, it was a modernised re-invention of a seventeenth-century house in East Hampton, New York, the house in which John Howard Payne, author of the song *Home Sweet Home*, was born (Hutchinson 1986). After the house's exhibition and extensive media coverage (especially in the pages of *The Delineator*, which maintained an active role in the movement), the house was relocated near the Corcoran Gallery, where it served as an education centre for the Girl Scouts of America. Young scouting girls were given instruction in home economics inside the walls of this ideal house (Hutchinson 1986: 173). Ten years later, in New York, the local chapter of the Better Homes movement in collaboration with CBS built 'America's Little House' at the corner of Park Avenue and East 39th Street. The inauguration of the house was a media event: participated in by New York Mayor Fiorello LaGuardia and Eleanor Roosevelt. CBS made weekly radio broadcasts from it, following its opening; the house was open for public tours until it was demolished (Schneider 1997). This historical context suggests the thoroughly mediated and mediatised circulation of the image of Colonial

Revival structures, both in Hollywood filmmaking and in the larger culture. 'America's Little House' and the set standing in for Barbara Stanwyck's fictional character's house in *Christmas in Connecticut* might be written off as fantasies or ideological projections but they both participated in and, in different ways and to varying extents, produced the social materiality of the Colonial Revival house and the values it seemed itself to house.

'America's Little House' was, of course, modest in size. The compactness of designs for the middle class Colonial Revival house, however, masks the enormous scale of its impact on the American landscape. We might think, for instance, of the 'Cape Cod' houses that were the preferred model for the first wave of construction in a mass suburb like Levittown, New York. The giganticism of so many small houses has as its counterpart the magically expanding Colonial Revival houses that we see in Hollywood musicals such as *Holiday Inn* (Mark Sandrich, 1942) and its sequel, of sorts, *White Christmas* (Michael Curtiz, 1954). The Colonial Revival house acts as the setting for both of these films.

When Jim Hardy (Bing Crosby) shows Linda Mason (Marjorie Reynolds) into his house, now being transformed into the 'Holiday Inn' of the film's title, Linda is momentarily at a loss: 'Oh! ... Well this is darling.' The ellipsis in my quotation of dialogue does not correspond to any contraction of time, but rather to time's dilation as the camera pans across the room, right to left, across the enormous expanse of the house-cum-inn. Hook rugs, stiff low sofas, an elaborately newelled double-landing staircase, wingback upholstered chairs, 'sack-back' Windsor chairs, a nearly baroque pedimented doorway, extensive dentillation along every bit of woodwork: the art department has larded this house with every signifier of Colonial Revival interior decoration. Linda asks, understandably, 'Was it as large as this when it was a farmhouse?', to which Jim replies, 'Yeah, it was built by a fellow who felt cramped in New York. He finally ran out of lumber, though.' The problem of the house's size needs to be established, processed (marvelled at, really) and settled, in terms of some minimum necessity of diegetic plausibility. As the house becomes a swanky country dinner theatre, and as its productions grow in size and elaborateness, the Holiday Inn appears to possess a magical expansiveness. The 'unrealistic' size and capacities of the stage in the Hollywood musical are, of course, common features of the genre. What gives us pause here is the way in which Linda, and therefore we, via the panning camera, all pause to consider the house's size and interior decoration. Slightly more textual energy than is generically necessary is expended to introduce the possibility that this space could really exist.

Here we see and look forward to the way in which property's inherent spectacularity offers the grounds by which this house becomes the staging-place of spectacle.

Holiday Inn derives its title from the fact that Jim's plan for the inn is that it would only open for holidays, with the inn's theatrical shows thematised around the iconography and music associated with a given holiday. We sense the ability of the Holiday Inn, and of *Holiday Inn*, to unfold themselves extraordinarily in the context of the first thematised holiday-performance, the one for President's Day. The number for this holiday, entitled 'Abraham', written by Irving Berlin, celebrates Abraham Lincoln by way of having Bing Crosby sing in blackface while wearing a Lincoln-esque stove-pipe top hat, looking like some cross between Uncle Tom and Honest Abe. The chorus singers and the orchestra all also appear in blackface; Linda emerges for her solo as a blonde piccaninny doing a soft shoe on a bale of cotton. Jim's African American domestic servant, Mamie, played by the black actress Louise Beaver, and her two children, Daphne and Vanderbilt (Joan Arnold and Shelby Bacon), are given a turn in the number: they sing a verse that is shown to us, the film audience, but that remains unintegrated into the spectacle staged for the audience in the inn. The casual racism of what we can only presume to think was intended as Hollywood liberalism is both shocking and unsurprising. Weirdly, the architecture and decoration of the house summon an image of a moment the past in which Mamie and her children (to whom we have been introduced before this number) would have most likely been slaves. The ambiguity of their presence in the Holiday Inn needs to be metabolised by the film's pseudo-patriotic and sham liberal investment in Lincoln. The song celebrates Lincoln's idiosyncrasies, as well as his ability to keep the country together and usher it, incidentally, into the first major, mass-mediatised phase of Colonial Revivalism. The Inn's magical capacity to expand itself beyond its already considerable dimensions runs parallel to its overweening appeal to Lincoln, which results in the recapitulation of the most egregious forms of racism that the Emancipation Proclamation and Civil War did little to eradicate, despite the official end to slavery that both achieved. The Colonial Revival ambience of *Holiday Inn* is, like the film and its spaces, remarkably capacious in its accommodation of conflicting impulses and attitudes. Both *Holiday Inn* and the Colonial Revival depend on our suspension of disbelief – that so much stuff could be fitted into the inn, or that the appeal to an idealised past will not churn up undigested cultural and historical materials – like the spectacle of Mamie, Daphne and Vanderbilt, who very clearly inhabit if not the legal

ARCHITECTURES OF UBIQUITY 25

Figure 1.2 The expansiveness of the colonial revival in *Holiday Inn* (1942). Film still.

status, then at least the iconography of the slave, singing along to a musical number that insults them. Like the Inn whose size Linda marvels at when first she enters, Mamie, Daphne and Vanderbilt constitute another spectacle of property (Rhodes 2017: 1–6).

By the time the Fourth of July show rolls around, the Holiday Inn's spectacular ambitions have overgrown the elastic capacities of its interiors. This number is located, the film shows us carefully, out of doors in the Inn's front yard. The new stage is crowned by three scroll pediments: colonial architecture, again, is the ground of national(ist) fantasy. It seems that the film wants to traffic in a kind of spatial realism (one credibly aligned what can or cannot be imagined to fit inside the house) while also superseding the limits it sets up (Figure 1.2). Case in point: this being a war film, the celebration of the Fourth of July most obviously summons the war context. As Jim sings his *Song of Freedom*, the stage's curtains momentarily close, only to open again: the scroll pediments have disappeared, and first the entire stage, and next, the entire film image are identified with an enormous film screen on which we see projected images of the war effort (war ships, fighter planes, munitions factories, etc.). This is one of those meta-moments in the Hollywood musical in which film and *this* film must make clear their abilities to astound over and above any capacity that would be creditable to the musical theatre (much less to a theatre housed in a country farmhouse).

Holiday Inn's Korean War-era successor, *White Christmas*, which trades shamelessly on the song first featured in the earlier film, is less concerned with its relation to the theatrical musical and more with its anxious relation to television. Here again we have a New England inn, this time the Columbia Inn in Vermont. Revivalism striates this film: extradiegetically, it attempts to resurrect a song, a medium, a genre; diegetically, it revives a general, his inn, and an ideal of American (wartime) values. Bing Crosby and Danny Kaye play Bob Wallace and Phil Davis, a singing act who accompany a pair of sisters, Betty and Judy Haynes (Rosemary Clooney and Vera-Ellen) to the Columbia Inn where the sisters are booked to perform over the Christmas season. Bob and Phil discover that their former commanding officer, General Waverly (Dean Jagger), is the proprietor of the inn, which is struggling financially due to a snowless winter. As a struggling proprietor and entrepreneur, the General's effeminised position excites the sympathy of his former soldiers who plot to save him from financial ruin. (The General has also been turned down in his application to return to active duty, a rejection which has added to his disgrace.) Their scheme involves importing their company to Vermont in order to attract business to the inn. To secure a paying audience Bob engineers an impromptu appearance on the 'Ed Harrison' (read 'Ed Sullivan') show in order to ask the General's former troops to come to the inn for Christmas and lift his spirits (and generate some income for him as well).

White Christmas was the first feature film to employ Paramount's VistaVision technology in that studio's bid to compete with Twentieth Century-Fox's CinemaScope. Whereas the CinemaScope image was incredibly wide, Paramount promoted the VistaVision technique's height; its publicity materials touted the idea that 'height was equally important as width' (quoted in Belton 1992: 126). A backstage musical might seem an odd vehicle for showcasing the possibilities of the VistaVision image, but *White Christmas* contrives several dance numbers whose set designs and athletic dancing explore the gigantic dimensions of the image: in one ('Choreography') Vera-Ellen's leg extends down into the image from off-screen space, while in the same number a male chorus dancer bounds (via an unseen trampoline) into the image from off-screen, below (see Rhodes 2006). The widescreen image was among Hollywood's desperate attempts to shore up an audience whose numbers were shrinking due to a variety of economic, technological and cultural shifts. Perhaps chief among these was the rapid growth of television broadcast and domestic television ownership in the early 1950s. The film permits us to watch the televised broadcast version of Bob's appeal to the General's former troops on the Ed Harrison show. At one point the film cedes the entire dimensions of its newly enlarged image to the television screen. Similar to the moment in *Holiday Inn* in which the projected intra-diegetic film image that is part of a theatrical spectacle subsumes the entire screen, here the momentary exhibition of television's black and white flickering graininess via the colourful and hypertrophied VistaVision image makes a plea for cinema's superiority to its competitor media form.

Bob's televised plea is, of course, successful, and the soldiers dutifully make their (implausible) way to the Columbia Inn on Christmas Eve. The show and *White Christmas*, therefore, enfold a nostalgic commitment to the nation (embodied by General Waverly) inside the confines of the Columbia Inn's Colonial Revival architecture. The inn's performance hall, and especially its stage and backstage areas, are fantastically large and seemingly infinite in size and possibility, not unlike the spaces of the Holiday Inn, whose interiors clearly influenced the design of the Columbia Inn. Commitment to the cinematic image and commitment to authority, especially in a period of wartime, require articulation, we might be led to think, through a medium as emptily expandable as that of the Colonial Revival itself.

While *White Christmas* was and remains one of the most financially successful films of all time, another VistaVision experiment has enjoyed a similar success, one measured more in terms of longevity than in strictly financial terms. This film is *Williamsburg: The Story of a Patriot* (George Seaton, 1957), the film that every visitor to Colonial Williamsburg must submit to as part of her orientation to the historic town and that has been shown at the Visitor Center continuously since 1957. The film stars Jack Lord as the fictional John Fry, a Virginia planter with weak Loyalist sympathies. The film begins in 1769 as John is setting out to serve his first term in colonial Virginia's House of Burgesses and narrates, across thirty-six minutes, his coming-to-consciousness as a sympathiser with the cause of revolution and war against Britain. The film was shot specifically for exhibition in specially designed cinemas called 'transcineums' by their architect and designer, Benjamin Schlanger, a prolific designer of movie theatres. The screens were at the time the largest indoor screens in the world, and the seating was raked in such a way that spectators' sightlines were not obstructed by the heads of others sitting below them.

Bosley Crowther, the film critic for the *New York Times*, evoked the effect thus:

> As one enters the semi-darkened interior, an illusory purple light, suffusing the whole forward area, attracts and bemuses the eye. The tiers of chairs, indirectly lighted from beneath, are separated by wide spaces and lacquered steel barriers (or row dividers) that mask the heads of viewers in the forward tiers. The illusion created is that of being under the dome of the sky at night. (Crowther 1957)

The intention was to immerse the spectator in the dimensions of the image – to effect a deep and sensual identification with the image of Colonial Williamsburg and the nation of which it was a privileged, sacramental metonym.

The decision to use VistaVision probably stemmed in no small part from the fact that the president of Paramount Pictures (the owners of the technology) sat on the board of the advisory board for the production of the film. Whatever the instrumentality involved in the decision, *The Story of a Patriot* markedly exploits the VistaVision image's height by way of two figures: the human body and colonial architecture. As Jocelyn Szczepaniak-Gillece has written, the 'relative height' of *The Story of a Patriot*'s VistaVision image 'could be awe-striking and monumental in a more substantial way than just width ... [it] meant a greater possibility of silent contemplation as opposed to the bodily thrills commonly associated with widescreen' (Szczepaniak-Gillece 2012). Indeed, the thrills are rather more sober. The film opens with a travelling shot through a forest path that opens onto a field leading up to the Fry plantation. As the lighting adjusts from the forest's dark to the daylight of open farmland, we realise that the shot is following a small black boy – a slave, part of John Fry's property – as he makes his way to the plantation, one of a handful of colonial-era houses (recently restored along with the rest of Williamsburg). The film's spectacle is already a spectacle of property, even before the camera settles on any image of domestic architecture. The sense of VistaVision technology's capacity for height is mostly derived from low-angle shots of standing human individuals or else from long shots that emphasise architecture, both interior and exterior. The Capitol, where the House of Burgesses meets, is especially favoured as a location. The large brass chandelier hanging from the centre of the House's chamber anchors the appreciation of the image's height, while shots of the Capitol's exterior use the building's height as an index of the image's dimensions (and use the image's dimensions as a means of communicating the building's interest). When John Fry is unexpectedly re-elected to the House of Burgesses, despite his increasingly unpopular loyalist politics, he decides to take his family to Williamsburg with him. 'We're going to Williamsburg!', his daughter exclaims. The segment that follows offers the Fry family's trajectory through the town's monuments – their itinerary would be the template for the tourist-spectators watching *The Story of a Patriot* who would have arrived in Williamsburg by automobile, not in the coach and four that conveys the Fry family from their country seat.

I mention the automobile because the rise in car ownership – itself a contributing factor to and by-product of suburbanisation – fostered cheap forms of tourism like the family driving vacation. Tourism to Williamsburg is primarily organised around the automobile, despite the fact that no cars are permitted in the historical core – what the Williamsburg Foundation now calls 'The Revolutionary City'. The film industry's decline in the 1950s was attributable not only to the rise of television, but also to the rise in automobile tourism of the sort that would have seen families driving to a destination like Williamsburg for a week's or a weekend's getaway. Money spent on trips like these would have been money not spent on movie tickets. *The Story of a Patriot*, then, in part, is also a complex trace of this contest between Hollywood and the competing forces that were dismantling its cultural hegemony. In a sense, it is a kind of indoor drive-in (or drive-to) cinema: an exhibition space entirely predicated on automobile travel; and yet, the film's technological and aesthetic form (those terms are inseparable) was the product of Hollywood's war against the automobile and the stay-at-home suburban consumption that the automobile encouraged and embodied.

The Ground of Televisual Iteration

Television sitcoms from this same period (the 1950s) offer yet another archive of images of Colonial Revival architecture. The Colonial Revival family house introduces, organises and locates almost every major family sitcom of the 1950s. *The Adventures of Ozzie and Harriet* (1952–66) *Father Knows Best* (1954–60), *Leave it to Beaver* (1957–63): each of these shows offers us – often in the credit sequence – an image of the Colonial Revival house that will be the location of most of the episode's diegetic action. The house in *Ozzie and Harriet* speaks a different historicity from that of the one we see in *Leave it to Beaver*. In the former show the house seems to have been built sometime before its fictional time, that of a 1950s present tense, contemporaneous with the show's production and transmission. It seems perhaps as old as the Colonial Revival's 1930s cycle of popularity. In the latter, the house seems spanking new, a part of a larger pattern of post-war construction. In all of these, as well as in in *Father Knows Best* (1954–60) or *The Donna Reed Show* (1958–66) – a late, transitional instalment in the 1950s family sitcom and which is more reticent about the exterior of the Stone family's house – the houses' interiors always bespeak a committment to Colonial Revival design. In 'A Day in Bed', an episode of *Ozzie and Harriet* from 1956, the signifiers and material indices of Colonial Revival taste pin the house's surfaces to the national imaginary. Ozzie and Harriet's scroll pediment headboard echoes the design of the house's exterior; 'ancestral' portraits (including a large one of woman hanging over the bed) punctuate the room; antique 'Paul Revere' candlesticks adorn the federal style dresser – and so on. All of these houses share a basic floorplan: a central staircase that rises from the first-floor entry hall, and some version of open-plan living room or den on one side of this entry hall, with a formal dining or living room on the opposite side. When shot from inside the house, the front door most frequently opens onto the outside world on screen right. The staircase leads up into the world of the second story – the world of bedrooms, bathrooms and other forms of more guarded privacy – while the front door opens onto the world of school and work. Both of these worlds that flank the entry hall are visualised consistently but less frequently than the interstitial world of the house's ground floor whose public-in-private front door and entry hall act as the literal hinge between the publicity of the outside world and the privacy of the world upstairs.

The difficulty of telling one 1950s family sitcom house from another underlines one of the impressive indicators of both television's and suburban architecture's bids for hegemony at mid-century. In her analysis of the function and ideology of domestic space in *Leave it to Beaver* and *Father Knows Best*, Mary Beth Haralovich has noted that 'Ward and June Cleaver [of *Leave it to Beaver*] raise two sons in a single-family suburban home which, in later seasons, adopted a nearly identical floor plan to that of the Andersons [of *Father Knows Best*]' (1989: 63).[3] The assent of these fictional houses to an already-agreed-upon vision of what middle class homes looked like was constituted in part by an unconscious (or at least unreflective) participation in national fantasy, but also by a concerted attempt both to imitate the real and, by doing so, guarantee its reality by way of its apparent conformity with the television fictions that would seem (or be seen to seem) merely to reflect its anterior substance. Haralovich notes that '[r]ealist mise-en-scène drew upon housing architecture and consumer products in order to ground family narratives within the domestic space of the middle-class

Figure 1.3 The ground of national fantasy in *Ozzie and Harriet* (1952). Film still.

home' (1989: 80–1). This mimetic fidelity to what already existed, however, was a fidelity to a world of proliferating suburban consumption that, as Haralovich's work demonstrates, was busy constituting itself as real during the same period in which 1950s family sitcoms were, in reciprocal and interdependent ways, consolidating their own market share of the television audience and the national imaginary. Every family sitcom was sponsored by a consumer product, one whose consumption might be witnessed in the show's diegesis, in addition to the obligatory advertisement that announced this corporate sponsorship. More powerfully, perhaps, these shows' houses were display cases for a new model of consumption whose logic was mouthed wordlessly by every object in the *mise en scène* and by the spatial disposition of the same (Figure 1.3).

Haralovich's work on the specificity of the domestic interior of 1950s family sitcom was pioneering, while Lynn Spigel's slightly later work on this subject has been indispensable in making clear the intense entwinement of the 1950s family sitcom and the real world of burgeoning suburbia that it represented. In *Welcome to the Dreamhouse*, Spigel argues that 'the central preoccupation in the new suburban culture was the construction of a particular *discursive space* through which the family could mediate the contradictory impulses for a private haven on the one hand, and community participation on the other' (2001: 32).[4] Her observation that the opening credit sequences of these sitcoms 'encouraged audiences to perceive television's families as neighbors' (Spigel 2001: 43) makes clear the difficulty in delimiting the discursive space of actual suburbia from the discursive space of its representation on television. Spigel suggests exactly this blurry distinction between the real and the representational in her earlier book *Make Room for T.V.* when she argues that domestic sitcoms of the 1950s 'offered viewers a sense of imaginary transport, promising to carry them into the homes of familiar television neighbours, who lived in a new electronic landscape where the borders between fiction and reality were easily crossed' (1992: 180). While it is too easy and too lazy to suggest that spectators and readers often fall into the trap of confusing the real for the 'merely' represented, the case of the 1950s sitcom presents us with a special case. The drama of 1950s suburbia expansion was paralleled by the similar dramatic growth of television in the same period. Both entailed the radical development of infrastructural and technological means (of production, transportation, transmission and habitation) and both were representational. That is to say, both were real *and* representational, in a very strong sense.

Both Haralovich and Spigel – the latter of whose work is both synoptic and particularising – pay attention to numerous specificities in the way in which the 1950s suburban home was evoked, constructed and metonymised in family sitcoms from this period. Their aims, rather different from mine here, do not lead them to reflect on the specificity of Colonial Revival architecture in providing so many identical links in the metonymic chain that was the 'realism' of these sitcoms. Spigel traces the way in which television's bid to become 'a national medium' entailed the relocation of sitcoms from the city (in shows like *The Goldbergs* and *I Love Lucy*) to the suburbs, as well as the ascesis of earlier sitcoms' non-white ethnicities and the privileging of the putatively unmarked all-white Anglo-American family (the Cleavers, the Nelsons, the Andersons, and so on) (Spigel 1992: 150–1). This suburbanised blanching of the television family is indissociable from the sitcoms' universalising of the Colonial Revival house as the medium and ground of both this family and the medium of television itself. The Colonial Revival 'Cape Cod' ranch houses built in Levittown, New York eventually became equipped with television sets built into the house itself (often installed under the stairs that led into the open-plan living room). This image, drawn from architectural history, is the counterpart of the images of the Colonial Revival houses that appeared inside the screens of these built-in televisions. As television went national, so did the architectural style of its fictional houses, each of which, apparently, needed to be built in the national idiom of the Colonial Revival.

Apart from apparently reflecting, neutrally, the built culture of American suburbia (that built from the 1930s up through the 1950s), these houses' dedicated exposition and exhibition of Colonial Revival architecture enjoyed a range of ideological and aesthetic advantages. The Colonial Revival, in its most diffuse operations and instantiations, offers on its exterior some specific (if nominal) reference to early American architecture (the clapboard facade with black shutters, the pedimented door, etc.), but this exterior grants to the interior a radical fungibility. The most that the interiors of the 1950s family sitcoms share – like their real-life counterparts – were the relatively open-plan disposition of their first-floor living spaces and the relatively consistent colonial character of the objects arrayed therein. Thus, the Colonial Revival offers a pointedly referential surface without and a neutral volume within; this volume, however, the sitcoms' art direction suggests, is best and most effortlessly filled with artefacts that provide the continuity from outside to in. The house must commit itself to a public iteration of the 'national idiom', but it must remain empty enough of reference within so that any given family's accumulation of smaller consumer durables might both assume the appearance of contingency (what has been inherited, perhaps – like the portrait over Ozzie's bed) and secure the exhibition of taste (what has been acquired). The relative neutrality of the interior's architecture, in turn, grants the appearance of contingency to the plenum of the objects it houses: somehow these all just happen to reflect a taste for the national idiom.

All that the Colonial Revival Allows

Although space does not permit me to do so here, Douglas Sirk's melodramas of the 1950s offer fertile territory for further exploring the vicissitudes of Colonial Revival architecture in cinema. In films such as *All That Heaven Allows* (1955) and *There's Always Tomorrow* (1956), Colonial Revival architecture provides the ambience and the key to reading these stories of middle-class, middle-aged stuckness, social conformity and erotic privation. In the former film, we are given the opportunity to admire both the exterior and the interior of the Scotts' family home, a solid and compact iteration of the Colonial Revival. In the latter, although views of the Groveses' house exterior are suppressed, the shots of the interior emphasise the architectural elements and decorating choices that fully place this house as yet another example of the national idiom. Victoria L. Evans has usefully explored the way in which the Scott house in *All That Heaven Allows* allegorises the close-minded conservatism of the film's suburban setting (2017: 162–8). The exteriors for the film were actually shot on Universal Studio's backlot, specifically on an artificial street of houses known as 'Colonial Street' (Teague). These film's desperate (and, depending on how we read Sirk's filmmaking, potentially ironised) attempts to shore up the white, heterosexual American family are just as iterative – film to film – as the 1950s sitcoms discussed above. In fact, neither the sitcoms nor Sirk's films can be fully understood in isolation from one another. (Surely as much is already suggested in *All That Heaven Allows* when Corey Scott's children offer her a television to replace her lover whom they have banished from her life.) Sirk narrates the family in the key of melodrama (and even brushing close to tragedy at times), whereas the sitcoms nervously manage conflict in terms of comedy. But both films and television sitcoms are housed in the same Colonial Revival architecture. Cinema's insistence on this architecture finds a latter day iteration in the teen comedies of the 1980s: in films such as *Risky Business* (Paul Brickman, 1983) and *Ferris Bueller's Day Off* (John Hughes, 1986), in which Colonial Revival architecture's (apparently inevitable) presence signals the necessity of summoning its iconography as a means of comprehending and making visible the stakes of the American family itself. These films from the 1980s stage the misbehaviour of (mostly male) teenagers as potentially catastrophic threats to the value embodied by the property of the family home. If we can claim that some cultural memory of Sirk and the 1950s family sitcoms continues to circulate in these comedies, it is in no small part because of their shared reliance on the reassuring iconography of the Colonial Revival. These films, however, make something critical appear. In their fraught anxiety over the financial damage that might be done to the family by doing damage to the house and the possessions housed therein, these silly films make us see the Colonial Revival itself as a kind of currency – infinitely fungible and infinitely durable. The appearance of the Colonial Revival house in these representations is not unlike the appearance of the same sort of architecture on the back of United States paper currency (Independence Hall appears on the back of the $100 note, Monticello on the back of the $2 note, the White House on the back of the $20 note ...). The representation of the American family and the architecture that grounds its representation are as obstinately real, as flimsily symbolic, and as infinitely repeatable and expansive as the abstraction of money itself, which might explain this architecture's purchase on the American imaginary.

Notes

1 Wilson (2004: 15). William Strickland, the architect for the project, first proposed a brick tower, which was judged to be unsympathetic to the building's original architecture. The final design was much taller, but classical in style, and made of wood; these last two elements seem to have secured its sense of homogeneity with colonial architecture. Thus, early on, Colonial Revival architecture, as Wilson argues, began its tendency not just to repeat but to 'improve on' the past.
2 On this subject, see William B. Rhoads (1976), 'The Colonial Revival and American Nationalism', *Journal of the Society of Architectural Historians*, 35, no. 4 (December), pp. 239–54. (The occasion of this article is obviously the bicentennial celebrations observed during the year it was published.) See also David Gebhard (1987), 'The American Colonial Revival in the 1930s', *Wintherthur Portfolio*, 22, no. 2–3 (Summer–Autumn), pp. 109–48.
3 Haralovich provides a useful summary of the typical ways in which these houses' interior spaces are arrayed and deployed in *Leave it to Beaver* and *Father Knows Best*. See especially pp. 75–8.
4 This book's first chapter, 'The Suburban Home Companion: Television and the Neighborhood Ideal in Postwar America', is a major point of reference for understanding the relations between the construction of suburbia and the fictional construction of the family and suburbia in 1950s television sitcoms.

Works Cited

Ames, Kenneth (1985), 'Introduction', in Alan Axelrod (ed.), *The Colonial Revival in America*, New York and London: W. W. Norton and Company.

Belton, John (1992), *Widescreen Cinema*, Cambridge, MA: Harvard University Press.

Crowther, Bosley (1957), 'Screen: Williamsburg; Information Center at Colonial Site Opens and Special Film Has Premiere There', *New York Times*, 1 April.

Evans, Victoria L. (2017), *Douglas Sirk, Aesthetic Modernism and the Culture of Modernity*, Edinburgh: Edinburgh University Press.

Gebhard, David (1987), 'The American Colonial Revival in the 1930s', *Wintherthur Portfolio*, 22, no. 2–3 (Summer–Autumn), pp. 109–48.

Haralovich, Mary Beth (1989), 'Sitcoms and Suburbs: Positioning the 1950s Homemaker', *Quarterly Review of Film and Video*, 11, no. 1, pp. 61–83.

Hutchinson, Janet (1986), 'The Cure for Domestic Neglect: Better Homes in America, 1922–35', *Perspectives in Vernacular Architecture*, 2, pp. 168–78.

Rhoads, William B. (1976), 'The Colonial Revival and American Nationalism', *Journal of the Society of Architectural Historians*, 35, no. 4 (December), pp. 239–54.

Rhodes, John David (2006), '*White Christmas*, or Modernism', *Modernism/modernity*, 13, no. 2 (April), pp. 291–308.

Rhodes, John David (2017), *Spectacle of Property: The House in American Film*, Minneapolis and London: University of Minnesota Press.

Schneider, Daniel B. (1997), 'F.Y.I.', *New York Times*, 12 January, <http://www.nytimes.com/1997/01/12/nyregion/fyi-100064.html?pagewanted=2> (last accessed 3 August 2019).

Scully, Vincent (1976), *American Architecture and Urbanism*, New York: Praeger.

Spigel, Lynn (1992), *Make Room for TV: Television and the Family Idea in Postwar America*, Chicago and London: University of Chicago Press.

Spigel, Lynn (2001), *Welcome to the Dreamhouse: Popular Media and Postwar Suburbs*, Durham, NC: Duke University Press.

Szczepaniak-Gillece, Jocelyn (2012), 'In the House, in the Picture: Distance and Proximity in the American Mid-Century Neutralized Theater', *World Picture 7*, <http://www.worldpicturejournal.com/WP_7/Szczepaniak-Gillece.html> (last accessed 24 October 2019)

Teague, Kipp, 'Colonial and New England Streets', <www.retroweb.com/universal_colonial_street.html> (last accessed 29 October 2017).

Wilson, Richard Guy (2004), *The Colonial Revival House*, photography by Noah Sheldon, New York: Abrams.

CHAPTER 2

No Down Payment: Whiteness, Japanese American Masculinity and Architectural Space in the Cinematic Suburbs

Merrill Schleier

This chapter examines the imbrication of spatiality, masculinity and race in the melodrama and social problem film *No Down Payment* (Martin Ritt, 1957), one in a cycle that explores the adverse forces that impinge on the mid-century cinematic suburbs. The cycle includes *The Desperate Hours* (William Wyler, 1955), *Bigger Than Life* (Nicholas Ray, 1956) and *Crime of Passion* (Gerd Oswald, 1957) among others that refer both overtly and obliquely to race and housing issues often because of the subjects they omit, films in which suburban homes are either under siege by undesirable others who 'move in' or 'inhabit' the domestic realm and are jettisoned in order to restore a provisional, normative, white suburban hegemony and insure private property. As Eric Lott asserts when discussing film noir – an assertion also applicable to the aforementioned domestic melodramas – the exclusion or marginalisation of others frequently prompts us to dismiss racial associations as coincidental or as the ruses of metaphor when 'in fact such metaphorical ruses and the presence of black, Asian, or Mexican bodies confirm the central symbolic significance of color to the black-and-white world of many noirs' (Lott 1997: 545). Extending Lott's analysis, I seek to recover such covert and overt racial themes, which displace the fear of minorities, the lower classes and others to a myriad of external and internal threats, especially the era's countless acts of the real, and what historian Arnold R. Hirsch refers to as the 'hidden violence' perpetrated against those who sought equal housing, especially in the white suburbs (Hirsch 1998: 40). I also examine the discrete experiences and representations of Japanese Americans seeking housing from those of other minority groups in cinema so as to avoid essentialising a generic raced other. With regard to real housing exclusions during the post-war period, African Americans and Japanese Americans shared the most reviled status behind Mexican Americans and Chinese Americans; the former were constructed as aggressive, overly sexual and criminal, while the latter were labelled inassimilable and disloyal, especially after Japan's attack on Manchuria (1931) and later, the bombing of Pearl Harbor (1941).

The Japanese Americans' relationship to actual domestic space in the United States is a singularly vexed one, both before and after the Second World War, from the Alien Land Laws of the late nineteenth to early twentieth century designed to forbid Asian Americans from owning land to Roosevelt's Executive Order 9066 in 1942, which forced thousands of Japanese Americans to abandon their homes, to the subsequent confiscation of those homes through escheat, to the continuing racist policies that prevented Asian Americans from purchasing homes through governmental policies and the collusion of private capital. The renditions of Japanese Americans in post-war cinematic domestic space began to change for a variety of reasons, including the presence of Asian war brides after the Second World War and the Korean War, the guilt over the dropping of the atomic bombs on Hiroshima and Nagasaki, and the fear that non-aligned Asian countries would fall into communist hands.

I will discuss *No Down Payment* in light of other renditions of Japanese Americans in domestic space in a variety of post-war American films, including *Go For Broke!* (Robert Pirosh, 1951), *Bad Day at Black Rock* (John Sturges, 1955), and *The Crimson Kimono* (Samuel Fuller, 1959), arguing that it is a transitional film that allows Japanese Americans to gain entry into the suburbs only by ellipsis without disturbing white hegemony. I explore the representation of race from a multipronged perspective, taking into consideration both the construction of whiteness and the various iterations of difference that inhabit the narrative. The formation of both raced and gendered ideologies are embedded in the architectural styles, spatial plans and appurtenances of the film's domestic realm, realised in the production design and then enhanced by the entire *mise en scène*. Moreover, while the Japanese American character Iko and his family are delineated as the identified other, the depiction of whiteness is normalised and opaque, seen in the white gaze and the construction of cinematic domestic architectural space and its material objects.

White Flight and Homogenised Architectural Style and Space

The point of view in *No Down Payment* (1957) is primarily through the trials and tribulations of four white married couples in a Southern California suburban town, under pressure to achieve the American Dream, which leads ineluctably to several acts of violence. Concurrently one of the film's prominent subthemes concerns the efforts of an exemplary Japanese American family to gain entry to Sunrise Hills, a uniformly white, middle-class enclave. The film begins strategically with its eager thirty-something main protagonists David (Jeffrey Hunter) and Jean Martin (Patricia Owens) moving from polyglot, urban Los Angeles to their new dwelling in suburban Sunrise Hills via one of Los Angeles's new serpentine freeways built to accommodate both the city's urban congestion and the new private and segregated residential developments. These freeways were built not only to alleviate crowding, but designed to forge a spatial barrier or wedge between what historian Eric Avila has called the increasingly chocolate city and the vanilla suburbs (Avila 2006: 1). Seen from their car interior, the Martins' drive maps the actual centrifugal spatial journey of white Angelinos, which is indexical of their mass migration to the southern and eastern outskirts of Los Angeles, which exacerbated and concretised racial segregation patterns. Wishing to raise a family in this suburban enclave, the Martins depart a city that was traditionally linked to crime, congestion and blight, often erroneously associated with racial diversity. The final script makes this division clear, employing adjectives that are redolent of such racial divisions, referring to their 'exodus from the dark heart of a cramped and strangling city' filled with grime and soot to 'spacious sun-filled suburbia' (Yordan 1957: 1). On their freeway drive accompanied by an upbeat musical score, an extended close-up shot focuses on the smiling couple who are greeted with a succession of welcoming billboards that line the roadside, with such utopian monikers as Fairview Ranchos and Enchanted Homes, promising advantageous terms for veterans. Since the Federal Housing Authority (FHA) and Veterans Administration's rules did not extend these loans to Americans of African, Mexican and Asian descent or to single women, the freeway signs also serve as an address to white middle-class spectators.

Government in an alliance with private capital were complicit in the construction of such post-war east coast and west coast segregated suburbs, through redlining, zoning ordinances and discriminatory covenants that excluded non-whites, or what FHA manuals from the 1930s until 1950 baldly referred to as 'inharmonious racial or national groups' (Jackson 1985: 208; Brooks 2009: 184). Refusing to underwrite houses threatened by an 'invasion', they argued that blacks and other minorities were bad loan risks (Wright 1983: 247). The FHA warned further that: 'If a neighborhood is to retain stability, it is necessary that all properties shall continue to be occupied by the same social and racial classes' or else property values would decline (Jackson 1985: 208; Wiese 2004: 101), thus promoting what Arnold R. Hirsch calls a policy of racial containment (Hirsch 1998: 170). As Andrew Wiese points out, by the mid-1950s, 'suburbia' had become a spatial metaphor for whiteness itself (Wiese 2004: 109).

White racial homogeneity in *No Down Payment* (1957) is even registered in its architecture and spatial geography. A high angle shot of the fictional Sunrise Hills development shot on location in the outskirts of Los Angeles surveys a row of identical, mid-century Ranch Style dwellings that seem to extend limitlessly to the mountain range in the distance, a decidedly non-urban location. The previous signage on the road indicates that the Martins are driving down Highway 39 to the segregated subdivisions of Orange County, the actual site of white flight. The pale stucco, almost identical homes spread horizontally outward from the street, meant to convey both sameness and inevitability, serving as the material embodiment of heteronormativity and the nuclear family. Yet in contrast to its material expansion, Sunrise Hills developers practice racial containment and white hegemony by refusing to sell homes to minorities while other dwellings are sold liberally to undesirable white denizens such as the lower-class Boones and the middle-class alcoholic philanderer Jerry Flagg (Tony Randall) and his complicit wife, Isabelle (Sheree North).

William Levitt, the largest east coast suburban builder, instituted a whites only policy in his several Levittown east coast developments, yet sold to diverse ethnic and religious minorities of various classes, thereby constructing a new type of whiteness that had been absent from heterogeneous cities in which diverse peoples traditionally lived with their own kind. Referring to African Americans, in a statement that referred implicitly to racial minorities, he claimed in 1954:

> I have come to know that if we sell one house to a Negro family, then ninety to ninety five percent of our white customers will not buy into the community. That is their attitude, not ours. We did not create it, and cannot cure it ... We can solve a housing problem or we can try to solve a racial problem, but we cannot combine the two. (Levitt 1954: 26–7)

The same is true of the suburban spaces in Southern California, particularly the Lakewood development near Long Beach, the largest of its kind on the west coast, which included 17,500 houses and 80,000 people, almost all white (Hayden 2003: 139).

Production designer Henry Blumenthal designed the interiors of the suburban Sunrise Hills dwellings in *No Down Payment* for ideological purposes as what Robert Beuka has termed in another context, places of 'surveillance and entrapment', which I argue further instantiates an enforced white conformity and a heteronormative gaze, while embedding the architectural style with ideological content (Beuka 2004: 89).

Blumenthal achieves the former by caricaturing typical features of west coast Ranch houses, to represent what social critic William H. Whyte referred to as the 'dormitory for the organization man' (Whyte 1956: 10). It is important to note that the FHA sanctioned only certain styles of architecture, such as various iterations of the Colonial Revival or Ranch Style dwelling on the west coast. Built in the suburbs of Los Angeles, the latter was viewed as a quintessentially regional American idiom that referenced both Spanish missions and western ranches, and thus redolent of nationalist and patriotic American values. They were open-planned with rooms connected to enclosed patios and floor-to-ceiling glass panels and sliding doors, providing unobstructed views of backyards, which afforded the illusion of increased spatiality and informal outdoor living. Promoted in the pages of *House Beautiful* and other shelter magazines, they were regarded as 'nativist, regional and humanistic' (Penick 2007: 79), serving as an intrinsically American rejoinder to the putative sameness of International Style modernism. Yet the FHA's own design guidelines for American housing developments included a low 'Adjustment for Conformity' rating for houses that digressed too much from their prescriptions, which unsurprisingly mirrored their policies on race, hence advocating a policy of stylistic containment (Wright 1983: 251). As Robert Beuka noted, 'homogeneity of architectural and landscape styles bespoke a desire to elide the very notion of difference among suburban residents' (Beuka 2008: 5).

The Sunrise Hills production designed Ranch Style houses, which are placed only a few feet from one another, are porous and prompt boundary transgressions, prompting neighbours to encroach on each other's space, reinforcing the ideological orthodoxy consonant with the open plans, the picture windows and the American nativism the architecture purports to represent. As social critic William Whyte noted in *The Organization Man* (1956), 'the picture (outside) the picture window is what is going on inside – or what is going on inside other people's picture windows' (389).

For example, shortly after the Martins move into their new home, Herman Kreitzer (Pat Hingle) and his wife Betty (Barbara Rush) observe the new occupants from their glass-walled living room and call out to welcome them, before walking through the Martins' yard uninvited, urging them to attend an evening barbecue. While ostensibly a friendly gesture, it also evinces easy intrusion and the implied expectation of heteronormative familial engagement and socialising. Likewise when the Martins, in turn, look through their large, un-curtained living room window, they witness Troy (Cameron Mitchell) and Leola Boone (Joanne Woodward) frolicking in their marital bed. The propinquity of their living arrangements leads to acts of sexual harassment and violence perpetrated against Jean Martin later in the film.

Compromised and Redeemed White Masculinity

Most of the modern appliances in Blumenthal's tiny, identically constructed kitchens have been purchased on credit as the film and its title repeatedly make clear. For example, neighbour Jerry Flagg says to Dave, 'Do you want to buy yourself a good used car? No money down. Nothing to lose.' Yet despite the putative material plenty, the houses' gloomy wallpaper and wood panelling further constrict the already circumscribed space, which acts as a cipher for the male breadwinners' failure to keep up with the rise of an ever-increasing consumerism. In the script, Troy Boone refers to them as 'cardboard houses fancied up with glass and gadgets' (Yordan 1957: 20A). As social critics such as William Whyte, David Riesman and Vance Packard lamented, spineless, conforming men who were more concerned with economic security replaced the stalwart business tycoons and individualists of yesteryear (Schleier 2009: 219). In view of such mid-century material prosperity, Catherine Jurca claims that it is ironic that social critics represented comfortable white middle-class men as the era's unlikely victims; while, as Nicolaides and Wiese point out, these self-same commentators were conspicuously silent on matters of race and its real victims (Jurca 2001: 18–19; Nicolaides and Wiese 2006: 291).

Two of the four Sunrise Hills husbands are this type of challenged white organisation men, but are redeemed by the film's denouement through absorption into the corporate system. Dave Martin is an ineffectual electronics engineer who is being pressured at work and at home to sell automation machines rather than follow his passion for design while passively sitting by and allowing his wife to be pawed by two of the other husbands. Martin finally rejects the corporate pressure and returns to his love of creative engineering, and violently confronts Troy Boone for assaulting his wife. Alcoholic Jerry Flagg, who is always in need of money, hawks used cars on commission and cannot seem to stop womanising. By the end of the film, Flagg has decided to take a salaried job, thus alleviating the pressure which it is implied has contributed to his drinking and bad behaviour. Swarthy lower class Troy Boone is also a philanderer; a Tennessean with a decidedly southern accent, who is often seen in dark-coloured sports jackets or uniforms, he serves as a stand-in for the feared racial minorities who haunted the white imaginary. A former Second World War hero who committed atrocities during the Japanese campaign, he is awaiting a decision on his application for the town's police chief. Troy suffers from PTSD, abuses his wife and eventually commits a rape. Herman Kreitzer manages an appliance store in the Sunrise Hills shopping centre, feeding the consumerist desires of his neighbours. He begins the film as a doubting Thomas, washing his car on Sunday in full view of his church-attending neighbours. The only male character in a supervisory role and a prominent position on the town council, Herman finally experiences an epiphany concerning racial integration, which restores his confidence in the church. Hence all of the white male suburban breadwinners begin with their masculinity in deficit, but by succumbing to the American Dream, three of the four preserve the capitalist suburban order of private ownership and the consumption of goods.

Japanese American Housing and Masculinity

Despite its prosperous consumer driven, material spaces, Sunrise Hills cannot contain the anger and dysfunction that is roiling underneath its physically walled-in and psychic surfaces. The threat to suburban domestic equanimity comes from both without and within – a combination of class envy, racism against the Japanese and Japanese Americans, and misogyny, which provide the flame that lights the powder keg. One of the film's largest repressions is the absence of the real harassment and violence that were perpetrated against non-white minorities who sought to challenge the nation's housing discrimination in the 1950s in the form of 'house bombings, arson, death, threats, physical assaults, and mob demonstrations' which became an ugly commonplace in post-war suburbia (Nicolaides and Wiese 2006: 322). Perhaps the most famous case involved the African American Myers family who moved into Pennsylvania's Levittown in 1957 amidst twenty-four-hour-a-day protests, harassment and vandalism.

During and after the Second World War, many West Coast Japanese Americans also experienced various acts of both governmental aggression and physical violence. After the attack on Pearl Harbor, more than 120,000 were forced to leave their homes and sell their possessions on short notice for pennies on the dollar. Housed initially in racetracks in dehumanising horse stalls, they were subsequently sent to internment concentration camps in various badland sites such as Manzanar, Tulelake and Topaz. While they were away, their homes were often confiscated by a process known as escheat, the state claiming that they had been abandoned. When they returned, many could not find replacement housing or were relocated to segregated trailer parks or compelled to move to crowded Japan towns. A Nisei family in all-white Glendale had their rental property burnt to the ground in 1948, as did others, a practice that continued throughout the 1950s in rural California.

As Marita Sturken points out, wartime battles and white middle-class families who struggled on the home front were often rendered in the visual arts, while the Japanese internment – and I would add the postwar domestic difficulties of Japanese Americans – have resisted certain kinds of representation, especially in Hollywood cinema (Sturken 2001: 38). An exception is the film *Bad Day at Black Rock*, which considers the violence perpetrated against Japanese Americans and their domiciles during and after the war, re-enacting 'the absent presence of the Japanese internment' reinforced by the fictional town's location in the Eastern Sierras near Manzanar (Tajiri in Sturken 2001: 40). The town bully Reno Smith (Robert Ryan) and his group of surly cowboys dominate the isolated location and harbour a murderous secret concerning the town's only Japanese American, Komoko. Soon after the arrival of stranger John Macreedy (Spencer Tracy) by train, they display their xenophobia by trying to bar his entry. Macreedy is there to deliver the fallen Japanese American hero's medal to Komoko, the father of the deceased, and the man who saved Macreedy's life, a fact which the ruffians are initially unaware of. Both Komoko and his son are dead, which serves further to underscore the idea of the erased Japanese American in both the California landscape and its domestic spaces.

When the town bullies discover later that Macreedy is looking for Komoko, they go to great lengths to sabotage his journey to preserve the town's racist underbelly – Reno's murder of the elder Japanese American who he refers to as a 'lousy Jap farmer' and 'a mad dog'. Supposedly Reno's own failure in being turned down for the military after Pearl Harbor prompted him to kill the Japanese American; but he also learned that there was water on Komoko's land, providing an opportunity to confiscate the property, much like white Californians did to Japanese Americans in the name of the state during their forced internment.

In accord with his Japanese American deceased army buddy who he comes to represent, the one-armed, war-wounded Macreedy is designated as other by proxy by the suspicious and inbred group of failed white men — one of whom calls him a 'yellow bellied Jap lover' — even using judo and karate to foil his adversaries in one scene. Almost immediately, they try to prevent him from checking into the town's only domestic lodging, the Blake Hotel, in accord with America's white suburban dwellers that sought to exclude minorities. There is a tension between the expansive Western landscape and the constricted interior spaces where most of the film's action takes place, referencing the inwardness and fear of all things foreign that characterised the 1950s (Polan commentary). Finally hiring a jeep, Macreedy drives to the edge of town to find Komoko, only to discover the latter's house burnt to the ground, a cipher of the violence perpetrated against Japanese Americans' domestic spaces before and after the war.

All Asian Americans experienced various types of domestic exclusions in the post-war period; Southern California realtors refused to show them houses for fear of losing their jobs; while homeowners declined to sell, convinced that their property values would plummet. One of the most prominent examples was the Korean American army doctor Sammy Lee, an Olympic gold medallist and a dinner invitee to the White House with President Eisenhower, who was refused homes in both Southern Garden Grove and Orange County (Brooks 2009: 218). Only through favourable publicity and the intervention of Vice President Richard Nixon was Lee able to acquire property in one of California's suburban neighbourhoods. Likewise Japanese American Iko is initially barred from Sunrise Hills in *No Down Payment*, but through the influence of his boss Herman Kreitzer, the town council and the church, he is finally admitted by ellipsis.

Japanese American Masculinity in *No Down Payment's* Suburbia

Sunrise Hills and the town's racist housing policies in *No Down Payment* are primarily explored in the film's delineation of Iko, the only major character who lacks a surname (he is referred to as Iko Matuko in the script) and whose appellation is feminine in the Japanese language. Seen initially in a close-up shot, crouching in the appliance store's picture window, he is arranging items reinforcing the stereotype of the 'oh-so-artistic Oriental' (Kelley and Ryan [1947] 2006: 13) seen from the point of view of the evaluative gazes of his white boss Herman and neighbour Jean Martin (Figure 2.1). Iko echoes the representation of Asian America male cinematic characters that are often seen in feminised, subservient positions 'lacking in the traditional masculine qualities associated with Anglo American males', and heir to the 'good' Asian men of the Charlie Chan stories and films (Xing 1998: 61). Asians and Asian Americans are often depicted as stereotypical houseboys or underlings, what Frank Chin refers to as the Asian 'house nigger type' (Chin 1972, quoted in

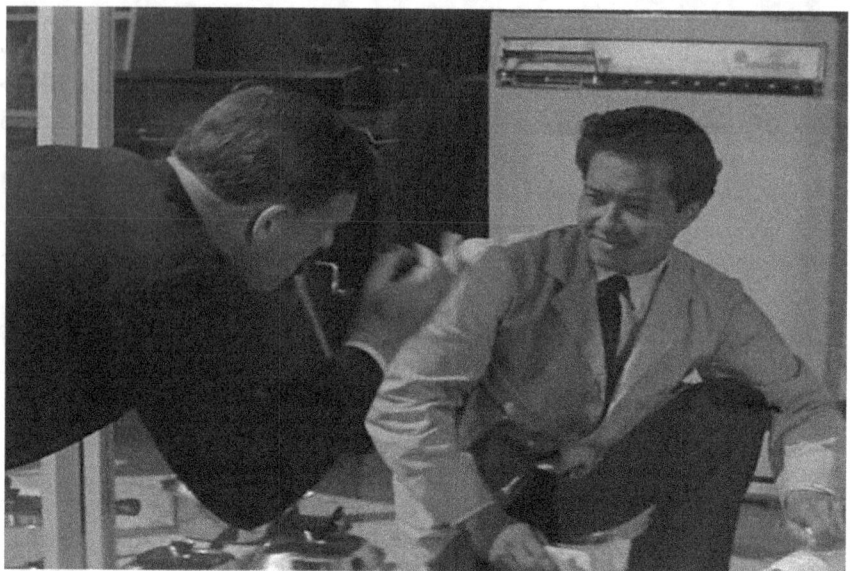

Figure 2.1 Iko in store window in *No Down Payment* (1957). Film still.

Xing 1998: 61). Physically constrained further like an object behind the store's transparent glass display, in accord with the appliances he assembles, the wavy-haired, feminised Iko performs the role of exhibited other or exotic curiosity. From his squatting posture, he looks up and smiles obsequiously at his admiring observers who comment favourably on his aesthetic talents.

In another scene, Iko requests a conference with his boss Herman, establishing a hierarchy of the white manager and subservient minority employee, a common trope in post-war films about Japanese American–Caucasian relations such as *Go For Broke!* (1951). We learn through their conversation that Herman has even dined at Iko's home but not vice versa, perhaps because of the constant surveillance exercised by the former's intrusive Caucasian neighbours; indeed, we never see them socialising in the same domestic environs, hence instantiating the same segregation patterns as its actual counterparts. When another dinner invitation is requested, Iko informs Herman that his wife is pressuring him to move to Sunrise Hills to be closer to his job – currently he must commute three hours per day – further depriving the feminised Iko of masculine agency.

Rather than seeking redress through legal or collective means, instead Iko implores Herman to intervene on his behalf because of the latter's position on the city council, further transferring authority to an individual white superior. When Herman equivocates, Iko employs legal and ethical rationale for his deserved inclusion while pointing to his similarity to white American veterans: 'I earn my money Herman. I have the right to live in a house that I can afford. I am a GI. I qualify under the same bill like all you GIs here.'

In addition, Iko appeals to their shared values in order to elicit Herman's sympathy, a concern for their children's welfare, thus establishing his ready assimilability. This is the reverse of the previous wartime stereotypes of Japanese Americans as exotic traitors that were part of the United States propaganda campaign to justify their forced evacuation and imprisonment.

Later in a conference with his wife in their living room, the formerly noncommittal Herman supports Iko because of his employee's loyalty and exemplary skills, identifying the latter as a model minority. It is significant to note that John McPartland's novel upon which the film is based featured an African American instead of an Asian American, perhaps because the latter minority was currently looked upon more favourably than the former. Historian Charlotte Brooks explains that the model Asian and Asian American are racist tropes that gained currency early in the Cold War, at a time when the United States 'sought to draw into its sphere the newly-independent, non-aligned nations of post-World War II Asia' such as Taiwan, the Philippines and Japan as a bulwark against international communism, hence the necessity of treating its own citizens fairly (Brooks 2009: 196). Naoko Shibusawa argues further that Japan's educated workforce, corporate infrastructure and centralised government bureaucracy, and its location near China and the Soviet Union rendered it particularly important to United States Cold War geostrategy (Shibusawa 2006: 259).

Although there were still barriers against Asian Americans gaining admittance to the suburbs in both Northern and Southern California in the early 1950s as previously mentioned, the tide began to turn in their favour because of such international policy at a time of the most intense racial conflicts between whites and blacks over housing (Brooks 2009: 197). Asian Americans are hence represented as able to successfully assimilate not only due to their supposed 'stoic patience, political obedience, and self improvement' but because they were not 'black', further explaining the decision not to employ an African American family in the film (Lee 1999: 145). Indeed one reviewer even accused the filmmakers of 'sidestepping the Negro vs. white social struggles' which characterised the nation (Gilbert 1957: 32).

Herman, as the film's ethical and legal conscience, serves to instantiate white liberal values, citing further the so-called fairness of the new American policy concerning domestic space by invoking the United States Supreme Court – probably a reference to the landmark case Shelley v. Kramer (1948), which recognised the unenforceability of racially based covenant agreements. Yet Herman's new-found advocacy indicates that Caucasian attitudes, especially toward Japanese Americans moving in to traditionally white neighbourhoods were changing, appealing to the film's audience to follow suit. But as his wife Betty reminds him, men like the alcoholic Jerry and the angry veteran Troy will never accept a Japanese American in their midst. Indeed in an unused line in the final script, Troy asserts belligerently that if it wasn't for his wartime service 'Sunrise Hills would be a Japanese rice field today!', which demonstrates his insurmountable racist attitudes (Yordan 1957: 86). But in a confrontational moment, Herman challenges Betty to seek higher council through the intervention of Reverend Norton, while implying that he will consult the town council. The consultation of Reverend Norton by ellipsis implies that Iko and his family are Christians, a fact corroborated later, and in keeping with US Cold War policy, which advocated the beneficial integration of Japanese Americans with their white neighbours.

Paradoxically the Japanese body is already contained within the walls of Sunrise Hills in degraded form, as the plundered remains of the Second World War, an absent presence seen in the diverse objects displayed in Troy's garage, including demonic masks, prints of courtesans and weaponry (Figure 2.2). In the new post-war suburban homes, the garage is a homosocial space where men fix their cars or engage in do-it-yourself projects, the mid-century version of the man cave. Thus, when Troy invites the flirtatious Jean Martin to see his wartime collection without her unassertive husband, she engages in a clear boundary transgression and subjects herself to danger. In the garage's masculinised interior, Troy informs her proudly that his war trophies were acquired through direct combat, foreshadowing the violence of which he is still capable. He offers her a sword which she mistakenly handles, and informs her that he confiscated it from 'a little Japanese colonel', whose bunker he blew up with a bazooka, foreshadowing his sexual assault of her. Revealing his PTSD and class resentment, Troy confides, 'If I didn't have my memories, I'd crawl into my car and turn on the exhaust. You think it makes me feel like a man greasing cars and cleaning toilets in gas stations.'

Later, when he is passed over for the police chief position because of his lack of a college degree, Troy rapes Jean Martin in an act of

Figure 2.2 Troy Boone in his garage in *No Down Payment* (1957). Film still.

retribution, transferring his racist violence and his class bitterness onto the female body. Significantly Troy dies later under the wheel of his car in the trophy-filled garage, a just punishment for his aggression against the Japanese during the war and against women – both Jean and his long suffering wife Leola. Filmed a little over a decade after the Second World War, *No Down Payment* portrays the cinematic Japanese – previously vilified in such films as *Destination Tokyo* (Delmer Daves, 1943) and *Guadalcanal Diary* (Lewis Seiler, 1943) – as the hapless victims of a sadistic American sergeant, while ushering in a new attitude toward Japanese Americans, seen in the implied inclusion of Iko into the suburban space that was once inhabited by Troy.

Changing Attitudes Towards Japanese Americans in Cinema's Post-war Domestic Spaces

Opinions towards Japanese Americans in cinema began to change with the release of *Go For Broke!* (1951), which celebrated the heroism of the segregated 442nd regiment made up almost solely of 'Buddhaheads', who were purportedly the most decorated small regiment for their size. The film instantiates the model minority trope that is later offered up in *No Down Payment*, representing Japanese Americans as loyal, brave and willing to go to any lengths to help their fellow soldiers. Released in the early years of the Cold War, *Go for Broke!* was meant not only to celebrate Nisei bravery, but also to combat the continued racism against Japanese Americans. Starring Van Johnson as Lieutenant Grayson, the film's other main plot is his journey from intolerant racist to understanding advocate of minorities. Grayson is not happy commanding 'Japs', as he makes abundantly clear to his superior in Mississippi, and requests that he be sent back to the 36th division from his home state, Texas. Through the course of commanding his platoon, Grayson comes to respect his charges and disavows his previous racist beliefs, telling former racist Sergeant Cully: 'They're not Japs. They are Japanese Americans – Nisei. Buddhaheads but not Japs. They don't like it and neither do I.'

Ultimately the 442nd division rescues the Texas division who are surrounded by Nazis, prompting even the respect of Sergeant Cully. The last scene shows some of the Nisei and their white counterparts locked arm in arm in a newfound demonstration of solidarity and trust as they head home from Europe, gesturing toward their ability to coexist in the same environs as they did on the battlefield.

In spite of the best intentions of the film, the 442nd regiment is housed in segregated domestic quarters, administered by their Caucasian superiors. There is almost no mention of the relocation camps where most of their relatives are housed except when one of the soldiers reads a letter from home or others send packages to their families. Their bunk is rendered as chaotic, dirty and undisciplined, gambling, unauthorised pets and unapproved food abound, and order is imposed by the Caucasian supervision of Grayson. When the Nisei are initially sent to the European front, they are likewise excluded from its domestic spaces, precluding any suggestion of fraternising or miscegenation. For example, when an attractive and flirtatious Roman lady opens her shutters, she spies the members of the 442nd leaning against her apartment building. Looking past the Nisei, whom she ignores as possible love interests, she discovers Lieutenant Grayson under her window and invites him inside, cooing '*que alto*' and calling him John.

Tall and blonde, Grayson provides a physical contrast to the much shorter Japanese Americans he is assigned to command, a staging device meant to underscore racial difference, establishing the white domination and the racial hierarchies the film presents. Male Japanese American bodies are initially rendered in stereotypically feminised, comedic or incompetent poses, which is frequently registered by Grayson's repulsion. As Takashi Fujitani points out, in *Go for Broke!* there is an overall emasculation of the Nisei soldiers that serves to domesticate them

(Fujitani 2001: 250). When Grayson arrives, he witnesses Hawaiian Buddhahead entertainment, consisting of a feminised, hip swinging hula dance accompanied by the ukulele. The film suggests that through Grayson's discipline and training, the Japanese American body has been masculinised and his spaces Americanised, preparing him for the rigours of war, thus supporting the idea of Japanese American assimilability.

Samuel Fuller's *The Crimson Kimono* (1959), completed two years after *No Down Payment*, goes a step further in showing the successful inclusion of Japanese Americans into formerly white domestic spaces, while still commenting on segregation practices in the United States. The plot revolves around the detective duo, Caucasian Charlie Bancroft (Glenn Corbett) and Japanese American Joe Kojaku (James Shigeta), who are assigned to solve the murder of stripper Sugar Torch (Gloria Pall). Significantly Sugar was in the process of incorporating *japonaiserie* into her striptease act, including a kimono, a samurai and a kendo performer, which leads the detectives into Los Angeles's segregated Japantown with its private cemeteries, Buddhist temples and Nisei celebrations. The fusion of Japanese and western cultural tropes is a prevalent theme throughout the film, serving as a plea for cross-cultural harmony and exchange.

While *No Down Payment* took the tentative step of including the model Japanese American family into the suburbs by ellipsis, *The Crimson Kimono*'s two detectives are roommates in the swanky Gaylord Hotel Apartments on Wilshire Boulevard, a bachelor pad that even provides room service. Significantly, production designer Robert Boyle, who gained fame working with Alfred Hitchcock, appointed the apartment with Korean wartime and military imagery and commendations and a plentiful array of tasteful Japanese figurines, prints and other works of art, demonstrating the harmonious integration of two diverse cultural traditions as ciphers of their gendered personalities, while pointing specifically to Joe's developed aesthetic tastes.

The detectives' cohabitation also builds on the implications presented in *Go for Broke!* and *No Down Payment* that Japanese Americans and Caucasian Americans who fought together as loyal confederates are compatible in domestic space, whether in a neighbourhood or an individual dwelling. Indeed, during the Korean War, Rifleman Joe saved Company Officer Charlie's life, even donating his blood to keep the latter alive, rendering them symbolic brothers, obviating the racist claims of difference and incompatibility that informed FHA-inspired housing exclusions. Japanese American loyalty is further underscored when Joe accompanies Mr Yoshinada, who may know one of the murder suspects, to the Japanese American cemetery to pay homage to his son who was awarded the Congressional Medal of Honor. A downward tilt shot enumerates the mass of graves before terminating on a plaque featuring the words of General Mark Clark who commanded the 442nd division, praising the loyalty and courage of the Nisei during the Second World War, before the camera moves to a commendation by President Eisenhower for those who died in Korea.

Despite the film's appeal for the integration of racial minorities in domestic space, much of the action takes place in the segregated environs of Japantown, a crowded warren of shops, run-down apartment buildings and seedy streets, which are contrasted with the clean modernist environs of police department headquarters and the upscale dwelling of Charlie and Joe on Wilshire, a tale of three cities. Yet even in the confederates' domestic space, the Caucasian–Japanese American wartime hierarchy is still entrenched, with white Charlie as sergeant and Japanese American Joe as minion and aspirant. The domineering superior even strides into Joe's bedroom while he is still asleep, dictating the day's investigative tasks while paternalistically offering to buy his subordinate a fancy breakfast.

Yet the homosocial coupling of Charlie and Joe serves as a prelude to the film's other theme, the love story between Joe and white artist Christine Downes (who painted a portrait of Sugar Torch in a kimono before her demise), thus presenting the previous tabooed subject of miscegenation. Although films such as *Japanese War Bride* (King Vidor, 1952) and *Sayonara* (Joshua Logan, 1957) dealt with the marriage between Caucasian soldiers and Asian brides, this film explores specifically the plight of Japanese Americans' interracial relationships, both fraternal and romantic, and their difficulties assimilating in their own country.

Subsequent to an attempt on Chris's life, the detectives provide her with police protection in their bachelor pad. Charlie has already fallen in love with her and Joe is about to, even spurning the advances of a Japanese American Kibei lady and her old-fashioned parents. During an intimate conversation, Chris discovers that Joe's father is an artist and that the detective has his own aesthetic opinions, even willing to critique her artwork. In his living room, she learns that Joe is also a talented pianist, playing her the traditional Japanese tune 'Red Dragon Fly' which concerns the longings for both Japanese traditions and a lost love. The mesmerising melody acts as a bridge to draw Chris closer, and she falls in love with Joe in return, spurning the mooning Charlie. The film thus makes a plea for emotional affinity instead of racial and ethnic similarity – here their joint interest in aesthetics and culture. Ultimately Joe must deal

Figure 2.3 Iko and family departing the church in *No Down Payment* (1957). Film still.

with his own Japanese American identity and the imagined racism of his partner Charlie and paramour Chris, before he can accept a heretofore forbidden love.

Conclusion

No Down Payment serves as a transitional film in the acceptance of Japanese Americans into post-war suburban domestic space, while maintaining white hegemony in its heteronormative relations, architectural style and spatial practices. In a symbolic reallocation of tenancy, 'darkened' Troy and the racism of the Second World War are symbolically expelled and replaced by the new model minority Iko. Yet we never view Iko at home in the white suburban space of Sunrise Hills; rather he and his family are seen leaving the town's church, implying that they are Christian, at a time when most Japanese Americans described themselves as either Buddhists or unaffiliated (Figure 2.3).

In 1957, Hollywood still considered it too challenging to show minorities transgressing private white suburban boundaries, when fears of miscegenation were prevalent. That would occur two years later in such films as *The Crimson Kimono* and *Take a Giant Step* (Philip Leacock, 1959). But the problem of suburban segregation and the exclusion of difference had not been resolved in either *No Down Payment* or the nation. Prior to Troy's death, his wife Leola decides to leave after years of verbal and physical abuse, reducing him to a blubbering weakling. The figure of a departing, now unmarried Leola Boone suggests that Hollywood, in collusion with US governmental policy, still advocated for the white normative nuclear family at the expense of single women, thus continuing to exclude otherness.

Works Cited

Avila, Eric (2006), *Popular Culture in the Age of White Flight: Fear and Fantasy in Suburban Los Angeles*, Berkeley and Los Angeles: University of California Press.

Beuka, Robert (2004), *SuburbiaNation: Reading Suburban Landscape in Twentieth Century American Film and Fiction*, New York: Palgrave Macmillan.

Beuka, Robert (2008), 'The View Through the Picture Window Surveillance and Entrapment Motifs in Suburban Films', in Andrew Blauvelt (ed.), *Worlds Away: New Suburban Landscapes*, Minneapolis: Walker Art Center, pp. 89–100.

Brooks, Charlotte (2009), *Alien Neighbors, Foreign Friends: Asian Americans, Housing, and the Transformation of Urban California*, Chicago: University of Chicago Press.

Chin, Frank [1972], 'Confessions of a Chinatown Boy', *Bulletin of Concerned Asian Scholars*, no. 67, now in Jun Xing (1998), *Asian America Through the Lens: History, Representation and Identity*, Walnut Creek, CA: Altamira Press.

Dombrowski, Lisa (2008), *The Films of Samuel Fuller: If You Die I'll Kill You*, Middletown, CT: Wesleyan University Press.

Fujitani, T. (2001), '*Go For Broke*, the Movie: Japanese American Soldiers in U.S. National, Military, and Racial Discourses', in T. Fujitani, Geoffey M. White and Lisa Yoneyama (eds), *Perilous Memories: The Asia-Pacific War(s)*, Durham, NC and London: Duke University Press. 239–66.

Gilbert, Justin (1957), 'No Down Payment', *New York Mirror*, 31 October, n.p. Clipping File. Margaret Herrick Library of the Academy of Motion Picture Arts and Sciences (AMPAS), Los Angeles.

Hayden, Dolores (2003), *Building Suburbia Green Fields and Urban Growth, 1820–2000*, New York: Vintage Books.

Hirsch, Arnold R. (1998), *Making the Second Ghetto: Race and Housing 1940–1960*, Chicago: University of Chicago Press.

Jackson, Kenneth T. (1985), *Crabgrass Frontier: The Suburbanization of the United States*, New York: Oxford University Press.

Kelley, Frank and Cornelius Ryan [1947], *Star Spangled Mikado*, New York: R. M. McBride, now in Naoko Shibusawa (2006), *America's Geisha Ally*, Boston, MA: Harvard University Press.

Jurca, Catherine (2001), *White Diaspora: The Suburb and the Twentieth-Century American Novel*, Princeton, NJ and Oxford: Princeton University Press.

Lee, Robert G. (1999), *Orientals: Asian Americans in Popular Culture*, Philadelphia: Temple University Press.

Levitt, William, interviewed by Craig Thompson (1954), 'Growing Pains of a Brand New City', *Saturday Evening Post*, 227, pp. 26–7, 71–2.

Lott, Eric (1997), 'The Whiteness of Film Noir', *American Literary History*, no. 9, pp. 542–66.

McPartland, John (1957), *No Down Payment*, New York: Simon & Schuster.

Nicolaides, Becky M. and Andrew Wiese (2006), *The Suburb Reader*, London: Routledge.

Penick, Monica Michelle (2007), 'The Pace Setter Houses: Livable Modernism in Postwar America', unpublished PhD thesis, University of Texas at Austin, Texas.

Polan, Dana (2005), Commentary, *Bad Day at Black Rock* (Sturges, 1955), DVD, WarnerBrothers.

Rowley, Stephen (2015), *Movie Towns and Sitcom Suburbs: Building Hollywood's Bad Communities*, New York: Palgrave Macmillan.

Schleier, Merrill (2009), *Skyscraper Cinema Architecture and Gender in American Film*, Minneapolis: University of Minnesota Press.

Shibusawa, Naoko (2006), *America's Geisha Ally: Reimagining the Japanese Enemy*, Cambridge, MA: Harvard University Press.

Sturken, Marita (2001), 'Absent Images of Memory: Remembering and Reenacting the Japanese Internment', in T. Fujitani, Geoffey M. White and Lisa Yoneyama (eds), *Perilous Memories: The Asia-Pacific War(s)*, Durham, NC and London: Duke University Press, pp. 33–49.

Tajiri, Rea (1991), *History and Memory*, Distributed by Electronic Arts Internix, New York, quoted in Sturken, above.

Wiese, Andrew (2004), *Places of Their Own: African American Suburbanization in the Twentieth Century*, Chicago: University of Chicago Press.

Whyte, William H. (1956), *The Organization Man*, New York: Simon and Schuster.

Wright, Gwendolyn (1983), *Building the Dream: A History of Housing in America*, Cambridge, MA: MIT Press.

Yordan, Philip (1957), 'No Down Payment', final revised script, 16 April, Martin Ritt Collection, Box 22, folder 221, AMPAS, Los Angeles.

Xing, Jun (1998), *Asian America Through the Lens: History, Representation, and Identity*, Walnut Creek, CA: Altamira Press.

CHAPTER 3

Resist, Redefine, Appropriate: Negotiating the Domestic Space in Contemporary Female Biopics

Victoria Pastor-González

In the last few years, there has been a notable increase in the number of female-fronted biopics, from *Hidden Figures* (Theodore Melfi, 2016), to *Jackie* (Pablo Larraín, 2016), *The Iron Lady* (Phyllida Lloyd, 2011), *Big Eyes* (Tim Burton, 2014) or *Queen of Katwe* (Mira Nair, 2016),[1] to name just a few. However, celebratory reports of this remarkable phenomenon are frequently punctuated with a sense of urgency. As veteran producer Alison Owen emphatically puts it: 'we're currently on the crest of a new wave. I've seen this wave before, and then it subsides' (Newland, 2017). Paying heed to the advice of experts, it seems that we must take advantage of this perhaps brief surge in production to take the pulse on the current situation of the female biopic. Moreover, it is not just numbers that should justify our interest, but more importantly the significant shift from narratives of victimisation and failure to ones of empowerment and triumph.

In his comprehensive study of the biopic genre, Dennis Bingham argues that whilst biopics about men have evolved from the early celebratory melodramatic formula to the postmodern and parodic, biopics of women 'are weighted down by myths of suffering, victimization and failure' (Bingham 2010: 10). Films about real women seem to revert with predictable regularity to the biome of melodrama and realism that defined the 'warts-and-all' biopic after the 1950s. A further legacy of that era was a taste for exploring 'the private lives and travails' of famous protagonists (Bingham 2010: 19), which in the case of the female biopic frequently implies – then and now – an insistence on the protagonist's inability to balance or to establish a clear distinction between the public and private spheres.

In the case of female artists this melodramatic formula 'reproduces the double standard of our culture concerning creativity – men create as a result of personal genius, but women come to do so through passionate love and loss' (Moine 2014: 63). For Moine, *Coco before Chanel* (Anne Fontaine, 2009) and *La Môme/La Vie en Rose* (Olivier Dahan, 2007) are contemporary examples of this tendency, where the creative forces of the two female protagonists are closely linked with personal tragedy and suffering. I would argue that in these two films, the connection is further emphasised by the *mise en scène* and editing, with public and private spaces merged in an almost seamless continuum. A clear example would be the flat where Coco Chanel conducts her love affair with the English businessman Arthur 'Boy' Capel in *Coco before Chanel*. Whilst our experience of this domestic setting is limited to a number of bedroom scenes, much attention is paid to the spiral staircase that joins this private space to the very public atelier downstairs. An iconic element in Chanel's brand image, the camera revels in the organic quality of the sinuous handrail, rendering it a sort of architectural umbilical cord, a symbolic reminder of the key role that 'Boy' played not only in the designer's personal life but also in her professional career.

Bingham argues that these recurrent patterns in the female biopic 'can be broken only by deliberate efforts to rethink them and a definite desire to undo and rework them' (Bingham 2010: 222). This call to resist rather than insist on the traditional patterns of grief and melodramatic excess may come at an auspicious time for, as Belén Vidal concludes in her analysis of performance in the biopic, the genre 'has become a metagenre: that is, a genre that intently reflects on its own form of life writing' (Vidal 2014: 15). This state of introspection may well be the reason why a number of films in the recent outpouring of female biopics engage with their subjects in innovative ways. In the particular case of the three films considered in this chapter, a conscious effort has been made to rethink the performance of the female protagonists in the context of the domestic space. *The Invisible Woman* (Ralph Fiennes, 2013), *To Walk Invisible* (Sally Wainwright, 2016) and *A Quiet Passion* (Terence Davies, 2016) could even earn a place in Bingham's canon of feminist biopics through their 'avoidance of the genre's usual melodrama, or of incidents that explain the protagonist or that fix her in a particular ideology' (Bingham 2010: 25).

On first impression, the protagonists of these three films – Charles Dickens's secret mistress Nelly Ternan, the Brontë sisters, and the American poet Emily Dickinson – seem the most unlikely candidates for a biopic that would favour a feminist point of view. The very titles, with their references to invisibility and silence, together with possible preconceptions about the characters' biographies and historical and social background – mid-nineteenth-century, non-working class – evoke almost immediately images of repressed female desire, unfulfilled professional ambitions and tragic deaths. However, that a little known female figure from the nineteenth century can be at the centre of a highly successful feminist biopic has already been established by the Australian director Jane Campion with her portrayal of John Keats's muse Fanny Brawne in *Bright Star* (Jane Campion, 2009). *Bright Star* is in many ways the precursor and companion piece of the three biopics analysed here. Like *The Invisible Woman*, the film seeks to rescue a forgotten female muse. Like *To Walk Invisible* and *A Quiet Passion*, it deals with the desire for recognition of a female author. Key to Campion's feminist intervention is a conscious depiction of Fanny's sewing as a creative process, thus subverting the traditional image of the passive muse. In the film 'the muse becomes an artist and occupies the authorial persona reserved for men' (Shachar 2013: 206). Ironically, by binding Fanny's authorial identity to an activity mostly done in the silence of a domestic space, the film reminds us 'of the nineteenth-century discourse on gender, which positioned women within the home and thereby denied them access to the outside world or to historical presence' (Shachar 2013: 208). However, whilst acknowledging this historical reality, the film establishes Fanny's sewing as an equal to Keats's poetic output, thus making it difficult to judge the latter as superior to the former. This non-judgemental attitude towards the female protagonists' actions or ideology is also at the heart of Bingham's appraisal of other films that try to reinvent the female biopic such as *Erin Brockovich* (Steven Soderbergh, 2000) and *The Notorious Bettie Page* (Mary Harron, 2005); and a powerful strategy that the three biopics considered in these chapter also display.

Both Bingham and Shachar agree that in order for a biopic not to pass judgement on its female protagonist, the male gaze must be reappropriated or even totally elided. In *Bright Star*, for example, Fanny is shown standing at her window, casting her desiring gaze at Keats as he lies on the grass, and she is 'here wholly active, casting a traditionally masculine gaze upon her beloved "other", while Keats, in a submissive position, is wholly passive' (Shachar 2013: 207). With their profusion of interior scenes, the three films discussed in this chapter create a space for the female gaze to explore, measure and construct its surroundings almost undisturbed. In addition to this, discourses around the domestic space in the three films are rarely defined by constraint, control or confinement; nor are there clear boundaries established between female and male spaces within the household. More importantly, the decision of the protagonists to remain in the private space and thus render themselves invisible may have been first determined by the conservative morals of society or by the misogynistic tendencies of the nineteenth-century publishing world, but in the films it is presented ultimately as a personal choice, an opportunity for the characters to display their agency. Confining the characters to domestic invisibility also deals with and brings to the fore the problematic encounter between the audience and characters about whom they may hold few documented historical facts. For most viewers Nelly Ternan is a mystery waiting to be discovered, the Brontë sisters exist shrouded in the Romantic myth of their oeuvre, and Emily Dickinson has come to be defined mostly by her reclusiveness. Placing these characters in a domestic and private arena engenders an extraordinary liberating dialogue between *mise en scène* and performance that in turn allows the characters to develop their own voices unencumbered, generates persuasive arguments about the protagonists and reveals essential truths behind these myths.

In *The Invisible Woman*, Nelly Ternan is mainly characterised by her stubborn resistance to the role that she is expected to perform. Her restlessness is mirrored in the transitional nature of most domestic spaces in the film, with inhabitants always in the process of leaving or arriving, and where corridors and hallways seem more important than enclosed rooms. In *To Walk Invisible*, the domestic space is fluid with no room out of bounds to the Brontë sisters, not even their brother's bedroom or their father's study. Thus, the entire Haworth parsonage is not only redefined as their personal creative space but also becomes an arena of performance where the audience is confronted with a demystified version of the historical characters. Finally, the exquisite cinematography in *A Quite Passion* transforms the Dickinsons' Homestead into an ethereal space, that it is progressively measured and plotted through Emily's poetry in a process of appropriation that culminates in a total identification between building and verse, as if the voice of the poet had become the very mortar that holds the edifice together.

The Invisible Woman, 'You see him, and he sees you'

Based on the book of the same title by the English journalist and biographer Claire Tomalin, *The Invisible Woman* (Ralph Fiennes, 2013) dramatises Charles Dickens's extramarital relationship with the actress Ellen (Nelly) Ternan. Lasting thirteen years until the death of the writer in 1870, it remained a well-kept secret until the early twentieth-century. Both book and film can be construed as attempts to bring the character of Nelly out from the colossal shadow of the Victorian author, and they both carry the promise of revealing the 'real' Nelly to a contemporary audience.

We first meet Nelly in the English coastal town of Margate in 1883 after she has reinvented herself as Mrs George Wharton Robinson, the young wife of a schoolmaster, 'beautifully spoken, well read, [...] fluent in foreign languages and a good musician' (Tomalin 1991: 218). Understandably reluctant to discuss her past with either her husband or her acquaintances, she claims that Dickens was nothing more than a family friend from her childhood. After this opening scene, the story of her romance with the writer will be told in a succession of flashbacks, beginning with an episode in Manchester twenty-five years earlier. It is here at the age of eighteen where she first meets Dickens, as she performs a minor role in one of his amateur plays.

Crucially, we first encounter Nelly in these public spaces, the school and the theatre, where she is required by professional duty or social convention to play a predetermined role in front of an overwhelmingly male 'audience'. Nelly's evident discomfort during these scenes – wonderfully conveyed by Felicity Jones in a mesmerising performance – signals that the 'real' Nelly cannot be found in these two public performances, but in the very private process of moving from visibility into invisibility. As the director Ralph Fiennes explains, he is not interested in the end result but 'in the story of how Ellen Ternan became the mistress, [...] the drama was a young girl becoming in a particular social world, the mistress of a famous man' (Ralph Fiennes interview, 2014).

Fiennes chooses to track this process by placing Nelly in a series of domestic spaces where she scrutinises and is scrutinised in turn by a number of female characters, each representing a possible reading or model for her relationship with Dickens.

The first domestic space is Park Cottage, where Nelly lives with her mother and sisters who are also professional actresses. Unbeknownst to Nelly, her sister Maria and her mother have both noticed Dickens's interest in the young girl, and they both discuss, half-ashamed, whether this would be a good way to ensure Nelly's future, for she lacks the talent and temperament to survive in the world of theatre. When Nelly overhears this conversation, she locks herself in the outhouse where she resists any attempts by her elder sister to define the nature of Dickens's advancements. The second domestic space is the house at Ampthill Square where Nelly receives the surprise visit of Dickens's wife, Catherine. During their conversation, Nelly realises that being married to a famous author may not be as fulfilling as she might think, for she would never be sure of whom Dickens loves the most, his public or her. Once the conversation is over, Nelly heads straight out into the garden, where she sits and waits for Dickens to arrive. The third and final domestic space is the house of the writer Wilkie Collins and his companion Caroline Graves who lived together openly as a couple but never married. When Dickens takes Nelly to the couple's house, she politely refuses to take off her hat and gloves, and remains seated in the hallway until they depart. Afterwards in the carriage, she accuses Dickens of callousness for exposing her to such a humiliating and shameful situation.

Nelly stubbornly resists all these possible roles offered to her – the poor, innocent girl rescued by the great author; the neglected wife, less important than his readership; or the public mistress, who does not seem to care about social conventions. Nelly's interaction with these domestic spaces is characterised by restlessness, her body ready to spring into action, her eyes permanently wandering in the direction of an escape route – the outhouse, the garden, the street. In the end she realises that the only role available to her is that of an invisible companion that somehow wields the power to make Dickens more real by her very existence. As Wilkie Collins tells her, 'you see him, and he sees you'. And this is what the film argues, that the real Dickens is not the public figure that his readers and his family see, but the man desperately in love captured through Nelly's gaze.

It is not known where (or even if) Nelly and Dickens became lovers, but in the film their first sexual encounter takes place at Dickens's house in Tavistock Square, right after the author completes the final chapter of his novel *Great Expectations*. Nelly's attitude as she walks into Dickens's domain is not that of a sacrificial lamb, but of a woman who is fully conscious of the consequences of her decision. As Dickens humbly seeks her approval of the novel's new ending, Nelly becomes his intellectual equal and is swiftly transformed from passive muse to active reviewer. Whilst Tomalin argues that we can only guess 'how the balance of power was held between him and her' (Tomalin 1991: 124), the film settles the matter by turning Nelly into the agent of her own destiny. Painfully aware of Dickens's emotional distress, it is finally Nelly that draws Dickens into her arms and the consummation of their relationship.

Although the film takes a number of liberties with historical facts – Claire Tomalin argues that 'as far as we know Dickens did not introduce Nelly to Wilkie's women' (Tomalin 1991: 132) – it ultimately manages to elevate the character of Nelly in the eyes of a modern audience, from a passive victim of social conventions to an active agent, reluctant to become Dickens's mistress out of her own sense of pride and dignity. It is in the end a persuasive portrayal of a forgotten muse that helps us reach an understanding of the 'real' Nelly, beyond the self-imposed invisibility of her lifetime, or the cold and mercenary woman portrayed by Dickens's early biographers (Tomalin 1991: 9).

To Walk Invisible: Reframing the Brontë Myth

Rather surprisingly considering the wealth of academic studies and fictional works devoted to their lives, the number of film biopics on the Brontë sisters is very limited and not particularly well-regarded. Most of the early biopics tend to romanticize and beautify the characters, as it is the case with the highly fictionalised British drama *Devotion* (Curtis Bernhardt, 1946), or the French costume drama *Les Soeurs Brontë* (André Téchiné, 1979). Only the 1973 ITV mini-series *The Brontës of Haworth*, directed by Christopher Fry, seems a better attempt at picturing the real life at Haworth parsonage. Compared to these three versions, Sally Wainwright's *To Walk Invisible* is far more muscular and thoroughly surprising.[2] The film refuses to romanticize the Brontës' hardships and succeeds in humanizing the sisters to an unprecedented extent, bringing them 'to fizzing life, equipped with robust Yorkshire accents and a furtive but furious determination to be heard' (Rees 2016).

Wainwright balances out this startling use of characterisation with reassuringly authentic costume and set design and a solid period reconstruction of the parsonage and the surrounding area. As with the characterisation of the sisters, Wainwright's depiction of the parsonage defies old myths; she films it as a working household proving that 'far from being the gloomy place of Brontë legend, Haworth parsonage was a vibrant powerhouse of intellectual activity' (Barker 2002: 30). Wainwright translates this creative dynamism to the screen by documenting the minutiae of the family's everyday life, and focusing on how the characters interact with this domestic space and the objects within it. Letters, manuscripts, furniture and clothes, '[a]ll these artefacts possess a certain fascination – not merely as relics, but also because of their ability to bring the members of this remarkable family to life by virtue of their very ordinariness' (Dinsdale 2012: 18). Didactic and revisionist in equal measure, the film provides an insight into the still fairly unknown domestic dynamics of the Brontës, which have been frequently obscured by the far more appealing Brontë myth that 'has developed through time, shifting its focus, collapsing lives with works and landscape with fiction' (Stoneman 2002: 238).

By concentrating on the domestic routine of the parsonage, Wainwright privileges the female gaze which in turn allows for a revisionist view of the men in the family, as their actions are consistently placed under the scrutiny of the three sisters. The characterisation of the father, the Reverend Patrick Brontë, owes nothing to the unfavourable portrait popularised by Elizabeth Gaskell in her biography of Charlotte Brontë

(Green 2012: 38), and much to contemporary studies of his life and correspondence that 'reveals a kindly and loving father who took a keen interest in his children's development' (Green 2008: 10). Deeply concerned about his troubled son Branwell, Patrick Brontë remains unaware of his daughters' artistic endeavours until Charlotte reveals to him that she is the author behind the controversial but highly successful *Jane Eyre*. His reaction is one of pride at the achievements of his daughters, but the film gives much more value to his indifference than to his praise. As Emily confesses, perhaps it was precisely because they were never under their father's scrutiny that they had the freedom to produce something remarkable, whilst Branwell suffers deeply from his inability to live up to Reverend Brontë's high expectations.

It is through the sisters' eyes that we experience Branwell's progressive collapse into drunkenness, illness and depression, but also observe glimpses of his intelligence and artistry. More importantly, with this historically accurate description of Branwell's demise, Wainwright challenges the conventions of the classic female biopic by transferring discourses of victimisation and emotional frustration from the female characters to the male. There is hardly any reference in the film to the sisters' desires or romantic attachments, most notably Charlotte's infatuation with her Brussels employer Constantin Héger that caused her to undergo 'two years of torment before her one-sided passion receded' (Lonoff 2012: 114). The character of Branwell on the other hand is mostly defined by his failed relationship with his ex-employer's wife Mrs Robinson. Branwell's progressive decline is triggered by a series of events related to this liaison, and he frequently confides in and seeks romantic advice from close male friends. Pity, rather than derision or mockery, characterises the sisters' reactions to Branwell's romantic misfortune, and Charlotte's friend Ellen Nussey later remarks that 'he has been very sadly used', an expression more commonly associated with young women seduced and abandoned by older men.

Branwell's physical collapse and increasing inability to work is paired with a rejection of the domestic space of the parsonage, as it gradually evolves from mere dwelling to an engine of creativity that both encases and multiplies the sisters' writing efforts. For him the parsonage is just a roof over his head, a place populated by people 'who are always looking at me with empty faces', reminding him of his failures and shortcomings. Unlike his sisters who are mostly seen arriving at the house, he is frequently on the way out, visiting pubs or simply walking along the road. Within the parsonage, there is a clear division between the orderly parlour where the three sisters methodically sit to write every day and the untidy bedroom where Branwell exiles himself to lament his misfortunes. Early in the film, he is shown asleep dangling at the edge of his bed, in a pose that is almost an exact replica of the 1856 Henry Wallis's iconic painting *The Death of Chatterton*, suggesting that he will share the tragic destiny of the Romantic poet. Wainwright's striking image is both affecting and amusing, and hints at one of the core themes in the film: that this is a literary biopic that interrogates the soundness of the male Romantic authorial persona through the construction of an alternative feminine artistic identity that marries the Romantic imagination with industry.

The fact that the film closes with Branwell's death stands as Wainwright's final assault on the conventions of the classic female biopic, a genre whose narrative thread 'is most often in the downward trajectory, with female subjects victimized by their own ambition, or the limitations placed on them' (Bingham 2013: 237). By refusing to recreate their final suffering and choosing instead to inform the audience of the sisters' deaths as a mere historical fact through a series of succinct notes, the film ends in an upward trajectory. There is even no mention of Charlotte's own death, and instead we are reminded of the further two books that she published after *Jane Eyre*. These notes accompany contemporary footage of the parsonage, now a museum and a research centre, in a show of resistance to 'the image that persists of Haworth Parsonage as a symbol of their [the Brontë sisters] tragic lives' (Burham Bloom 2016: 548).

Ultimately, *To Walk Invisible* succeeds in presenting a domestic space that nurtures rather than hinders creativity, an element that is also central to the film *A Quiet Passion*, Terence Davies's biopic on the American poet Emily Dickinson.

A Quiet Passion: 'Myself was formed – a Carpenter'

It is not surprising that Terence Davies would choose a poet for his first, but not last, venture into the biopic genre.[3] A lifelong admirer of T. S. Eliot, Davies like the poet 'is exploring in his work the nature of time and memory in relation to identity' (Everett 2004: 38); concerns that resonate with Dickinson's oeuvre. One of the most surprising moments in the film is a simple transitional device. The sixteen-year-old Emily, played by Emma Bell, has sat down to pose for what would become the only authenticated photograph of the poet, taken in 1847. As the camera closes up on her face, the image morphs almost imperceptibly into the face of the actress Cynthia Nixon who plays the older Emily. The film closes with a similar shot, only this time, the face of Nixon dissolves into the face of the original portrait. Although Davies justifies this noticeable use of CGI as a money saving decision (Rizov 2017), it is also an example that merges in a single image two of the director's most idiosyncratic techniques: long motionless takes and fluid tracking shots. For Wendy Everett, these visual strategies define the way that spectators engage with Davies's work:

> They draw the spectator's attention to the materiality of the film, the nature of the shot and its duration. In other words, by stretching time visibly, they involve the spectator directly in their exploration of time and space, and in so doing demand a creative reading not only of the images that are shown but of the hidden, invisible spaces behind and beyond them. (Everett 2004: 4)

As the face of the older Emily emerges, almost three dimensional thanks to the play of light and shadow, it draws our attention to two key aspects of the biopic genre. First, that what we see is a construct, a fact-based fiction that demands an active engagement from the audience, constantly negotiating between the narrative in the film and their previous knowledge of the subject. Second, that this filmic experience bestows upon the spectator a privilege that very few enjoyed in Dickinson's life: the pleasure of gazing upon the 'Hidden Face' that remained unseen for almost a quarter of a century.[4] Costumes, period dialogue, and the striking similarity between the actors and the real characters are a number of warrants of truth that Davies adopts in his depiction of the poet and her historical context, but, as in *To Walk Invisible*, it is the house that claims central space as both a marker of historical accuracy and a tool in the characterisation process of the protagonist.

In *A Quiet Passion*, action rarely ventures outside the confines of the Dickinson Homestead, in Amherst, Massachusetts. When Davies visited the original house, he noticed that 'what's lovely about it is that in both parlors there are lots of windows, so lots of light is coming in. And gradually throughout the film the light disappears' (Rizov 2017). In the film, architectural elements such as walls and apertures (windows and doors) seem to function less as markers of the physical boundaries of the house and more as features whose primordial function is to enable the play of light. This construction of the house as a translucent space, emphasising its porosity rather than its impenetrability, mirrors Dickinson's own complex understanding of interior spaces and demands a rethinking of the popular view of Emily residing in a prison-like environment. As the scholar Diane Fuss suggests:

> For Dickinson, interiority was not only a matter of physical enclosure. Interiority was a complicated conceptual problem, continually posited and re-examined in a body of writing that relies heavily on spatial metaphors, to advance its recurrent themes of joy, despair, death, time and immortality. (Fuss 2004: 9)

Fuss adds that 'architectural, rather than decorative references shape Dickinson's poems. Hers is a vocabulary of plane, beam, and dome, of angle, slant and degree, of plan, scale, and latitude' (Fuss 2004: 9). Davies captures this concept strikingly by incorporating disembodied recitations of Emily's poetry, the off-screen voice of Nixon acting as a musical soundtrack to long lyrical tracks across rooms and corridors. During these poetic interludes, where the voice of the poet seems to emanate from walls and objects, time collapses, and viewers are simultaneously encountering the poet in the then and the now. As modern readers we connect with the poet through her texts, but by virtue of being inside the Homestead, we also meet the poet as a contemporary guest would, particularly in the last years of her life, when 'Dickinson spoke to friends, visitors, and even a doctor from behind the safety of a door or curtain' (Martin 2007: 22). In *A Quiet Passion*, rooms appear uncluttered and spare, a feature shared with Davies's other foray into the life of the nineteenth-century American bourgeoisie, *The House of Mirth* (2000). Whilst Davies may again claim that this is exclusively due to budget constraints,[5] it implies that certain objects become loaded with meaning. In *The House of Mirth*, the protagonist Lily Bart's imperfect assimilation to the decor 'is highlighted by objects whose meaning keep treacherously shifting. Teacups, books and cigarettes signpost the relationships between characters and are wielded in significant gestures' (Vidal 2012: 104). Nixon's performance as Dickinson takes the character closer to the volcanic imagery of poems such as *On my volcano grows the Grass*, where 'she fears that the fire "below" her suppressed passions, will come to the surface, shocking "the General though"' (Farr 1992: 215). Davies relays the poet's emotional turmoil through her handling of a number of domestic objects. At one point in the film, Dickinson's father complains about a stain on a plate. Emily, who is sitting next to him, proceeds to smash it against the table as she states it 'now is no longer dirty'. Whilst the scene presents an accurate view of the way Dickinson 'could sometimes be the only member of her family who has the courage to stand up to her father' (Waxman 2017), it also crystallises in a single gesture Dickinson's earlier concerns about the fragility of her soul and her increasing rejection of Edward Dickinson's Puritanism. This issue of the fragility of the inner self resonates throughout the film, in a soundscape composed of the clink of fine glasses, the swish of curtains and silks, and the brushing of parasols.

Similarly to Wainwright's experiments with the genre in *To Walk Invisible*, the use of a domestic space in *A Quiet Passion* allows for a revisionist portrayal of the character of Dickinson, and provides an opportunity to reframe the myth. Despite Davies's complex understanding of time and space, this biopic is quite traditional in the way it presents Dickinson's timeline, with major personal and historical events – marriages, deaths, the American Civil War – dutifully ticked off in, unusually for Davies, chronological order. But within the privacy of the Dickinson Homestead, Davies chooses to depict the facts in a way that would suit his characterisation and dramatic purposes.

Critics and viewers expressed their surprise at how funny the film is, a term not normally associated with a filmmaker who confesses that he is 'really good at death and misery' (Hoffman 2016) and a poet for whom mortality was 'a riddle she could never solve but which she always explored' (Martin 2007: 97). In order to emphasise Dickinson's sharp wit, her sense of fun and her lifelong passion for language, Davies decides to foreground the poet's friendship with the high-spirited Vryling Buffam with whom Dickinson shares 'a mischievously humorous sense of aphorisms that range from gleeful absurdity to fierce irreverence' (Brody 2017). Although Davies takes great liberties in the portrayal of the character – she was in fact a friend of Lavinia Dickinson and 'looks very bored' in pictures (Kilkenny 2017) – it can be argued that in choosing to emphasize this fictional friendship rather than perhaps the well-documented but more loaded relationship with her sister-in-law Susan Gilbert, both filmmaker and subject are granted the freedom to explore lesser known aspects of the character, and as such both 'that friendship, and the film as a whole, is faithful to the inner facts – to a truth about the poet that's revealed only through fiction' (Brody 2017).

Davies does not seek to hide his departures from the documented facts of Dickinson's life. For example, it is the conviction amongst Dickinson scholars that the poet never met Mabel Loomis Todd,[6] the young faculty wife who had a scandalous affair with the poet's married brother Austin, and who was responsible for the first edition of Emily's poems. In the film, Davies has Emily walking in on Austin and Todd as they consummate their affair in the Homestead living room. Davies justifies this invention as being 'dramatically much more interesting' (Macnab 2016), conveying quite effectively that this is a moment of crisis for Dickinson as a character.

Like Nelly Ternan's and the Brontë sisters' invisibility, Dickinson's reclusiveness leaves space for Davies to take full advantage of the hybrid nature of the biopic. *A Quiet Passion* may take some liberties with a number of historical facts, but it is powerfully persuasive in its rendition of Dickinson's poetic voice.

Conclusion

In his appraisal of *The Notorious Bettie Paige* and *Marie Antoinette* (Sofia Coppola, 2006) as films that deliberately attempt to rethink the female biopic, Dennis Bingham stresses that both films feel fresh 'because the filmmakers, working within the framework of the facts, leave the subjects alone, basically, with us, allowing them to discover themselves as we learn about them' (Bingham 2010: 350).

This description fits perfectly with the three examples considered in this chapter, where characters are frequently placed in the privacy of their domestic spaces with only the audience to keep them company. Moreover, the three films also demonstrate an uncommon understanding of the hybrid nature of the biopic and its unique possibilities. By confining the characters to the domestic space, the films keep true to biographical facts, but they also adopt an arena of performance primed for reinvention and dramatic reconstruction, which eventually leads to an understanding of an essential truth about the characters. In *The Invisible Woman*, Nelly is never engaged in any domestic tasks and, whilst this is a documented fact,[7] it makes it easier for the director to emphasise her resistance towards complying with the traditional Victorian roles of domestic angel or fallen woman. In *To Walk Invisible* we see a domestic space redefined, where a kitchen table can serve both as a place to peel onions and as a place to compose verse. It is a known fact that after the death of Aunt Branwell it was Emily who took over responsibility for running the household (Pykett 2012: 70–1). In her furiously energetic hands, baking bread and sweeping the floor do not come across as home making activities, but simply as tasks that need to be completed in order to ensure the good running of the creative engine of the Brontë Parsonage. Relieved of household chores by an ensemble of domestic servants, Emily Dickinson's well-documented baking efforts are presented more as a leisure activity than as a duty.[8] The film never seeks to justify Dickinson's disengagement with domestic or social obligations, for it essentially argues that Emily's role within the household was to write poetry, a view supported by her sister Lavinia who saw Dickinson's withdrawal from society as 'a logical outcome for the one family member whose main job was to think' (Fuss 2004: 22).

The three examples in this chapter provide a glimpse of what the future may bring to the female biopic. Even though it requires some effort on the part of artists and the industry to step away from the melodramatic formula, there is much to be gained from testing the limits of the genre and engaging with female protagonists in innovative and surprising ways.

Notes

1 *Hidden Figures* narrates the story of three women, all African American mathematicians who worked at NASA during the space race in the early 1960s. *Jackie* is a searing portrait of the iconic First Lady Jackie Kennedy focusing on her experiences in the aftermath of her husband's assassination. *The Iron Lady* depicts the career and later struggle with dementia of the British politician Margaret Thatcher. *Big Eyes* is a film about the American artist Margaret Keane and her fight for recognition as the real author of the portraits with big eyes, popular in the 1950s and 1960s. *Queen of Katwe* documents the progress of Ugandan teenager Phiona Mutesi from street seller in Kampala to international champion chess player.
2 Wainwright, who was born and raised in the proximity of Haworth and spent almost two years researching the project, approached the subject with a myth-busting spirit. As she explains in an interview: 'I may be wrong but I was worried there would be a preconception out there that the Brontë sisters were a little bit like Jane Austen or a little bit like Louisa M. Alcott, these little ladies who wrote nice novels. And I wanted to show the reality of their lives in somewhere like Haworth' (Sally Wainwright interview, 2016).
3 In a recent interview, Terence Davies discusses his ongoing project on the life of the British poet Siegfried Sassoon (Rizov 2017).
4 Judith Farr opens her book on Emily Dickinson with a chapter entitled 'The Hidden Face', where she describes the events immediately after Dickinson's death, and collects the reaction of mourners as they gaze upon the poet's dead features (Farr 1992: 1–2).
5 Although Davies was certainly relieved when his recreation of Dickinson's interiors received the approval of academics and curators of the Emily Dickinson Museum in Amherst (Macnab 2016), he also comments on the budgetary constraints and creative decisions that would shape his portrayal of the character and her surroundings: 'I said to them, look it is not a documentary. It is going to be a subjective fictional idea of this woman. I can't have everything in it, I can't' (Macnab 2016).
6 According to Farr 'Mabel Todd never achieved a meeting' with Dickinson (Farr 1992: 2), and Fuss adds that Mabel 'who never actually saw Dickinson while she was alive, came to know her principally through the sound of her voice' (Fuss 2004: 20).
7 As Tomalin observes, Nelly 'was always totally undomesticated; household management and cookery were of no interest to her at all' (Tomalin 1991: 124).
8 According to Wendy Martin, Emily Dickinson 'mastered the art of baking bread' and her father 'refused to eat any loaves' but those that she made. Also, bread 'provided Dickinson with a wealth of metaphors' (Martin 2007: 56).

Works Cited

Barker, Juliet (2002), 'The Haworth Context', in Heather Glen (ed.), *The Cambridge Companion to the Brontës*, Cambridge: Cambridge University Press, pp. 13–33.

Bingham, Dennis (2010), *Whose Lives Are They Anyway?: The Biopic as Contemporary Film Genre*, Piscataway, NJ: Rutgers University Press.

Bingham, Dennis (2013), 'The lives and Times of the Biopic', in Robert A. Rosenstone and Constantin Parvulescu (eds), *A Companion to the Historical Film*, Chichester: Wiley, pp. 233–54.

Brody, Richard (2017), Terence Davies's truthful fictions about Emily Dickinson, *The New Yorker*, 9 April, <http://www.newyorker.com/culture/richard-brody/terence-daviess-truthful-fictions-about-emily-dickinson> (last accessed 18 May 2017).

Burham Bloom, Abigail (2016), 'The Brontës in Popular Culture', in Diane Long Hoeveler and Deborah A. Denenholz (eds), *A Companion to the Brontës*, Chichester: Wiley, pp. 547–63.

Dinsdale, A. (2012), 'Domestic Life at Haworth Parsonage', in M. Thormahlen (ed.), *The Brontës in Context*, Cambridge: Cambridge University Press, pp. 9–17.

Everett, Wendy (2004), *Terence Davies*, Manchester: Manchester University Press.

Farr, Judith (1992), *The Passion of Emily Dickinson*, Cambridge: Harvard University Press.

Fiennes, Ralph (2014), interview in *The Invisible Woman* DVD bonus material, UK: BBC Films.

Fuss, Diana (2004), *A Sense of an Interior, Four Writers and the Rooms that Shaped Them*, New York and London: Routledge.

Green, Dudley (2008), *Patrick Brontë; Father of Genius*, Stroud: Nonsuch.

Green, Dudley (2012), 'The Father of the Brontës', in Marianne Thormahlen (ed.), *The Brontës in Context*, Cambridge: Cambridge University Press, pp. 36–43.

Hoffman, Jordan (2016), Terence Davies on avoiding Hollywood A-listers: 'I don't cast big names', *The Guardian*, 9 May, <https://www.theguardian.com/film/2016/may/09/terence-davies-british-film-director-sunset-song-agyness-deyn> (last accessed 10 May 2017).

Kilkenny, Katie (2017), 'The Quiet Firebrand Feminism of Emily Dickinson', *Pacific Standard*, 17 April, <https://psmag.com/news/the-quiet-firebrand-feminism-of-emily-dickinson> (last accessed 18 May 2017).

Lonoff, Sue (2012), 'The Brussels Experience', in Marianne Thormahlen (ed.), *The Brontës in Context*, Cambridge: Cambridge University Press, pp. 107–14.

Macnab, Geoffrey (2016), 'Interview with Terence Davies', *The Independent*, 4 October, <http://www.independent.co.uk/arts-entertainment/films/features/a-quiet-passion-terence-davies-interview-emily-dickinson-london-film-festival-cynthia-nixon-a7344021.html> (last accessed 10 January 2017).

Martin, Wendy (2007), *The Cambridge Introduction to Emily Dickinson*, Cambridge: Cambridge University Press.

Moine, Raphaëlle (2014), 'The Contemporary French Biopic in National and International Contexts', in Tom Brown and Belen Vidal (eds), *The Biopic in Contemporary Film Culture*, New York and Oxford: Routledge, pp. 52–67.

Newland, Christina (2017), 'After the Success of Hidden Figures, Are Female-fronted Biopics on the Rise', *Esquire Magazine*, 23 February, <http://www.esquire.com/entertainment/movies/a53175/rise-of-female-fronted-biopics/> (last accessed 2 March 2017).

Pykett, Lyn (2012), 'Emily Brontë', in Marianne Thormahlen (ed.), *The Brontës in Context*, Cambridge: Cambridge University Press, pp. 68–74.

Rees, Jasper (2016), '*To Walk Invisible: Review*,' The Telegraph (online), 29 December, <http://www.telegraph.co.uk/tv/0/walk-invisible-review-Brontë-sisters-brought-fizzing-furious/> (last accessed 10 February 2017).

Rizov, Vadim (2017), 'The Language is Being Destroyed: Terence Davies on *A Quiet Passion*', *Filmmaker Magazine*, <http://filmmakermagazine.com/102033-the-language-is-being-destroyed-terence-davies-on-a-quiet-passion/> (last accessed 2 May 2017).

Shachar, Hila (2013), 'Authorial Histories, The Historical Film and the Literary Biopic', in Robert A. Rosenstone and Constantin Parvulescu (eds), *A Companion to the Historical Film*, Chichester: Wiley, pp. 233–54.

Stoneman, Patsy (2002), 'The Brontë Myth', in Heather Glen (ed.), *The Cambridge Companion to the Brontës*, Cambridge: Cambridge University Press, pp. 214–41.

Tomalin, Claire (1991), *The Invisible Woman: The Story of Nelly Ternan and Charles Dickens*, London: Penguin.

Vidal, Belen (2012), *Figuring the Past: Period Film and the Mannerist Aesthetic*, Amsterdam: Amsterdam University Press.

Vidal, Belen (2014), 'Introduction: The Biopic and Its Critical Contexts', in Tom Brown and Belen Vidal (eds), *The Biopic in Contemporary Film Culture*, New York and Oxford: Routledge, pp. 1–32.

Wainwright, Sally (2016), Open Learn interview, <http://www.open.edu/openlearn/history-the-arts/culture/literature-and-creative-writing/creative-writing/walk-invisible-interview-sally-wainwright> (last accessed 12 January 2017).

Waxman, Olivia B. (2017), '*A Quiet Passion* and the Real Emily Dickinson', 14 April, <http://time.com/4717501/emily-dickinson-quiet-passion/> (last accessed 18 May 2017).

CHAPTER 4

Liminal Spaces, Lesbian Desire and Veering off Course in Todd Haynes's *Carol*

Anna Backman Rogers

It is given that the straight world is already in place and that queer moments, where things are out of line, are fleeting. Our response need not be to search for permanence ... but to listen to the sound of the 'what' that fleets. (Sara Ahmed 2006: 106)

The very frequency with which the lesbian has been 'apparitionalized' in the Western imagination also testifies to her peculiar cultural power. Only something very palpable – at a deeper level – has the capacity to haunt us so thoroughly. (Terry Castle 1993: 7)

For Olivia Gragnon

Introduction: 'What a strange girl you are – flung out of space'

Set in the 1950s and based on Patricia Highsmith's novel *The Price of Salt* (which was originally written in 1952 under a pseudonym because of its subject matter), Todd Haynes's *Carol* relates the story of an illicit love affair between two women socially divided by age and class. Upon its release, critics noted the film's tasteful and chaste treatment of its literary source material; indeed, Haynes's implicit and subtle delineation of the central love story serves to ground the film in political and historical authenticity (namely, as the film makes clear, such a relationship is considered impossible, unthinkable and a moral abomination that must be impeded by law). However, this essay contends that this sublimation of lesbian desire is figured in the film not only as a trope of authenticity, but more profoundly as an affective and emotional history that plays out in liminal spaces between the social and domestic stratifications determined by patriarchal law. The radical nature of lesbian desire is adumbrated as a force that cannot exist or thrive within, and thus refuses, the hierarchical spaces of power structures (the patriarchal family home, the public space, the place of work) that are associated with masculinity in the film; yet the betwixt and between the nature of this love works fundamentally to decentre and trouble these spaces of power. In essence, I will argue that *Carol* traces a phenomenology of lesbianism through affective orientation towards objects and spaces that render lesbian desire as a powerful, disruptive and liminal – rather than utopian – force that refuses forms of regulation and conventional domesticity. That its depiction is subtle and implicit makes the force of this desire all the more potent and destabilising; for if, as we shall see, the lesbian is apparitional, as Terry Castle (1993) has argued, this is not merely because she is written out of visual culture and hegemonic narratives, but because she *haunts* dominant fictions precisely as an absence – an absence upon which patriarchal hegemony is predicated and therefore relies for its own existence. I will argue in what follows, then, that *Carol* does more than offer a compassionate portrayal of the lesbian relationship since it works to reveal the ways in which both public and domestic spaces are harnessed as sites of control and containment. Such films are rare since, as Teresa de Lauretis sets forth: 'films that portray or are about lesbian and gay subjects may provide sympathetic accounts, "positive images", of those subjects without necessarily producing new ways of seeing or a new inscription of the social subject in representation' (1991: 224). There is a difference between films, then, that seek to depict or represent, and those that tackle the problematic of representation in itself; again as de Lauretis remarks, it is: 'never just a problem of the film, but of the whole cinematic apparatus as a social technology and of the much larger field of audiovisual representation' (1991: 257). In my view, *Carol* falls into the latter category of challenging the field of audiovisual representation at large, despite or perhaps because of its chasteness. It is a film that actively works to place the viewer within queer and in-between spaces and posits one's outlook onto the world as askance and awry.

The film poses as a question of production design what is it like to be a ghost or to be made to disappear within public space or to be trapped within a domestic space that rejects the very core of one's being, and thus, by extension, how one's desire is lived out always in the interstice. That Carol marvels at Therese's 'strangeness', that she is a girl who seems to be 'flung out of space', speaks volumes of not only the ineffable nature of all human desire (why and how do we come to love whom we love), but also of her queerness: that she cannot be made to fit within the places that are set out for her. She comes from and exists elsewhere.[1] This, the film contends, is radically troubling to patriarchy, its official spaces, such as the domestic family home, and its attendant values.

This is a story about two women who cannot be made to fit and who veer off course in order to survive.

The Apparitional Lesbian and Public Space: A Theoretical Preface

The lesbian is made manifest as absence because she refuses: 'to undergo the symbolic emasculation that Western society demands of its female members – indeed depends upon' and thus, 'the woman who desires another woman has always set herself apart (if only by default) as outlaw and troublemaker' (Castle 1993: 5). The lesbian, in other words, may be consigned to an 'off-space', but she never seeks to occupy the strict and contained social spaces set out for her by patriarchy. Her sexuality is – or may be, politically speaking – an active refusal of the dominant social order and its coterminous norms and values; indeed, Monique Wittig has infamously argued that for this reason, the lesbian is not a woman:

> (t)he refusal to become (or to remain) heterosexual has always meant to refuse to become a man or a woman, consciously or not. For a lesbian this goes further than the refusal of the role of '*woman*'. It is the refusal of the economic, ideological, and political power of a man. (1992: 13)

Lesbian desire and existence is therefore often wilfully obscured, ignored or absented from social space; it is frequently conflated with a continuum of female friendship (see Rich 1980 and Stacey 1987) or wholly denied through the assumption that lesbian desire is physically, and carnally, impossible;[2] as Castle has somewhat humorously remarked:

> (g)iven the threat that sexual love between women inevitably poses to the workings of patriarchal arrangement, it has often been felt necessary to deny the carnal *bravada* of lesbian existence. The hoary misogynist challenge, 'But what do lesbians do?' insinuates as much: *This cannot be. There is no place for this.* It is perhaps not so surprising that at least until around 1900 lesbianism manifests itself in the Western literary imagination primarily as an absence, as chimera or *amor impossibilia* – a kind of love that, by definition, cannot exist. (1993: 30)

That there can be 'no place for this' is telling: it is not that it is impossible to imagine or to think – and by extension to depict – lesbian desire, but that in doing so one opens up a site of contestation that runs against the grain of patriarchy and the notion of the heteronormative nuclear family.

The imagining – and imaging – of lesbian desire (outside of the distortion of the male gaze)[3] from this perspective, then, is highly subversive.[4] In addition to Castle (1993), theorists such as Monique Wittig (1992),

Teresa de Lauretis (1991) and Judith Mayne (1991) have argued that there is a vehement political agenda behind this dismissal of the lesbian because of the threat she poses to the dominant order, which in the case of the female body is too often associated with domesticity of a heteronormative order; which is to say, then, that the lesbian body holds the power to disrupt and decentre this most sacred of spaces by subverting the patriarchal order. She is therefore removed not only from visual culture, but is also ignored or remains unseen in public space (outside of the domestic). As Castle puts it:

> (w)hy is it so difficult to see the lesbian – even when she is there, quite plainly, in front of us? In part because she has been 'ghosted' – or made to seem invisible – by culture itself. It would be putting it mildly to say that the lesbian represents a threat to patriarchal protocol: Western civilisation has for centuries been haunted by a fear of 'women without men' – of women indifferent or resistant to male desire. Precisely because she challenges the moral, sexual, and psychic authority of men so thoroughly ... (she) has always provoked anxiety and hatred. (1993: 5–6)

A very powerful way of controlling, containing and exorcising the threat that lesbian desire poses to patriarchal order is by rendering it either as ghostly and non-existent, or as a derivative and lesser version of male (homo)sexuality – a theoretical position that even Julia Kristeva has maintained.[5] Conflating female and male homosexuality is a way to disregard the specificity of lesbian desire, though; whilst both (homo) sexualities certainly disrupt dominant narratives of heteronormativity, it is specifically female homosexuality that problematises and decentres the allegiance of masculinity with activity and femininity with passivity, domesticity and orderliness. Therefore, as Luce Irigaray has suggested: 'the problem can be minimised if female homosexuality is regarded merely as an imitation of male behaviour' (quoted in Mayne 1991: 128; but also see Irigaray 1985 and 1993). However, that lesbian desire cannot be reduced to or made to fit easily within dominant patriarchal (and domestic) fictions (without rendering it as a parody of itself) means that in terms of narrative space, it cannot be assimilated to any generic formulation. That is, both the lived, embodied reality of female homosexuality and its narrative counterpart must, in essence, centre on deviation from normative heterosexual desire – a veering off course from domestic, contained space – in order to depict the problematic of representation itself.

Yet to stray from the normative route, to take the path less travelled, is exceptionally hard labour. *Carol* depicts the struggle to come to the moment of choosing to choose and the fractious and anxious consequences of choosing to love otherwise. Living outside of the confinements of dominant social space entails sacrificing traditional narratives that centre on happiness as a pre-given life script – a task which the film makes clear often requires 'abandoning happiness for life' (Ahmed 2010: 75). In what follows, I contend that *Carol* centres on the problematic of representing lesbian sexuality as a form of desire that exists between the possible and the impossible, the figurative and the invisible, the public and the private. Moreover, I will argue that the film painstakingly adumbrates a phenomenology of lesbian desire and queer domesticity that, in the words of Sara Ahmed, would help us: 'to consider how sexuality involves ways of inhabiting and being inhabited by space' (2006: 67). That is, *Carol* delineates the manifold ways in which shifting course is about learning how to re-orient oneself in the world and how to extend one's body into spaces that refuse to hold us or that even reject us. This in part requires and assiduous re-ordering of the domestic space, in particular the association of the female body to an ability to shore up a heteronormative order. Again, as Ahmed argues:

> (s)exuality would not be seen as determined only by object choice, but as involving differences in one's very relation to the world – that is, how one 'faces' the world or is directed toward it. Or rather, we could say that orientations toward sexual objects affect other things that we do, such that different orientations, different ways of directing one's desires, means inhabiting different worlds. (2006: 28)

Lesbian desire, then, as *Carol* renders clear, involves a recuperation of social and bodily action in the world through which we re-learn how to inhabit our skins in relation to others and the world. To veer off course, is to change fundamentally our relation to space. It is a film that manifests 'the work of reorientation' (Ahmed 2006: 100) precisely as a process of labour.

Veering off Course: 'I'm going away for a while … somewhere … wherever my car will take me'

Choosing a different path that takes one off an established and well-trodden line of trajectory is hard graft: it requires going against the grain; yet in doing so, one opens up new lines of flight and sites of contestation that can generate alternative ways of living and loving. To choose deviance or to deviate, as Ahmed puts it:

> leaves its own marks on the ground … which cross the ground in unexpected ways. Such lines are indeed traces of desire; where people have taken different routes to get to this point or to that point. It is certainly desire that helps generate a lesbian landscape, a ground that is shaped by the paths that we follow in deviating from the straight line. (2006: 20)

Lesbian desire, then, precipitates a new cartography that does not predetermine how a person should be or exist in this world, in direct contrast to heteronormative domestic space. This is, in part, because the lesbian (as a political body) does not seek to occupy the stratified spaces of patriarchy, but also because lesbian sexualities are not accorded the right to determination within spaces that are already codified through patriarchal law: therefore, the lesbian produces her own relation to geographical space out of necessity. Again, Ahmed states that:

> (t)he lesbian body does not extend the shape of this world, as a world organized around the form of the heterosexual couple. Inhabiting a body that is not extended by the skin of the social means the world acquires a new shape and makes new impressions. (2006: 20)

Indeed, to choose to live against the grain of the socially accepted or sanctioned, to take up the path less travelled, opens up new relations of space whilst it delimits or closes others, for:

> the sex of one's object choice is not simply *about* the object even when desire is 'directed' toward that object: it affects what we can do, where we can go, how we are perceived, and so on. These differences in how one directs desire, as well as how one is faced by others, can 'move' us and hence affect even the most deeply ingrained patterns of relating to others. (2006: 101)

From the outset of *Carol*, the viewer is introduced into a space that demands we look askance at the world. The florid metal work over which the film's title appears helps to emblematise the film's motif of deviation from the straight path. Moreover, it is Therese's viewpoint that generates the central focalisation; as a photographer, she is characterised as a person who is an observer, someone who is detached from the world and looks in on public space and human interaction as opposed to intervention (for to observe is not to act).

Todd Haynes has remarked that Vivian Maier's photographic archive was a source of aesthetic inspiration for him in designing the highly specific *mise en scène* for *Carol*.[6] Maier herself was somewhat of an 'outsider' figure, only lately discovered, who used her camera as an implement of observation or barrier between herself and the world whilst she remained so unremarkable that she could pass unnoticed in public space. Her invisibility, in fact, facilitated her considerable ability to capture quotidian existence in both its banality and its eccentricity. It is my contention that this link to Maier is, in fact, a direct inspiration for the character of Therese. That Therese is a theatre stage set designer in Highsmith's original novel, but is recuperated as an observer/photographer for her on-screen incarnation is telling. For *Carol* also plunges us into a world of female desire – an alternate universe indeed for most Hollywood productions – in which that desire is shown to function as much through tropes of distance, projection and idealisation as it does later through hapticity (the smell of one's lover's neck, the timbre and texture of her laughter). Therese is a woman who is obsessed with observing the world around her, but she cannot bring herself to insinuate herself into that world. She does not fit anywhere. It is through Therese's eyes that we come to understand that Carol, too, despite her upward mobility and glamour, is someone who only passes within public space because she has been conditioned to. In contrast to the muted and grey tones of the New York City landscape and her suburban, upper-class surroundings, Carol is nearly always depicted through Therese's eyes as an impossibly glamorous and elegant woman dressed in varying shades of red (Figure 4.1). Thus, she is marked out visually as not only the object of Therese's as of yet unnamed desire (in this earlier part of the narrative) but also as a woman who does not fit in with or assimilate into her environment. When Harge, Carol's entitled husband, with whom she is in the middle of divorce proceedings, callously and deliberately denigrates her by saying 'I would put nothing past a woman *like you*', it is not merely her sexuality he expresses contempt for, but her refusal or inability to fit within the confinement of the spaces patriarchy has set out for her, in particular her roles as mother and wife within the domestic space. The film, by allying us with the viewpoint

Figure 4.1 Carol (Cate Blanchett) dressed in red in *Carol* (2015). Film still.

of difference, renders clear the violent form of control that Harge – and by extension patriarchal law – wields over those who cannot be made to submit (indeed, their aforementioned conversation results in a physical altercation). That Carol is a woman who refuses to make herself smaller in order to fit makes her all the more troubling for the men around her.

Harge's presence on screen is characterised by intrusion, aggression and entitlement; male physicality tends to push the female body to the periphery of the film frame in *Carol*. According to Abby, Carol's best friend and former lover, Harge has spent the duration of his marriage to Carol making sure that he is her 'only point of reference'. As such, Harge, who invokes the aid of a coterie of men who stand in for patriarchal law (lawyers, detectives, doctors), casts himself as the maker of meaning and truth: he seeks to be the fulcrum of Carol's life. As her husband, he invokes the law to shore up his sense of entitlement. Likewise, the men whom he employs are entreated to find evidence of Carol's moral permissiveness, her lackadaisical attitude towards parenting and her profoundly disturbed psyche. Carol's doctor, employed by Harge and his upwardly mobile family, is, we are told, 'a Yale man' and therefore eminently qualified to diagnose her 'queerness' and eradicate it. When Carol lashes out at the man she discovers Harge has paid to spy on her, the gun she brandishes for her protection proves to be unloaded and thus functions metonymically – she is impotent to defend herself against the priapic narrative that is being woven tightly around her. She cannot fight back against the legal and medical process by which she is being brought under control. This control of public space and one's identity within it extends into the domestic space and determines and delimits what is possible and permissible within such spaces – a limited repertoire of marriage and motherhood. Both of these spaces, which function under the codes of patriarchal law, ensure that women 'like' Carol and Therese are unable to thrive and thus, to extend themselves within space. Indeed, it is especially the domestic space and its coterminous ritualistic codes and conventions from which they must flee in order not to suffocate. Accordingly, it is this confrontation with patriarchal law (the will and rule of her husband) that precipitates Carol's disappearance from public space, Therese's life and her retreat back into the hermetic order of the domestic; unlike Harge, however, who has chosen to mark Carol with the most egregious form of emotional ownership by enforcing the legality of her duties as his wife, Carol chooses to 'release' Therese whom she refuses to view as a form of property and, thus, as a mere extension of herself. Carol shuts herself up within her suburban home (a domicile that represents a very specific bourgeois notion of success and happiness), isolates herself socially and submits to the diagnosis of her doctor and the pernicious infringements of the legal system. The extreme reaction of patriarchal law to Carol's 'morally questionable' behaviour which results in her self-imposed incarceration in fact suggests the fragile and fractious nature of a law that is based on compulsory heterosexuality and the shoring up of the domestic, heteronormative, nuclear family; the necessity of such violent forms of control suggests by contradistinction that what is taken as given and natural is in fact purely contingent and evinces only the interests of those whom it serves best. As Ahmed reminds us:

> (f)or something to be required is, of course, 'evidence' that it is not necessary or inevitable. Heterosexuality is compulsory precisely insofar as it is not prescribed by nature: the heterosexual couple is 'instituted" as the form of sociality through force ... This enforcement does not mean that women are 'victims' of heterosexuality (though they can be), rather it means that to become a subject under the law one is made subject to the law that decides what forms lives must take in order to count as lives 'worth living'. (2006: 84)

It is this enforcement of patriarchal law that results in Carol realising that she cannot live a life that requires she 'shut' herself away and 'live against' her own 'grain'. To lead a life of such reduced expectation and hope is akin to internal death. In other words, her decision, which is not lightly made since it requires acquiescing to the deeply offensive and erroneous prognosis her doctor has made and admitting being 'unfit' for the role of motherhood, signals a rejection of what has been deemed by a very narrow constitution as a 'good' life or a life 'worth living'. In choosing to choose, Carol enacts a will to gain sovereignty and determination over her own existence: she chooses to live her life, but this is a life that ushers in a form of queer domesticity that is not recognised by patriarchal law. In other words, Carol chooses a form of ghost life in order to survive in a world that casts her as aberrant. It is in this moment that the clear discrepancy between notions of the domestic abode (a clichéd idyll) and home (and its concomitant signification of belonging) are rendered startlingly clear. Carol must remake her home by recognising her love for Therese and rejecting the clearly defined spaces of patriarchal law: the domestic cannot contain her.

By contrast with spaces controlled by patriarchal law, Carol and Therese, of their own volition, choose to occupy inherently liminal spaces that are designed for fleeting and ephemeral encounters. These spaces, largely speaking made up of cafes, motels, hotels, diners and a vast series of interconnecting roads set within nondescript and expansive countryside, are generally places through which one passes but does not definitively stop. These are not situations of identity and determination, but rather spaces in which one inherently becomes a passenger, divested of identity. Indeed, anthropologist Victor Turner (1995), taking his cue from the earlier work of Arnold van Gennep (1960) on liminal space, states that the ritual subject in such a space is: 'betwixt and between the positions assigned and arrayed by law, custom, convention and ceremonial' (1995: 95). Identity, here, is ambiguous, fluid and cannot be cleaved to or contained by exhaustive categorisation or definition. Moreover, the hegemonic norms and values of stratified, social society are not applicable to the liminal situation and participant. These in-between spaces, therefore, reflect the indeterminate, ambiguous nature of their relationship. In these spaces, they cannot or should not be pinned down – which in part may explain Carol's violent reaction to the private investigator's intrusion into their liminal space. In essence, *Carol* is a road movie: a genre which has – especially in its American iteration – worked to foreground notions of losing and remaking one's 'self' specifically in relation to one's environment or surrounding landscape. It has also often centred on the figure of the outsider who rejects norms and constrictions of 'the good life' and its coterminous laws. That *Carol*, as a queer iteration of the road movie genre, visually foregrounds motifs of reflection and refraction and readily utilises violations of screen direction cues the viewer to infer that this is a desire that drives identity off the straight and narrow in favour of deviation; this is a space in which one easily loses one's coordinates. It cannot be contained via a linear trajectory for to veer off track once is to veer forevermore; indeed, Carol deliberately leaves the details of her trajectory highly nebulous: 'I'm going away for a while; somewhere; wherever my car will take me', she states before inviting Therese to accompany her. At the centre of its narrative, after all, are two women who refuse, in essence, to fall into line with the governing norms of the society in which they live. Theirs is a comprehensive rejection of the priapic narrative that is forced upon them.

Likewise, Carol and Therese rebel against the men who determine how and with whom they must live by choosing to take to the road; notably, in answer to Richard, the man who wishes to marry her, Therese responds that she has never seen 'so clearly' when he contends that she has fallen into a 'trance' because of her relationship with Carol. As such, she enunciates in this moment her desire to see the world and her place within it for herself, through her own eyes, rather than through the male gaze that would determine a very limited narrative for her life. This manoeuvre into liminal space signals a wholesale rejection of the constricting space and vision of patriarchal law. Carol's car is much more than a vehicle that facilitates the promise of freedom for it is a mode of transportation in and of itself; by transportation, I mean to say that it designates a zone of betwixt and between in which possibility and transformation can play out. Many of the scenes set inside the car are conveyed through an oneiric *mise en scène* that employs superimposition, slow motion, delay, fade, heightened use of a green and golden colour palate, overlaid reflections and sounds (Figure 4.2). These dream-like images help to cocoon the female protagonists within their environment – a world which seems to exist outside of the space and time of the narrative set within public space. In fact, the places they pass through, though named (Ohio, Chicago, Iowa) remain non-specific and anonymous with few distinctive or defining characteristics. However, this is not a utopian space but rather a moment in which the limitations, if not the impossibility, of lesbian desire are played out. Carter Burwell's score, which is featured prominently within the scenes set in the car, is marked by a melancholic and yearning tone; the main piano theme is notably plaintive in its use of the minor key since even as the musical motif carried by the left hand rises, the melody performed by the right hand falls – a counterpoint that foregrounds and contrasts notions of expansion, growth and possibility with sorrow and diminishment. This melodic line blends seamlessly with the car radio that plays the romantic ballad *You Belong To Me* – a sentiment to which neither of them is able to lay any claim or articulation. These moments between Carol and Therese are bittersweet and convey what cannot be spoken between them in open space. The private and

Figure 4.2 The car as a liminal space of lesbian desire in *Carol* (2015). Film still.

enclosed space of the car, which carries them away from stratified social space, functions metonymically then to convey both the displacing effect of love (that one suddenly feels apart from the world, out of space and time) and the painful limitation of choosing a form of love that is not socially recognised (that one must choose, in essence, invisibility).

Carol is structured around a circular motif; as such, the main body of the narrative is conveyed through Therese's memory that relates the chance encounter that caused her to deviate off the straight and narrow path set out for her by patriarchal law. Central to this is Carol's letter to Therese (which is conveyed in voice-over at the midpoint of the film) in which she explains that she cannot sustain their relationship because of the sacrifices she is being forced to make. Devastatingly, their desire, admits Carol, can only exist in relation to an imaginary utopian ideal – a notion that is pre-figured in the film's single sex scene which is facilitated and envisioned through a mirror image of the lovers as they gaze at themselves (as an idealised and cohesive image). In this moment, their love becomes symbiotic, their limbs merging into one, suggesting that this desire resides in relation to the imaginary, pre-symbolic realm that precedes the symbolic mode of articulation. As such, their love-making remains chaste (for which the film was criticised) because it cannot exist carnally within the symbolic realm, governed as it is by the phallic Law of the Father; indeed, it is this encounter which the private detective captures on tape as evidence of Carol's supposedly wanton and morally permissive behaviour. This is, to be sure, a tragedy and it is this realisation that causes Carol to tear asunder her love for Therese. It is Carol's absence, or her lack of material presence, that haunts Therese. The film's central narrative, as such, is Therese's attempt to understand what it is that has happened to her – to grasp how this desire for another woman has incontrovertibly altered her. Their love exists in the mode of romantic memory, apart from the space and time of the social world. That the body of the film is crafted from 16mm film adds a further layer of poignancy to Therese's quest to understand herself since its material register is marked by disintegrative, friable and ephemeral qualities. The very form of the film, as such, reflects the fragility of their happenstantial affair and its primarily subjective viewpoint that is marked by Therese's desire; indeed, time in *Carol* is characterised by modes of protraction (waiting and duration) and expansion (slow motion and close-up) that are common to the experience of love. It is within Therese's internal and intensively felt monologue that she is able to bring herself 'full circle' to the moment of choosing to choose a love that will mean she must always live otherwise.

Conclusion: Everything Comes Full Circle

In her parting letter to Therese, Carol articulates the profound, yet impossible nature of their desire as she sees it; her vision of their future together is both tender and heartrending since it seems to exist purely in relation to a utopia that cannot be incorporated into the social world. She writes:

> (d)earest, ... everything comes full circle – and when it happens, I want you to imagine me there to greet you. Our lives stretched out ahead of us, a perpetual sunrise. But until then ... I do the only thing I can: I release you.

The circle that Carol intimates is manifest within the very structure of the film as the process by which both women arrive at a point of deeply painful and courageous compromise. In order to take up any place within a world that is resolutely governed by patriarchal law, they must yield to condemnation and invisibility. To be sure, the film offers this as an indictment of patriarchal law itself by giving Carol the space within which she can articulate powerfully the position into which she has been forced by Harge and his offensive assemblage of lawyers, doctors and investigators. She demands that she is allowed to speak; that she does this in a space marked out as distinctly male (a lawyer's office in which she is surrounded by men) in which the aim is to disarticulate her is crucial because her words, her naming of the injustice that has been forced upon her, concretises the way in which the film itself has explored the problematic of articulating and representing lesbian desire. She says of her love for Therese: 'I want it and I will not deny it ... what use am I being forced to live against my own grain?' The film has already prefigured this realisation by shifting subtly the focalisation from Therese to that of Carol; as she is passing through a crowded street in New York in a taxi, she catches sight of Therese crossing the road. This time, it is Therese who is elegantly clothed in red and posited as the object of desire from a female viewpoint.

Carol, therefore, suggests that both female protagonists have struggled to come to the point in which their desire can be inscribed into the fabric of the world because this comes at such a heavy psychical and physical cost. As such, the film employs the notions of futurity and utopia as a way of critiquing patriarchy from the perspective of an as of yet unrealised future (a place of perpetual sunrise). It is in this moment that Carol recognises Therese's struggle as her own. Her maturity and experience cannot save her from the reality of an environment that seeks to whittle down her ability to thrive and flourish; her only recourse is to choose her desire in the face of a culture that will force her to forsake her social legitimacy and live out her desire within confinement. Her choice entails electing a way of life that rejects the dominant narrative of happiness, it means losing the pre-ordained coordinates that designate one mode of living as legitimate to the exclusion of anything else. As Ahmed reminds us:

> for a life to count as a good life, then it must return the debt of its life by taking on the direction promised as a social good, which means imagining one's futurity in terms of reaching certain points along a life course. A queer life might be one that fails to make such gestures of return. (2006: 21)

In choosing to refuse to 'return the debt' and to veer off course, Carol and Therese incur the wrath and indignation of patriarchal law. The queer path is one that orients us towards bodies that are put out of reach by convention (and law). By extension, *Carol* is a film that does not seek to recuperate and calibrate its queerness – that is, it does not seek out a state of equilibrium. Its exploration of the difficulty of lesbian choice is borne out through the characters' relation to space; namely that if 'heterosexuality shapes the contours of inhabitable or liveable space' (Ahmed 2006: 106) it is also given that: 'the straight world is already in place and that queer moments, where things are out of line, are fleeting' (Ahmed 2006: 106). In its complication of the relation of lesbian desire to utopian (and impossible) space, *Carol* posits the liminal space as one in which the radical encounter changes the course of a life, a reorientation from which we cannot return or re-assimilate ourselves. To name one's queerness (as Carol names – or rather, sees – Therese as a 'strange girl, flung out of space') is also to acknowledge that one cannot undo one's unravelling. *Carol* is a film that refuses to recalibrate strangeness and disorientation. It asks that we inhabit the difficulty and intensity of such a reorientation. It brings us, in its concluding moments, to the meaning of 'I love you.'

Notes

1 This position of utopian lesbian politics (especially writing that has taken its cue from Wittig) is not without detractors. Anna Marie Jagose (1994) outlines the problematic of placing the lesbian as elsewhere/outside or as radically Other: in affirming the lesbian's transgression or subversion we also enforce her assumed and constructed position within hegemonic patriarchal system. Moreover, Jagose suggests that such theories invoke an essentialist notion of what the lesbian is (based on unpacked notions of 'woman'). In fact, the contradictory theoretical positions between essentialism and liminality mean

that by definition there cannot be, for Jagose, any definitive closure to or definition of the term lesbian. As Jagose argues: '(t)he tendency to figure "lesbian" as utopic and outside dominant conceptual frameworks essentializes that category as transgressive or subversive. The inherent revolutionary character of "lesbian" demonstrates the foundational flaw in its utopic figuration: that the exteriority of the utopic category is phantasmatic and conceals that category's position within the networks of power' (1994: 5). Therefore, for Jagose, because there cannot be any fixed or exhaustive definition of the lesbian body, we cannot claim a politics of lesbianism since the lesbian does not enact or possess anything essential: 'contrary to the logic of lesbian utopics subscribed by Wittig. [...] The category "lesbian" is not essentially radical or subversive. Indeed, the category "lesbian" is not essentially anything. It does not have a fixed valence, a signification that is proper to itself' (1994: 9). This, in turn, poses profound difficulties for any politics based on the notion of woman – namely, feminism. As Jagose argues: 'the category "women", which once seemed so solid and dependable in relation to the hesitant fluctuation of "lesbian" has been similarly destabilized. With this destabilization of the ontological foundations of the category "women", the relations between other apparently stable categories of chromosomal and anatomical sex, gender and sexuality are no longer naturalized' (1994: 14). Recent attempts by feminist theorists to recuperate and reincorporate difference into its politics has been, though well intentioned, tokenistic as far as Jagose is concerned because this gesture has not included a fundamental re-evaluation of the term 'woman'. She therefore argues that: 'the feminist goal of specifying precise location within a general category of identification, while politically strategic, is ultimately unattainable due to the infinity of possible specifications as well as the impossibility of the subject articulating herself in a closure of self-location ... for while dominant discourse, what is being challenged is the production of an identificatory category – no matter how complex – on which to establish a politics an articulation of the category "women", sensitive to difference, is infinitely superior to one which replicates the priorities of liberation. Nor is this fundamental indeterminacy peculiar to the category "women". It is associated with any attempt to found a liberatory politics on a category of identification – any misrecognition of a coherent identity as the basis of politics' (1994: 16–17). It is not my intention in this essay to contradict or seek to cast as erroneous Jagose's sophisticated argument that is highly attuned to minute calibrations of difference. However, as someone who has laboured hard to understand my own identification with the terms feminist and lesbian, I cannot eschew a position from which I am able to articulate my difference. These terms, rather than being seen as closed and exhaustive categories in service of a hermetic identity politics, should, in my view, be regarded as strategies through which we may express our difference. Moreover, it is quite clear that we *do* experience the world as divisively and harmfully gendered; much as I not only agree with, but celebrate the work that has come in the wake of Judith Butler's theory of performativity, then – of which Jagose's thesis is but one example – I do not believe that rendering the socially constructive basis of gender evident detracts from or attenuates habitual, embodied experience in the world – a world that subjects the LGBTQ community to horrific forms of violence and control. Indeed, the Chechen government have recently denied reports of the mass incarceration and torture of homosexuals on the basis that it would be logically impossible to imprison people who do not exist in Chechnya – perhaps the most extreme and pernicious example of what denial of an existence can be put in service of.

2 As Teresa de Lauretis argues persuasively, the figure of the lesbian has even posed problems for feminist theorists such as Julia Kristeva: '(l)esbian sexuality, in other words, (according to Kristeva), is a non-relationship, or a *non-sexual* relationship: unless it is an adjunct, a sideline, an added attraction to the cutting edge of masculine sexuality ... sex between women is a bland pre-oedipal soup. From it only two paths are open: return to the eroto-logic of the master-slave relationship, or death – loss of identity, psychosis, suicide' (1991: 254).

3 Films such as Abdellatif Kechiche's *Blue is The Warmest Colour* (2013), Peter Strickland's *The Duke of Burgundy* (2014) and Park Chan-Wook's *The Handmaiden* (2016) have been roundly criticised for objectification of the female body and recuperating lesbian sexuality in order to uphold a form of visual pleasure dominated by, filtered through and intended for the male gaze.

4 Especially since, as de Lauretis contends: 'heterosexuality is a ubiquitous institution in our culture, pervasively embedded in practices of daily life as well as in the media, language, art, science, literature, and the very structures of thought and knowledge ... the social contract and symbolic exchange that establish culture and society itself are *founded* on the presupposition, or as I prefer to say the presumption, of heterosexuality' (1991: 241). To depict love as lived otherwise is to destabilise the predominant narrative of happiness, its concomitant set of images and its attendant values. In doing so, it reveals the contingency of what we take to be natural and normal and moreover, the social structures that benefit from upholding this dominant fiction.

5 Another alternative to ridding female homosexuality of its charge is to conflate it with male (homo)sexuality since, as de Lauretis argues: 'sexuality in the dominant forms of Western culture is defined from the frame of reference of "man", the white man, who has enforced his claim to be the subject of knowing, and woman – all women – his object: object of both his knowledge and his desire ... sexual desire belongs to the other, originates in him' (1991: 253). In this vein, lesbian desire is read as a drive to access phallic power. Yet, this overlooks the specificity and complexity of female homosexuality since, as Judith Mayne argues: 'male and female homosexualities occupy quite different positions, and given the masculine logic of the "same" that dominates the patriarchal order, female homosexuality cannot be ascribed functions that are similar to male homosexuality' (1991: 128).

6 See Anna Leszkiewicz (2015), 'Behind Carol: the photographers who influenced Todd Haynes' award-winning film', *New Statesman*, 27 November. Available at <http://www.newstatesman.com/culture/art-design/2015/11/behind-carol-photographers-who-influenced-todd-haynes-award-winning-film> (last accessed 1 May 2017).

Works Cited

Ahmed, Sara (2004), *The Cultural Politics of Emotion*, Edinburgh: Edinburgh University Press.
Ahmed, Sara (2006), *Queer Phenomenology*, Durham, NC: Duke University Press.
Ahmed, Sara (2010), *The Promise of Happiness*, Durham, NC: Duke University Press.
Butler, Judith (1990), *Gender Trouble*, London and New York: Routledge.
Castle, Terry (1993), *The Apparitional Lesbian*, New York: Columbia University Press.
de Lauretis, Teresa (1991), 'Film and the Visible', in Bad Object-Choices (eds), *How do I Look? Queer Film and Video*, Seattle: Bay Press.
Haynes, Todd (2015), *Carol*, Studio Canal.
Highsmith, Patricia (2010 [1952]), *The Price of Salt* or *Carol*, London: Bloomsbury.
Irigaray, Luce (1985), *This Sex Which is Not One*, Ithaca, NY: Cornell University Press.
Irigaray, Luce (1993), *An Ethics of Sexual Difference*, Ithaca, NY: Cornell University Press.
Jagose, Annamarie (1994), *Lesbian Utopics*, London and New York: Routledge.
Kosofsky Sedgwick, Eve (1985), *Between Men: English Literature and Male Homosocial Desire*, New York: Columbia University Press.
Leszkiewicz, Anna (2015), 'Behind Carol: the photographers who influenced Todd Haynes' award-winning film', <http://www.newstatesman.com/culture/art-design/2015/11/behind-carol-photographers-who-influenced-todd-haynes-award-winning-film> (last accessed 1 May 2017).
Mayne, Judith (1991), 'Lesbian Looks: Dorothy Arzner and Female Authorship', in Bad Object-Choices (eds), *How do I Look? Queer Film and Video*, Seattle: Bay Press.
Rich, Adrienne (1980), 'Compulsory Heterosexuality and Lesbian Existence', *Signs: Journal of Women in Culture and Society*, 5, no. 4, pp. 631–60.
Stacey, Jackie (1987), 'Desperately Seeking Difference', *Screen*, 28, no. 1, 48–61.
Turner, Victor (1995), *The Ritual Process*, New York: Aldine de Gruyter.
van Gennep, Arnold (1960), *The Rites of Passage*, Chicago: University of Chicago Press.
Wittig, Monique (1992), *The Straight Mind and Other Essays*, Boston, MA: Beacon Press.

CHAPTER 5

A Home on the Road in Claire Denis's *Vendredi soir*
Maud Ceuterick

Home often appears in opposition to travel. Throughout the road movie genre in particular, we encounter male protagonists who undertake self-reflective quests *away from home*, with 'home' often representing a conservative lifestyle that they hope to escape. In their *Road Movie Book*, editors Steve Cohan and Ina Rae Hark write that 'the road movie promotes a male escapist fantasy linking masculinity to technology and defining the road as a space that is at once resistant while ultimately contained by the responsibility of domesticity: home life, marriage, employment' (1997: 3). Home becomes at once a space of conventions and one of lost intimacy that the protagonist hopes to regain on the road. The road thus becomes an alternative to 'home' where the main character searches for the self and for a more authentic space of intimate relations.

In contemporary cinema, and in road movies in particular, the notion of home often signifies a familiar domestic space associated with women, and that stands in opposition to mobility and the 'masculine' (see de Lauretis 1984; Frederick and Hyde 1993; Robertson 1997; Bruno 2002; Rollet 2003; Mazierska and Rascaroli 2006; Royer 2011; Fullwood 2015; Blum-Reid 2016). Giuliana Bruno describes how the notion of home, of one's origin, of *domus* – domesticity, domestication – in male narratives of travel 'continues to be confused and gendered feminine' (2002: 86). As such, home has acquired a meaning of 'the womb from which one originates and to which one wishes to return' and has become 'the very site of the production of sexual difference' (Bruno 2002: 86). In travel narratives, returning to and 'repossessing' home often emerge as repossessing the feminine subject or 're-housing gender' in Bruno's words.

In Claire Denis's subversion of the road movie genre *Vendredi soir* (2002), I argue that the domestication of place happens through the film's haptic aesthetic, which disentangles home from a gendered conception of travel. Spaces such as the home and the road carry a whole different meaning when we consider the mobility of women in films. When

Virginia Woolf wrote *A Room of One's Own* (1929), she expressed the difficulties women experienced when they sought to inhabit both 'public' and private spaces (whether a public library, a park or a private house), as all were dominated and ruled by men. In a way that recalls Woolf's essay, women protagonists in road movies tend to leave the domestic space to find a space for themselves elsewhere; outside of confining gendered binaries situating women into stasis, passivity and dependance, in opposition to men's mobility, activity and independence. In *Vendredi soir*, the main character, Laure (Valérie Lemercier), creates a 'home' on the road as she reconnects to her spatial environment, *domesticating* it through sensations, desire and intimacy. This chapter first shows how the film uses magical realism to challenge our idea of home as we know it from other travel narratives, as fixed, gendered and immutable. Second, I argue that *Vendredi soir* invites the viewer to observe and analyse how the characters' bodies *micro-relate* to space, re-creating thus home as *domus*, as a space of intimacy.

In line with the notion of space in contemporary social geography, *Vendredi soir* portrays domestic spaces as fluid and evolving with social relations. Following the work of geographers Henri Lefebvre, Gillian Rose, Doreen Massey, Linda McDowell, Nigel Thrift and Tanu Priya Uteng and Tim Cresswell, places must be regarded as processes in constant transformation through practices, relations and representations. Massey asserts that places are not neutral, 'fixed and unproblematic in [their] identity' but are instead evolving sources of meaning and social relations, produced and reproduced within power configurations (1994: 5). As such, any place – the household, the workplace, the street – is an 'ever-shifting geometry of social/power relations' (Massey 1994: 4). In *Vendredi soir*, as Laure is moving from her own apartment to her (male) partner's one, the film places emphasis on the gendered power relations of the household. Laure rediscovers her spatial environment through body sensations and affective relations, and extends her *spaces of intimacy* into other spaces, her car and a motel room.

Putting in dialogue social geography and affect theory, I consider that human bodies inhabit, create and transform space through social relations, themselves affected by power-geometries (in Doreen Massey's terms). Following Spinoza, contacts with other bodies influence how we perceive and experience space, through our accumulative memory of the ways in which our 'body's power of activity [has been] increased or diminished' (1982 [1677]: 104). It is due to the negative impact of patriarchal and misogynist attitudes towards women that 'women's mobility, for instance, is restricted – in a thousand different ways, from *physical* violence to being ogled at or made to *feel* quite simply "out of place" – not by "capital", but by men' (Massey 1994: 148, emphasis mine). In a first instance, for being made to feel out of place in the past, Laure moves through Paris with the fear of violence. However, when a giant traffic jam immobilises the whole city, mobility loses its gendered significations. This allows Laure to inhabit the city more playfully and affirmatively, and to open up to affective exchanges with the male 'other'.

While cinema tends to produce and reinforce social and spatial dichotomies, I argue that Denis's haptic aesthetic contributes to dismantling them. I refer to haptic aesthetic following Laura U. Marks's work, as triggering the sense of touch through the textures of images and sounds. By creating a 'habitable world' that emphasises the *lived*, textural and affective dimensions of space, the film invites the viewers to *touch* and *experience* what is being shown. As Marks writes, 'haptic images can give the impression of seeing for the first time, gradually discovering what is in the image rather than coming to the image already knowing what it is' (2000: 178). The haptic aesthetic of *Vendredi soir* functions as a political strategy that takes viewers beyond what they already know of gender, mobility and the domestic space.

When watching *Vendredi soir*, viewers experience a sensory world that is in continual production and transformation through their own and the characters' senses. In *Carnal Thoughts*, Vivian Sobchack asserts that films create a 'habitable *world* ... a space that is deep and textural, that can be materially inhabited' (2004: 151). For Jennifer Barker, drawing on Sobchack's work, the film's body is a lived-body (not a human one) that exists

> haptically, at the screen's surface, with the caress of shimmering nitrate and the scratch of dust and fiber on celluloid; kinaesthetically, through the contours of on- and off-screen space and of the bodies, both human and mechanical, that inhabit or escape those spaces; and viscerally, with the film's rush through a projector's gate and the 'breathing' of lenses. (2009: 3)

Barker asserts that attention to texture, space and rhythm allows us to determine 'the fleshy, muscular, and visceral engagement that occurs between films' and viewers' bodies' (2009: 4). In order to understand how the woman protagonist in *Vendredi soir* makes a space for herself, I argue that the film asks for a micro-analysis; looking at the scratches of the screen's surface, the micro-movements of bodies into space, and how the film 'breathes', creating thus the rhythm of the film. As the haptic aesthetic of *Vendredi soir* invites viewers to experience the film through their senses, it redefines the home as a domesticated space and a space of intimacy.

A Liminal Domestic Space

It is by bringing Paris to a standstill that *Vendredi soir* challenges the gendering of mobility and the domestic space. The paralysis of traffic reduces both men and women to a state of *im*mobility. In this 'exceptional' static state (or crisis of mobility) the commonly gendered narrative of travel is suspended, or of limited value. The car, which is ordinarily an index of 'masculine' power within the logic of mobility, converts into a space in need of re-appropriation and re-definition. The car becomes an instrument for appraising the urban space as one's own.

Claire Denis challenges the idea that the road quester finds a space for himself or herself through mobility, and assimilates it instead into the 'domestication' of space. If *Vendredi soir* echoes Jean-Luc Godard's *Weekend* (1967) in the absurd immobility and strangeness of human contacts, the cars stuck in traffic do not epitomise the purposelessness and meaninglessness of human existence. On the contrary, Denis's camera affirmatively converts the modern apocalyptic imaginary about immobilised cars into an opportunity for embracing one's desires and transforming the power-geometries of space.

Several recent filmic examples also convert the car into a space of dwelling whose 'inhabitants' somehow challenge gender binaries, such as *Night on Earth* (Jim Jarmusch, 1991), *No Sex Last Night* (Sophie Calle and Greg Shephard, 1996), *Crash* (David Cronenberg, 1996), *Ten* (Abbas Kiarostami, 2002), *Lluvia* (Paula Hernández, 2008), *Wendy and Lucy* (Kelly Reichardt, 2008), *Drive* (Nicolas Winding Refn, 2011), and *Locke* (Steven Knight, 2013). Denis's car in fact turns into a 'poetic' vehicle – a medium of *poiesis*, or else 'story-making', in which intimacy and connections are generated. Domesticating space emerges as inhabiting space through one's senses, through a body that affects and is affected.

When the film begins, Laure is packing up boxes: she is moving, we find out, to her (male) partner's house the following morning. She is leaving her 'home', that is her 'space of her own', to live with her partner in *his* apartment, which, as she admits, she has not yet learned to call 'home'. After a day by herself packing up boxes, she takes a bath and drives to a friend's house for dinner. As Laure leaves the security of her apartment, from where she could look at the city unobserved, she is immediately confronted with the 'dangers' that a city like Paris represents for a woman who is on her own at night.

Soon after Laure enters her car, a man slaps his palm on her window, startling her. Only slightly lit by street lights, the white face of the man contrasts with his dark outfit and the darkness of the street, which endows him with a frightening appearance. Instead of opening the car as the man wanted, Laure locks the doors and starts the engine. Even though we come to understand that the man was in fact only asking for a lift (because of a general transport strike), the chiaroscuro lighting, the strident musical phrase and the rapid montage of the scene portray him as a threat, aesthetically conveying how Laure perceives the urban space as dominated and controlled by men. For a moment, the immobility of the car lets the 'threats' of the 'public' space penetrate its private sphere and reminds us of Godard's film.

As soon as she leaves her street Laure is caught in a gigantic traffic jam, which blocks the whole city of Paris. An array of cars are at a standstill, cold people wrapped up in their winter jackets and looming out of the mist overrun the pathways and walk on the road in between cars. Stuck in traffic, Laure treats her car like an extension of her apartment: she dries her hair with the ventilation and sits in the backseat as she goes through boxes that she packed earlier. On the one hand, the car protects Laure from the world outside. Her hostile relation to the city as well as close-ups, tight narrow shots of Laure (imposed by the exiguity of the car), and frames-within-the-frame convert the car into a space of intimacy, albeit one of containment. Laure's car fulfils the role of a familiar space that is no longer to be found in her 'old' home or indeed in her new one with her partner. The car provides her with a refuge (in a moment of home-lessness) and protects her from the patriarchal city that negatively affects her capacity to inhabit space fully.

On the other hand, the car functions as a liminal space that opens onto the outside. At various times, the camera wanders off from Laure's car and explores the city, which appears through fog, fumes and neon lights. Instead of a familiar view of Paris, gaseous textures, bright lights and slow movements invade the screen. Rather than a solid material 'house', the haptic aesthetic of the film converts the car into a poetic gaseous object; a liminal space that comes into existence through social contacts and affective relations. Through haptic images and sounds, *Vendredi soir* encourages the viewers to establish an 'embodied and multisensory relationship to the image', in Marks's words (2000: 172). By portraying cars and windows of shops as forms, colours and textures, the film invites us to experience the city through other senses that go beyond cognitive functions.

In opposition to Laure's stationary body, the film's body is a mobile one. While Laure is stuck, the camera and editing create movement in the image. As the camera escapes and 'wanders' out of the confines of

Laure's car, it connects Laure with a collectivity of car-bodies similarly affected by the traffic jam, a connection that is reinforced by the close-ups on other cars and passengers. More permeable than the windows of Laure's apartment through which she is a distanced observer, the windows of the car appear as 'soft screens', at once marking the boundary of the domestic space and facilitating imaginative travel through the city.

Denis creates a world that merges realist and magical elements, stimulating both our cognitive and sensory functions, and opening up possibilities to reinterpret differently the gendered vision of private domestic space. As the camera films parts of cars, roofs, bright lights, smoking hoods, sleeping passengers and drivers getting busy in their cars, it draws us little by little into a world of textures and sensations, a 'habitable world'. The wandering camera merges human bodies with their cars and creates a lyrical city in which cars almost become characters themselves that move and dance. Fixed a little above the ground, the camera films in close-up the lights of slowly moving cars shrouded in mist from car fumes and winter fog. In combination with Dickon Hinchliffe's classical music, these abstract images, with the cars' and the camera's very slow movements, produce a magical atmosphere, a *ballet of cars*, that transforms modern purposeful objects of transport into poetic abstractions. This representation disconnects the car from its construct in the road movie as a symbol of man's freedom, violence and desire. Instead, in this dance, car-bodies establish a relationship with others while keeping a space for themselves. The traffic jam creates a unique situation that *resets* the power-geometries of space, producing thereby a possibility for the woman protagonist to domesticate the urban space from a place of relative safety.

Laure's car, containing and protecting her from the outside, also becomes permeable through the soundtrack of the film. When Laure sings along to a 1980s French hit 'Manureva', the diegetic song becomes a soundtrack somehow magically. Although the volume of the song lowers when the camera leaves Laure's car, filming her through the driver's lateral window, the score remains at the same volume – as if still outside Laure's window – when the camera wanders and films other drivers and passengers. The song, evoking a boat that went missing in the 1980s, has a nostalgic affect to it; it is through its popularity and the sound editing that it unites drivers and passengers in their desperation with the heavy traffic. In a similar way to the ballet of cars, the soundtrack interrupts the realist aesthetic as it creates a spatial atmosphere based on affects. This reinforces the domestication of Laure's car, as a space that is open to the other and to intimate connections.

Magical Realism and Lived Spaces

The exceptional immobility of cars in the city creates a pause in Laure's journey and a moment (a Friday night, hence the title of the film) in which the 'magical' (or the unthinkable) can meet the real. The formal aspects of *Vendredi soir* introduce magical elements into the realism of the film. As magical realism brings about Laure's subjectivity and imagination, it also challenges the gendered portrayal of the domestic space by establishing a connection with the many possibilities of the real. When the song 'Manureva' finishes, a female voice announces 'you all know by now ... that Paris is at a complete standstill due to the public transport strike'. The presenter seems to address Laure personally, who has been packing up all day and is probably 'the only one who did not know' ('Y en a peut-être encore deux qui sont pas au courant'). The magical realism of this address is reinforced by the presenter's intimate-sounding voice, almost like a sensual whisper, playfully suggesting that drivers offer a lift to cold stranded pedestrians.[1] A little later, the camera, in one of its 'wanderings' from Laure's car, suddenly stumbles over Jean (Vincent Lindon). As if in response to the radio announcement, Jean walks towards Laure's car and asks if he can come in. As Laure accepts, she learns to domesticate space, make it her own, outside the safety of her apartment. Her change of attitude and the change in the aesthetic of the film since Laure's first encounter with the frightening man invalidate the gendered binaries that represent women as nurturer of private spaces and men as explorer of so-called 'public' spaces.[2]

In the film, two places take the form of potential homes, of *spaces of intimacy*: the car and a motel room that Laure and Jean occupy together. As Laure inhabits these spaces through the sensations that her encounter with Jean provokes, she rehearses the founding of a shared home with her partner François. Oscillating between living as a single woman and living as part of a (heterosexual) couple, Laure's habitation of space through seemingly fixed gendered norms is in fact both reiterated and challenged through Jean's presence.

When Jean enters Laure's car, the film seems to start again. Sitting mostly in silence, Jean and Laure make slow progress through the heavy traffic. As Jean steps into Laure's car his presence changes the film's body; its spaces, textures and rhythm. Writing on Claire Denis's cinema extensively, Martine Beugnet asserts that Laure instantly *feels* Jean's presence: she can smell him, and his body comes with its weight (2004: 194). Haptic images and sounds in particular create an atmosphere (in Ben Anderson's words)[3] and a space of sensations, a lived space.

Phenomenologist Maurice Merleau-Ponty writes that we only exist *in space* through sensory experience: 'our experience is the experience of a world ... a particular manner of being in space and, in a certain sense, of *creating space*' (2012 [1962]: 230). The silence of the scene punctuated by highlighted diegetic sounds, in particular, give a materiality to the space (Donaldson 2014). The emphasised sounds of the door opening and closing, Laure turning off the inside light, Jean closing the window, his movement on the seat and the clearing of his throat both serve the realism of the film and create a space of contact and intimacy. Progressively in the film, the gendered aspect of the city disappears. If the urban space previously emerged in opposition to the safety of a closed space, a home, the home now takes a whole new meaning that is produced through the textures of the screen, the characters' sensory experience of space and the rhythm of the film.

The domestication of space happens through both physical interactions and the negotiation of power. The car and, later in the film, the motel room oscillate between the social and physical exchanges within them, and their 'housing of gender' (in Bruno's terms, 2002: 86) determined by heteronormative patriarchal norms. When Jean climbs into Laure's car uninvited, asking a rhetorical question ('Can I come in?'), his sense of entitlement comes to light: as a man he feels it is legitimate to enter this woman's space as if it were his own. A micro-analysis of the film's *mise en scène* and the characters' movements reveals the tensions between affects and social power that come with the domestication of space. While Jean looks towards Laure with steady movements of the head, Laure glances at him repetitively with jerky movements of the head. The short takes that characterise the characters' first interaction express Laure's nervousness at having a male stranger in her car.

Through absurd elements that invade the realism of the film, Denis ridicules the machismo of the city and denounces the patriarchal heteronormativity of space. Echoing the overtly masculinist and theatrical tone of the opening scene of Godard's *Weekend*, two men involved in an accident fight while the female partner of one of them hits the other with her handbag and is ordered to 'shut up'. Given the greater immobility caused by the accident, Laure steps out of the car to call her friend Marie and cancel their dinner as she starts feeling desire for Jean. However, when she returns she cannot find her car. Denoting the gendered power-geometries of space, Jean too demonstrates a patronising attitude towards Laure. Although he himself moved the vehicle, he blames Laure for leaving it in the middle of the street (an absurd comment since nothing else has moved since she left). Jean takes Laure by the arm, physically guiding her back to the car, and sits in the driver seat without hesitation, even though the car belongs to Laure. These gestures point to a male control over women's bodies and men's overall domination of space.

A micro-analysis of the film allows us to observe the liminality of the domestic space and its constant transformations. With Jean behind the wheel, the car magically overrides the traffic jam and fully regains, for a moment, its aspects of speed, freedom and travel, which have for long been deemed 'masculine'. The cinematography and editing of the scene, as well as a change in the music with its speedy violins, both produce the synesthetic sensation of the rapid motion,[4] and invite the viewer to live through Laure's physical sensations. When she panics and asks Jean to stop the vehicle so she can get out, Jean points out that he is the one who should get out since the car is hers. Her reaction and his remark, made significant by the scarcity of dialogue in the film, emphasise that gender norms condition Laure's relation to space (the driver often being the male protagonist in road movies). If Jean brings in the patriarchal aspects of the city to the safety of Laure's car – her 'home' – his presence also transforms the concept of home. From a place that is fixed and above the city such as Laure's apartment, home becomes a space in '*transito*' (in Bruno's words, 2002: 86), which is continually created through the desires, and positive and negative affects of its inhabitants.

Vendredi soir illustrates how power dynamics and sensory experiences have affective impacts on both the body and one's making of a space for oneself. After Jean has left the car, Laure drives around looking for him. From outside through the window of a cafe, she sees him interacting with a younger woman. The haptic sound and images again reveal the subjectivity of the scene. Before Laure enters the cafe, she watches the young woman and Jean playing pinball. While the words of both Jean and the woman are muffled, as Laure comes closer, the sounds of the pinball grow louder and Jean's words become clearer. The cinematography and editing of this sequence underline the two women's internalisation of sexual norms and their play of power to *get to touch* Jean. When Laure comes in, the young woman appraises her, looking her up and down (Figure 5.1). Then, a close-up of Jean slightly touching Laure's hand with intention highlights the desire between the two protagonists. The camera films the young woman's gaze towards their hands and then her own hand on the pinball, in a close-up that blurs her uncovered belly in the background (Figure 5.2). Like many scenes in the film, this one requires the viewer's active vision of the characters' micro-relations to uncover how Laure's capacity to re-create a space for herself outside the

Figures 5.1 and 5.2 *Vendredi soir/Friday Night* (2002): focus on a younger woman's gaze and hands in a cafe. Film stills.

walls of her apartment happens as much through a play of power and sensory experiences.

Re-writing Home: The Haptic as Feminist Statement

Whereas Laure at first appears negatively affected from inhabiting the city as a woman, she reaffirms her right to a home on the road through renewing with her body and desire. Sensuous connections transform the car and the motel room, where the lovers spend the night together, into homes, spaces of intimacy. In a point of view shot from Laure's perspective, Jean's hand in close-up enters the opening of his shirt and makes contact with his own skin. This simple gesture, filmed in close-up, emphasises both the texture of Jean's skin and Laure's desire for him. Similarly, when Laure watches Jean extend his legs, putting himself at ease, another series of close-ups edited together shows the tights on her feet rubbing against each other, her knees extending and her fingers lightly stroking the steering wheel. By constantly drawing attention to textures and sensations, the haptic aesthetic of *Vendredi soir* illustrates how the domestication of space builds on micro-relations between bodies rather than on gender norms.

In the car and in the motel room, the intimate connection between Laure and Jean brings to mind Laure's imminent reconstruction of a home with her partner. When Jean gets into Laure's car, he immediately lowers the passenger seat so that he can lie down comfortably. Through this overly familiar gesture, Jean 'makes himself at home' almost as if he were Laure's partner François. Denis also nourishes this confusion by giving very little information on either man, making them indistinguishable from other men (the only signs of François's existence are his keys left with a short note in Laure's apartment, we neither see him nor hear him speak).[5] Jean's magical appearance on screen, almost coming out of Laure's fantasy, and the possible confusion between the two men support an interpretation of the film as a rewriting of an ideal domestic space.

Figure 5.3 *Vendredi soir/Friday Night* (2002): Laure's and Jean's faces almost become indistinguishable as they kiss. Film still.

Rather than moving into François' apartment, Laure imagines moving into a *neutral* place, and so not losing her space but reconstructing one anew with a man, from an equal position.[6] The motel room, marked as pre-personal and undefined, forms an adequate space for Laure to make her own. By noticing the same objects as in her old apartment into the motel room, Laure appropriates the space. Laure and Jean take possession of the motel room through embracing on the bed and placing their personal objects on the tables and in the closet. From being dark, cold-lit and blue-hued (similar to Laure's empty apartment), the room becomes golden hued and inviting. As such, Laure's apartment has ceased to be a domestic space since it has lost its aspect of space of intimate contacts. Objects from Laure's apartment resurface in the motel room, such as her electric heater and a red lamp that she threw away. Bathed in the warm orange lighting from the heater and the lamp, images of the motel room and the apartment merge. The common objects, colours and textures of both places mingle, and establish a material and sensory parallel between Laure's apartment and her new home. In fact, these objects enclosed Laure's sensory memories, and leaving them behind amounts to being left without a place to call home. In *Vendredi soir*, creating a home develops into creating new sensory experiences. When Laure and Jean kiss for the first time in the street, the *mise en scène* and cinematography blur the characters' (gendered) identities and convey the reversibility of their touch (Figure 5.3). There is no relation of subject–object anymore, no one 'possesses' the other with their gaze, as the camera films the characters' faces in extreme close-up, illuminating them with a warm light while leaving all the rest in utter darkness. For Merleau-Ponty, there is always a *reversibility* of the touching experience; as he explains, two hands of one's body, or another's body, touching each other always simultaneously touch and are being touched (1964: 183). Foregrounding the rustling of their clothes and the faint sounds of their kisses, the direct sound of the scene creates an oneiric and tactile atmosphere. In contrast to the male domination of the city described earlier, the two characters now inhabit the street from an equal position, of touching and being touched. As the *mise en scène* focuses on the tactile, it erases the social, the 'real', and leaves the habitation of space up to reinterpretation.

Lived experiences and sensations come to the fore, leaving behind gender norms and power structures. Instead of filming the characters' faces during intercourse, Denis's camera shatters the mainstream cinematic conventions of sexual encounters. A shaky handheld camera films body parts in extreme close-up, a hand on a knee or on a back, upper and inner thighs, parts of a leg, a hand taking off underwear (Figure 5.4). As Martine Beugnet writes in her book *Claire Denis*, the 'tactile gaze of the camera establishes an intimacy with [the characters] as physical beings' (2004: 192). Extreme close-ups and chiaroscuro lighting disrupt the attributability of body parts to one specific sexed body. Both Laure and Jean have dark brown hair, dark clothes, very similar skin complexion

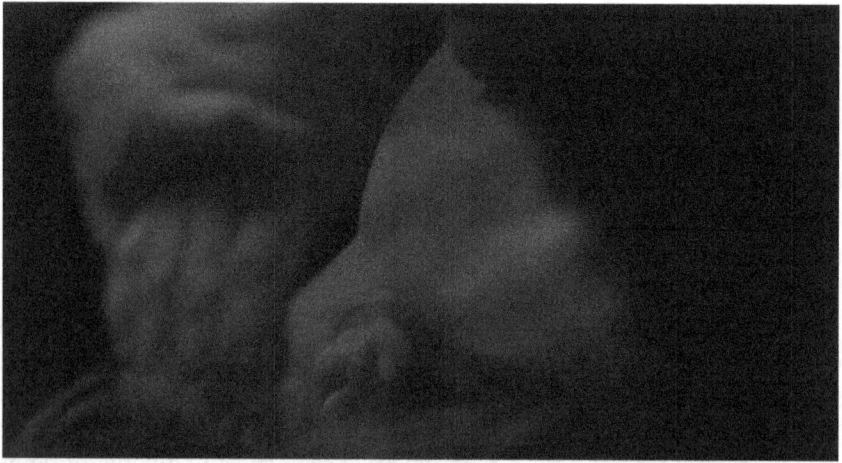

Figure 5.4 *Vendredi soir/Friday Night* (2002): close-up of the lovers' erotic encounter. Film still.

and body proportions, all of which facilitates their appearance as one androgynous body. Denis in fact recognises the haptic dimension of her filming techniques: 'In the end, we knew the very texture of their skin' (cited in Beugnet 2004: 193), and avoids giving 'feminine' or 'masculine' attributes to her characters.[7] Gender norms are continually counteracted by the mutual desire and the contagiousness of affects between Laure and Jean. The haptic aesthetic of *Vendredi soir* produces spaces that are lived and embodied, domesticated through intimate contacts, possibly beyond gender.

In this chapter, I have argued that a micro-analysis of bodies' relations to space helps uncover how home becomes a lived space rather than being gendered and associated with the feminine as in male travel narratives. For the woman protagonist, instead of escaping 'marriage, employment, and responsibility' through mobility (in Cohan's and Hark's words), finding a new home of the road signifies renewing one's desires and affirmation of oneself. As such, the film serves a feminist strategy. Contra Judith Butler, who argues in her early work that there is no escape from gender other than through its re-iteration (1993), I maintain that considering the body as a 'lived body' and gender as a situation which is dynamic and constantly being negotiated allows for transformations at the level of both spatial habitation and gendered discourse.[8]

In a way that is reminiscent of Godard's *Weekend*, the traffic jam situates individuals as part of a multitude within which social power is to be discussed and renegotiated. As the magical realism of Denis's film disturbs our perceptions of urban spaces and cars, it places emphasis on the malleability of space. From being structured by the gendered binaries woman/man and stasis/travel, the city and the home become spaces that are lived and produced through affects and sensory experiences. Jennifer Barker's description of the haptic particularly resonates with Claire Denis's film:

> [The haptic] is a clever kind of political activism, in that it invites us not only to consider from a distance the film's feminist celebration of female desire but also, and more important, to partake in it, to experience this desire for ourselves in the act of watching the film. The power of the film's feminist political statement is thus not merely rhetorical, but profoundly tactile. (2009: 24)

By connecting viewers to the characters' micro-relations to space, the haptic aesthetic draws us into a domestication of space that is sensory and affective. Through its dream-like world and the characters' intimate connection, *Vendredi soir* in fact invites us to perceive home from an alternative perspective.

Acknowledgement

I am very grateful to Dr Catherine Fowler for her invaluable support, insight and advice.

Notes

1. This way of presenting the traffic is characteristic of the (exclusively) female announcers of France Inter Paris radio (FIP), among whom is Jane Villenet who plays the radio announcer in film. Jane Villenet has in fact made a short video titled *How to deliver traffic info on radio in a Fipette's way?* Available online: http://www.dailymotion.com/video/xp3100_jane-villenet-radio-france-comment-faire-un-bulletin-trafic-a-la-maniere-d-une-fipette_creation (last accessed 8 April 2018).
2. Women's bodies have often been paired with childbirth, mothering, nurturing and nature, and conflated with the domestic sphere. In opposition, the public sphere became constructed around notions of 'rationality, individuality [and] self-control' associated with the 'masculine' (Rose 1993: 35). These considerations have long unproblematically shaped and legitimated gender roles and power relations (Spain 1992; Rose 1993; Massey 1994; McDowell 1999).
3. Borrowing from Mikel Dufrenne, Anderson describes an affective atmosphere as 'how the "expressed world" overflows the representational content … as "[a] certain quality which words cannot translate but which communicates itself in arousing a feeling"' (2009: 79).
4. About the synesthesia of cinema, Merleau-Ponty writes that 'the ambiguity of experience is such that an auditory rhythm fuses cinematic images together and gives rise to a perception of movement whereas, without an auditory contribution, the same succession of images would be too slow to provoke the stroboscopic movement' (1962: 237).
5. In Emmanuèle Bernheim's eponymous book (1998), from which the film is adapted, the stranger Laure meets (Jean) is called Frédéric, thus sharing the two first letters of his name with Laure's partner François. Laure also compares the two men in inner monologues. She wonders why François does not dress the way Frédéric does and imagines moving in with Frédéric just as she will (we suppose) with François.
6. The paratextual elements of the film also support this interpretation. For example, if one looks at the DVD menu, this part of the film is entitled 'Back home'. Additionally, Bernheim's book makes it very clear that Laure fantasises about the motel room as her home: 'Small, square and with a low ceiling, this room looked like hers. Laure stopped. It was hers. She was at her place with Frédéric [(Jean in the film)]. And just as every night, before going to bed, he would turn down the heating. Because together at night, they would never get cold' (Bernheim 1998: 92–3, translation mine).

7 When she meets Jean, Laure wears androgynous clothes and not the red sexy skirt that she wears in Bernheim's book. This is a change that I interpret as the film's will to shatter the boundaries of gender, in addition to the fact that Laure wears no make-up and is filmed from the back when showering. For his part, while Jean embodies, at least in part, the heterosocial dynamics of power, his masculine appearance is 'queered' by his soft voice and his availability as Laure's fantasy. Narratively, the story of *Vendredi soir* could in fact be interpreted as a reversal of the gendered practice of 'kerb crawling'.

8 Whereas for Butler the subject does not prefigure gender but is already born in gender, for Simone de Beauvoir and Toril Moi drawing on de Beauvoir's work, the lived body is a process rather than linked to sexual anatomy, the 'ongoing interaction between the subject and the world' (Moi 2001: 63).

Works Cited

Anderson, Ben (2009), 'Affective atmospheres', *Emotion, Space and Society*, 2, pp. 77–81.

Barker, Jennifer M. (2009), *The Tactile Eye: Touch and Cinematic Experience*, Berkeley, Los Angeles and London: University of California Press.

Bernheim, Emmanuèle (1998), *Vendredi soir*, Paris: Gallimard.

Beugnet, Martine (2004), *Claire Denis and the Cinema of the Senses*, Manchester: Manchester University Press.

Blum-Reid, Sylvie (2016), *Traveling in French Cinema*, Basingstoke and New York: Palgrave Macmillan.

Bruno, Giuliana (2002), *Atlas of Emotion: Journeys in Art, Architecture, and Film*, London and New York: Verso.

Butler, Judith (1993), 'Critically queer', *GLQ: A Journal of Lesbian and Gay Studies*, 1, no. 1, pp. 17–32.

Calle, Sophie and G. Shephard (1996), *No Sex Last Night*, France: Bac Films.

Cronenberg, David (1996), *Crash*, Canada and UK: Alliance Communications Corporation.

de Beauvoir, Simone (1949), *Le Deuxième sexe I: Les Faits et les Mythes*, Paris: Gallimard.

De Lauretis, Teresa (1984), *Alice Doesn't: Feminism, Semiotics, Cinema*, Bloomington and Indianapolis: Indiana University Press.

Denis, Claire (2002), *Vendredi soir*. France: Bac Films.

Donaldson, Lucy F. (2014), *Texture in Film*, Basingstoke and New York: Palgrave Macmillan.

Frederick, Bonnie and V. Hyde (1993), 'Introduction', in B. Frederick and S. H. McLeod (eds), *Women and the Journey: The Female Travel Experience*, Washington, DC: Washington University Press, pp. xvii–xxxiii.

Fullwood, Natalie (2015), *Cinema, Gender, and Everyday Space: Comedy, Italian Style*, New York: Palgrave Macmillan.

Godard, Jean-Luc (2012 [1967]), *Weekend*, France: Criterion Collection.
Hernández, Paula (2008), *Lluvia*, Argentina: Buena Vista International.
Jarmusch, Jim (1991), *Night on Earth*, France, UK, Germany, USA and Japan: Pyramide.
Kiarostami, Abbas (2002), *Ten*, France and Iran: MK2 Productions.
Knight, Steven (2013), *Locke*, UK and USA: Lionsgate Home Entertainment.
Lefebvre, Henri (1974), *La Production de l'espace*, Paris: Anthropos.
McDowell, Linda (1999), *Gender, Identity and Place: Understanding Feminist Geographies*, Minneapolis: University of Minnesota Press.
Marks, Laura U. (2000), *The Skin of the Film: Intercultural Cinema, Embodiment, and the Senses*, Durham, NC and London: Duke University Press.
Massey, Doreen B. (1994), *Space, Place, and Gender*, Minneapolis: University of Minnesota Press.
Mazierska, Ewa and L. Rascaroli (2006), *Crossing New Europe: Postmodern Travel and the European Road Movie*, Film Studies. London and New York: Wallflower Press.
Merleau-Ponty, Maurice (1964), *Le Visible et l'Invisible; suivi de Notes de travail*, Paris: Gallimard.
Merleau-Ponty, Maurice (2012 [1962]), *Phenomenology of Perception*, New York and London: Routledge.
Moi, Toril (2001), *What Is a Woman?: And Other Essays*, New York: Oxford University Press.
Reichardt, Kelly (2008), *Wendy and Lucy*, Collingwood, VIC: Madman Entertainment.
Robertson, Pamela (1997), 'Home and away: Friends with Dorothy on the road in Oz', in S. Cohan and I. R. Hark (eds), *The Road Movie Book*, London: Routledge, pp. 271–86.
Rollet, Brigitte (2003), 'Women directors and genre films in France', in J. P. Jacqueline Levitin and V. Raoul (eds), *Women Filmmakers: Refocusing*, New York and London: Routledge, pp. 127–37.
Rose, Gillian (1993), *Feminism and Geography: The Limits of Geographical Knowledge*, Cambridge: Polity Press.
Royer, Michelle (2011), 'The hijacking of a genre: French female film-makers and the road movie', in M. Allison and A. Kershaw (eds), *Parcours De Femmes: Twenty Years of Women in French*, Oxford: Peter Lang, pp. 243–56.
Sobchack, Vivian (2004), *Carnal Thoughts: Embodiment and Moving Image Culture*, Berkeley, Los Angeles, London: University of California Press.
Spain, Daphne (1992), *Gendered Spaces*, Chapel Hill: University of North Carolina Press.
Spinoza, Baruch (1982 [1677]), *The Ethics and Selected Letters*, Indianapolis and Cambridge: Hackett.
Thrift, Nigel J. (2008), *Non-Representational Theory: Space, Politics, Affect*, New York: Routledge.

Uteng, T. P. and T. Cresswell (2008), *Gendered Mobilities*, Farnham: Ashgate Publishing.
Winding Refn, Nicolas (2011), *Drive*, USA: FilmDistrict.
Woolf, Virginia (1945 [1929]), *A Room of One's Own*, London: Penguin Books.

CHAPTER 6

Acoustic Ectoplasm and the Loss of Home
Beth Carroll

Between 1969 and 1972 the British composer Gavin Bryars put pen to paper and composed a piece of music called *The Sinking of the Titanic*. In this minimalist piece, Bryars acknowledged something that the horror genre has been engaging with for decades; namely, that sounds never die. They mutate, transform and move as sound waves lengthen, but they do not disappear. Unlike images, they do not require a copy to prevent their absence. In *The Sinking of the Titanic*, Bryars imagines the musicians of the infamous vessel playing as the ship sinks: the sounds shifting and warping as water and distance, both temporal and spatial, alter the sound waves; the music becoming a memory, an echo of a past time, which is doomed to forever repeat itself. The sounds become artefacts and a tangible connection to the past. They are an ectoplasm that exteriorises what the source has left behind once it has faded. There is nothing static about sounds; whether in their creation or transmission, sounds require movement. This movement has the possibility of either transporting us to another time, or rooting us to a specific location. We are so accustomed to sounds, which accompany us throughout both life's mundane and its momentous events, that we sometimes forget to listen. Careful consideration of a soundscape, whether real or imagined, can, as Kendall Wrightson (2000: 10) states, allow us to be 'transported to another time, another place'.

Every location will have its own unique shape and sound, waiting to be heard. This sense of sonic entrapment, of sounds waiting and caught in an endless utterance, is a key motif within a certain subsection of the horror genre, specifically those that deal with haunted houses. How do spaces so familiar to us, containing sounds so commonly heard, become so alien and hostile? In this chapter I want to explore how the sounds of the horror genre both shape and respond to common notions of domesticity and associated discourses on the home. Here we have a genre that plays on core beliefs of safety and ownership, but which highlights the transitory nature of 'home'. The haunted house film illustrates that we are but custodians of domestic spaces; spaces that have their own histories, stories and memories, many of which would rather not be disturbed, and that ultimately assault our sense of self. In the haunted house genre sounds arguably become the dominant conveyor of information and certainly the primary instigator of both diegetic characters' and audiences' fearful responses. As Peter Hutchings (2014: 132) argues, in horror films, sounds no longer need to parallel their source. Sounds are ventriloquistic in manner and mismatched. The sounds have morphed through time and space; they are the ectoplasm left behind. Sounds clearly demonstrate that the walls we build around us and call a home are permeable; they let sounds in but make it hard for them to leave again. Houses are brought to life through the entrapped sounds; the house is no longer some inanimate object, but a living, breathing entity in its own right, which resists ownership and possession ... by the living.

The idea of home is multifaceted, both in general and in terms of its representation on film. The articulation of 'home' as a concept includes discussion on architectural space. Christian Norberg-Schulz (1971, 1980), for example, spent his career exploring the nuances of architecture, from the existential space it creates to the phenomenology of architecture. Whereas Anne Buttimer (2015) discussed the role various technologies can have in shaping the home. David Morley's (2002) exploration of the home, conversely, encompasses issues of power, safety and comfort. Where and when are you safer than in your own home? Indeed, core aspects of our Western way of life are rooted in notions of the home. Our families are bonded by it, our identities inscribed by it, our lives geared towards it. But what is 'it'? As this edited collection suggests, the notion of home holds an ambiguity that language is not always fully able to elucidate. Here, though, I am rooting the idea of home to a specific location: a house. The bricks and mortar of the home and a site that is fixed, even if its inhabitants are not.

Representations of the home on film are wide ranging. We see it in family films such as *The Little Mermaid* (John Musker, Ron Clements, 1989) with Ariel's yearning to move beyond the staid confines of her childhood home to the more exotic other of dry land. We see it in British realist films such as *Distant Voices, Still Lives* (Terence Davies, 1988) where the home becomes a site of both love and trauma. Films such as *The Lord of the Rings* trilogy (Peter Jackson, 2001–3) and *The Hobbit* trilogy (Peter Jackson, 2012–14) evoke a sense of home as utopia, with Bag End representing comfort and safety. Films such as *The Wizard of Oz* (Victor Fleming, 1939) illustrate how home is a nebulous concept that one yearns for but that can be understood in various ways.[1] From these limited examples, what is clear is that the concept of home is not always reduced to a specific place or even a building; however, they share a common trope in that the 'home' is central to the construction of the sense of self. But, what role might the house, more specifically, play in this?

A house is a physical location that has become a site of psychological layering in order for it to become a home. After all, not every house is a home. The house is a tangible manifestation of the imaginary concept of home. As soon as something as conceptual as a home is made concrete in the shape of a house, issues of delimitation arise. Where is the boundary of the house? Who has control over it? As Brandon Labelle (2010: 48) describes,

> the home can be appreciated as a counter-balance to the dynamics of exposure. The experience of coming home gives comfort and reprieve from the demands of the exterior world [...] It operates as a space of physical safety, an image of comfort, to extend the security and stability found in notions of homeland. To be home is to belong. (2010: 48)

In short, the home is supposed to be a sanctuary from the stresses of everyday life. Clearly, the home is more than a roof and four walls, and yet we continue to attach ambiguous feelings and symbolic meaning to a tangible space. Indeed, it is worth noting the overwhelming positive associations that Labelle connects to the notion of home. Home is a place of safety, belonging, relaxation and recovery, and the house is the locus for those feelings. An Englishman's home is his castle, goes the adage; the home is a marker of wealth and status, but also sovereignty. You are untouchable in the house and the house is to bend to your wishes and whims.

But what happens when those feelings are encroached upon? This is the focus of the haunted house trope in horror films. In these films the safety and security of the home is called into question, and in so doing, so too is the stability of our sense of self. Our identity and sanity are shown to be tenuous, open to the influence of external forces. Any power and control we might have over ourselves and our surroundings are shown to be illusionary and temporary.

The subgenre had a long history before it reached the medium of film, incorporating both a strong aesthetic and psychological dimension. As Dale Bailey (1999) argues, the haunted house genre or narrative bridges historical and national frameworks, permitting it to adapt to changing contexts. For Bailey,

> [t]he house is our primary marker of class and our central symbol of domesticity, touching upon everything from women's rights (the angel in the house, not to mention the homemaker) to the deterioration of the nuclear family (the broken home). (1999:8)

In short, the haunted house has appeared to symbolise struggles with representation for a long time. Strongly attached to a Gothic aesthetic and sensibility, the haunted house becomes the emblem of things we consider best forgotten, but that we should not forget. A haunted house has its own history, whether it has stood through familial strife such as in *The Others* (Alejandro Amenábar, 2001) or been built where it ought not, such as in *Poltergeist* (Tobe Hooper, 1982), the building is marked by its past. Indeed, as Barry Curtis (2008), states, how '[t]he house mediates between geological time and human time and this slippage from the contemporary to the timeless encounter with danger is a feature of haunted house films'. It is this slippage that is so important to the landscape of the haunted house. For Hutchings,

> sound in horror is far from being meekly subservient to the image. Particular sounds do not just underline or augment images but can also anticipate them and sometimes stand in for them altogether. [... T]here is a sense that sound and image are operating in relation to different registers. (2014: 134)

Images of previous inhabitants can be removed, crime scenes can be cleaned, records of past events can be wiped, but the sounds the previous inhabitants made cannot be lost. The house contains them, as whilst their source may be long gone, the sound waves continue however warped, however much an echo.

These are the sounds that we want to ignore, to deny and to dismiss, but that disturb characters in haunted horror films the most. They are the sounds that are familiar to us, for instance a door closing or a stair creaking, but that make us most uncomfortable and first signal the house as delinquent in some way. Yet these sounds are completely mundane. For this reason, the haunted house cuts to the heart of Freud's notion of the uncanny and it is here, in particular, that sound plays a crucial role. Freud describes the uncanny as something that is at once familiar and unfamiliar, a projection of the self and a threat to it. The uncanny, he states, 'There is no doubt that this belongs to the realm of the frightening, of what evokes fear and dread' (Freud 2003: 123). This horror, or the feeling of the uncanny, however, is not universal but varies from individual to individual, depending on tolerances or nature. Despite this mutability, the thread that runs throughout the uncanny is that 'the uncanny is that species of frightening that goes back to what was once well known and had long been familiar' (Freud 2003: 124). The uncanny is the expression of those repressed memories or feelings, unique to the individual or part of a shared consciousness, that for some reason we no longer remember. In essence, the uncanny is a reflection of our self in some way or other. It reveals much about ourselves that we would wish to remain hidden. The home is not only that concept most fundamental to us in terms of our memories and construction of our sense of self, but also most central to the uncanny, for the very term uncanny derives itself from the concept of home. The term *unheimlich* is at the heart of the uncanny and Freud presents in detail some of the nuanced definitions of the term *heimlich* and how it varies in different languages. For instance, Freud details how the term *heimlich* is a German adjective meaning 'belonging to the house, not strange, familiar, tame, dear and intimate, homely, etc.' and yet another definition of *heimlich* is that things are 'kept from sight and withheld from others' (Freud 2003: 126, 133). In short, inherent to the term *heimlich* is a double meaning that exists simultaneously.

> [T]he most interesting fact to emerge [...] is that among the various shades of meaning that are recorded for the word *heimlich* there is one in which it merges with its formal antonym, *unheimlich*, so that what is called *heimlich* becomes *unheimlich*. [...T]he term 'uncanny' (*unheimlich*) applies to everything that was intended to remain secret, hidden away, and has come into the open. (Freud 2003: 132)

Thus, a haunted house would be described as *unheimlich*, or in the English translation 'uncanny', because it is a familiar place that is concealing something. The nature of the subject of concealment can vary from house to house, but what becomes clear is that what is hidden cannot remain so. It has a desire to be released; one might describe it as having a life of its own. The home then is not only central to the construction of our psyche, but also the site where we are most vulnerable to it being assaulted. This vulnerability not only comes from within, perhaps we might understand this as the superego's need to hide the primitive desires of the id, but also from the house itself.

At this juncture it would be wise to turn to a case study that allows us to imagine the haunted house as a sentient character in its own right. Rather than looking at the classic haunted house films, such as the aptly named *The Haunting* (Robert Wise, 1963) or the remade *The Amityville Horror* (Andrew Douglas, 2005), the film I want to turn to first is the rather less well-known *I am the Pretty Thing that Lives in the House* (Oz Perkins, 2016). It begins with the following evocative monologue by its protagonist, Lily Saylor, played by Ruth Wilson:

> I have heard myself say that a house with a death in it can never again be bought or sold by the living. It can be only be borrowed from the ghosts that have stayed behind, to go back and forth, letting out and gathering back in again, worrying over the floors in confused circles. Tending to their deaths like patchy weathered gardens. They have stayed to look back at a glimpse of the very last moments of

their lives. But the memories of their own deaths are faces on the wrong side of wet windows, smeared by rain, impossible to properly see. There is nothing that chains them to the places that their bodies have fallen. They are free to go, but still they confine themselves, held in place by their looking. For those who have stayed, their prison is their never seeing, and left all alone. This is how they rot.

Here we have a first-person reflection on the nature of ghost filled houses, but I would expand its relevance to houses more broadly. Houses are the vessels of our memories, and we are their custodians. A contract is drawn up whereby the house will retain our memories for us, will record them and make them a part of the house, but in so doing, the house will become more and more alive through the palimpsest of memories. The sounds of the 'ghosts', whether vague memories without form or the more tangible poltergeist, become the expressions of the house. The house must hold onto these sounds and contain them in order to continue 'being'.

What the opening monologue of *I am the Pretty Thing that Lives in the House* does so well is demonstrate that there is an essential contradiction at the heart of my exploration into the sound of haunted house horror films. Namely that, on the one-hand, sound is trapped within the house, echoing the previous inhabitant's lives, and on the other, that the sounds cannot be contained. A specific example of this is in the film's use of music. About a third of the way through the film the song *You Keep Coming Back to Me like a Song* is performed quietly in the background. In addition to the song title's allusion to repetition and returning sounds, the song evokes memories of previous horror films, of dead performers and of family too. This is due to the performer of the song being Anthony Perkins, the father of Oz Perkins, the director of the film, and famous for his role as the disturbed killer Norman Bates in Alfred Hitchcock's seminal horror film, *Psycho* (Alfred Hitchcock, 1960).

The sonic allusion to Perkins's previous role acts as an uncomfortable intrusion into what should be a relaxed and safe place. Walls and doors will not contain sound. The sounds will make the spatial boundaries permeable and highlight the temporal component to homes. You are not the owner of a house, merely its custodian. The reference to Bates encourages the interpretation that the safety of a house is but an illusion. As *Psycho* demonstrated, you are not safe in the shower, in your bedroom, in fact anywhere in a house. The danger comes from within and the sonic ectoplasm demonstrates how those sounds cannot be removed, but linger. However, in order for the house to act out our fears and be a danger to us, it must first take on board the sounds of the past.

The uncanny is expressed sonically in *I am the Pretty Thing that Lives in the House*. The sounds provide a link to both the particular house's past, as well as a circular reference to common horror tropes or death and murder. We can see the uncanny as allowing us to understand the movement between two states and as an illustration of the permeability of boundaries: the boundaries between the past and present, consciousness and unconsciousness, and inside and outside. Sound is the perfect conveyor of penetrable borders. It is for this reason that it can so conclusively instigate our fears.

Besides the use of the song *You Keep Coming Back to Me like a Song*, much of the music in *I am the Pretty Thing that Lives in the House* is reminiscent of a drone. The constant hum blurs the boundary between time and space. The sound of the drone is endless and lacking in melody. Drone music is a temporal form, in which the sound is looped and at times layered. In short, it is unclear where the sound starts and stops, but rather it continues endlessly, much like Gavin Bryars's *The Sinking of the Titanic*. In describing the drone music of Phill Niblock, Greg Hainge places it within the context of Gilles Deleuze's work on time and states that

> Niblock's music manages to remove those listening to it from the punctual coordinates of the time of *chronos* where time can be regimented and 'known' by the imposition of arbitrary units of measurement, instead to plunge the listener into the time of *aeon* where the capacity of those very same units to measure time fails utterly. (Hainge 2004: 6)

Though not the music of Niblock, the use of the drone in *I am the Pretty Thing that Lives in the House* has a similar effect. The lack of harmony for the audience to lock onto and follow the logic of provides uncertainty and anxiety. Yet, there is also familiarity with the sound and the inducement of a meditative state in which the boundaries between consciousness and unconsciousness are indistinct. The unchanging nature of the drone music highlights the idea of sounds lingering long after the source has gone. It creates a link between the past and present, however uncomfortable or anxiety-inducing.

The house in *I am the Pretty Thing that Lives in the House* creaks, hums and plays music from another time. It creates a link with the past occupants that cannot be ignored, however much protagonist Lily Saylor would wish to. Often in the haunted house genre, the sounds become conduits through which the ghosts of the past create links with the living. It is as Lily states, 'a house that holds a seat for a memory of a death. The stained place of a rotten ghost.'

These ghosts use sounds to copy themselves into existence, forcing history to repeat itself. We could see this as a form of entrainment whereby the protagonist's body becomes aligned with the sounds.[2] This copying and repetition reinforces a sense of the uncanny for it blends the familiar with the unfamiliar. This can be achieved in a number of ways, whether through diegetic sounds or extra-diegetic voice-over. A clear example of this can be seen in Robert Wise's classic tale *The Haunting*. The film shows how doubling becomes a key component of the haunted house's *raison d'être*; there is a need to repeat the past in order to secure the ghost's (and house's) future. Again, much like in *I am the Pretty Thing that Lives in the House*, the music in *The Haunting* often lacks melody, beginning with drones and cymbal clashes. When the melody does begin it is played on high-pitched strings before being broken up by percussive instruments at a much lower pitch. Unlike in Perkins's film, there is a sense of melody, but it is uncomfortable. As the audience begins to become familiar with the tune, the percussion and woodwind instruments break it. Full musical resolution, therefore, does not happen. Often accompanying the music throughout the film is a series of voice-overs, shared between Richard Johnson as Dr Markway and Julie Harris as Eleanor Lance. In the introduction to the film, Dr Markway provides, via voice-over, a history of Hill House, which includes the following:

> The story goes that the old lady died calling for help in the nursery upstairs while her companion fooled around with a farm hand on the veranda. The companion inherited Hill House and occupied it for many years. The local people believed for many years that, one way or another, she had murdered her benefactor. She lived a life of complete solitude in the empty house, though some say that the house was not empty and never has been since the night old Miss Abby died. They say that whatever there was and still is in the house, eventually drove the companion mad.

Again, much like *I am the Pretty Thing that Lives in the House*, the voice-over in *The Haunting* is used to highlight repetition of events, and the possibility of it continuing to do so. It is therefore not just diegetic sounds within the home that convey a sense of entrapment or foreboding, but the extra-diegetic sounds of the voice. Indeed, the voice becomes a central factor in the sense of sonic entrapment and the uncanny. Clear examples can be seen in films such as *The Shining* (Stanley Kubrick, 1980) and 2005's *The Amityville Horror*, whereby the male protagonists – Jack Torrance and George Lutz respectively – take on the personas, including vocally, of previous inhabitants of the house. Entrainment is made manifest in these moments.

When we think of sonic entrainment and the idea of the sounds of the house, or its previous inhabitants, being 'taken on' by the building's new occupants, be it Jack Torrance, George Lutz, Regan in *The Exorcist* (William Friedkin, 1973), Father Lucas Trevant in *The Rite* (Mikael Håfström, 2011), or Anne Stewart in *The Others*, what becomes clear is that the borders of the body are penetrated by sound. Indeed, in order to hear sound, the sound must enter the ear. It goes further than this, however, and can be felt on a more multisensory level.[3] One need only think of a trip to a musical performance during which the bass sounds coming through the speaker could be felt in your chest to know this to be true. The sounds enter us and change us. These changes are made more possible as a result of their taking place in a house. This becomes clear when we look at *The Amityville Horror* of 2005.

In Douglas's 2005 version of *The Amityville Horror* the Lutz family slowly take on the characteristics of the previous inhabitants. George Lutz even unconsciously begins to attempt to recreate horrific past events that would lead to the murder of his family; a form of ventriloquism and entrainment. As the film progresses, the audience, and the Lutz family, begin to understand that history is repeating itself, a vicious cycle that others have also fallen victim to. What this shows us is that as much as the home is a reflection of ourselves, we also become a reflection of our home. The home is rarely inherently evil, rather generally taking on the characteristics of past inhabitant's actions. It becomes clear that the home is not immune to seepage from external sources. But what role does sound have in terms of the home?

An assessment of the role of the haunted house subgenre, whilst important, does little to explore the more focused uses it has for sound. Indeed, the focus on the Gothic and visual extends the usual ocularcentrism. The central point of examination should therefore be the role that sound plays in conveying, and indeed, challenging these tropes associated with the haunted house. It is clear that sound is at the heart of not just the horror genre, but also the home. Indeed as Brandon Labelle (2010: 52) explains, there is a long history of trying to remove external sounds from the home whilst still wanting the home to be 'an elaborated "sonorous envelope" keeping safe, or functioning to replicate, an imaginary of primary aural warmth'. At the heart of the home, therefore, there is a conflict; in particular, as Karin Bijsterveld (2008) has described, between the noise of the outside world and the desire to extend the borders of domestic space. Bijsterveld (2008: 166) details how in the early 1900s legislation needed to be passed in the Netherlands to allow the government to step in if people were proving a nuisance with their use of gramophones.

The desire to control encroaching noise into the home even influenced suburban planning. Labelle nicely explicates how in the US, in particular, there was a desire to organise housing development so that there would be minimal sound interference, particularly in suburban areas. The drive to reduce noise pollution led to an ironic situation, however. For, as Labelle states,

> [k]ey to suburban planning is the establishment of community life, which is understood as the free expression of common values. To maintain this, the suburb requires a set of design strategies, notably within street layout, for securing and controlling access. (2010: 57)

This led to the increased use of 'lollipop' designs, or, in other words, cul-de-sacs that 'specifically [dissuade] free access by limiting the movement of the random passer-by (Labelle 2010: 57). As such, the designs often became uniform, thus reducing social interaction in what was intended to be a developing community.

The irony of this situation notwithstanding, there is an inescapable fact that it seems to ignore; namely, the sounds of the house or home itself. Beyond the sounds made by the occupiers of the home, the building itself will make its own sounds and tell its own stories of rusting pipes, creaking doors and unsealed windows. In the haunted house film these sounds take on new meanings, namely that the new occupier, and it is almost always a new occupier, is unwelcome to both the house and the previous inhabitants.

From the above exploration into haunted house films, we can see that it is sound that makes us particularly vulnerable to whatever is contained by the house. It is no coincidence that the haunted house is a recurring trope in the horror genre, for it is in the home where we are at our most vulnerable. The home is central to our construction of our sense of self; it is where our borders have been extended beyond our body. But in opening ourselves up to this extension, our boundaries are made more porous. Despite the perceived safety of the home, we become more susceptible, rather than less, to the echoes of the past. The home is where we let our guard down. When something alters the landscape of the house, be it demonic possession, the house being built on a burial site or the house being the site of a grizzly murder, it alters us materially too. It is sound, however, that instigates the changes and indicates the loss of the home and consequently the self. For sound is materially different to the image. Sound does not require a copy for it to linger; light or walls do not bound sounds. In short, sounds become tangible manifestations of the past. An echo of an event long finished whose presence can still be felt, and felt in significant ways. We feel the impact of sound. In order to hear sound, the waves must hit our eardrum and in the haunted house film, when this happens, it enters and alters us. Sounds make us penetrable. The home is the vessel and container of our memories. The house lasts longer than the living, becoming a palimpsest that holds the reminiscences of past inhabitants.

Sounds and the home are the same. As Gavin Bryars's piece *The Sinking of the Titanic* demonstrated, sounds are altered by their location. Time changes them. They shift and morph and cannot remain the same, but maintain a patina of the past. They are acoustic ectoplasms that require and seek out new life to refresh them, even if it comes at a cost. The home too remains but a house until it is imbued with meaning and new life. It remains a shell or an echo of the past, a monument to past lives. Sound and the home are intimately linked: both are central to how we define ourselves ... and both are central to how we might be lost.

Notes

1 Alexander Doty (2000), for instance, argues that Dorothy recreates a parallel home in Oz in order to cope with her realisation of her queer persona. Salman Rushdie (1992), conversely, argues that Oz offers an interesting take on utopian spaces.
2 Entrainment has been considered in a number of ways, across a number of disciplines. For instance, Michael Menaker and Arnold Eskin (1966) explore how sparrows' circadian rhythm has been influenced by sound. Whereas Kia Nobre (2010) has explored how attending to sound can alter the listener's understanding of time. In short, we might define entrainment, as William Condon (1979) does, as the synchronising of rhythms.
3 See Beth Carroll (2016), for more information on the multisensory approach to understanding film sound.

Works Cited

Bailey, Dale (1999), *American Nightmares: The Haunted House Formula in American Popular Fiction*, Bowling Green, OH: Bowling Green University Popular Press.

Bijsterveld, Karin (2008), *Mechanical Sound: Technology, Culture, and Public Problems of Noise in the Twentieth Century*, Cambridge, MA: MIT Press.

Buttimer, Anne (2015), 'Home, Reach, and the Sense of Place', in Anne Buttimer and David Seamon (eds), *The Human Experience of Space and Place*, London: Routledge.

Carroll, Beth (2016), *Feeling Film: A Spatial Approach*, Basingstoke: Palgrave Macmillan.

Condon, William S. (1979), 'Neonatal Entrainment and Enculturation', in M. Bullowa (ed.), *Before Speech: The Beginning of Interpersonal Communication*, New York: Cambridge University Press.

Curtis, Barry (2008), *Dark Places: The Haunted House in Film*, London: Reaktion Books.
Doty, Alexander (2000), '"My Beautiful Wickedness": The Wizard of Oz as Lesbian Fantasy', in *Flaming Classics: Queering the Film Canon*, London: Routledge.
Freud, Sigmund ([1919] 2003), *The Uncanny*, London: Penguin Classics.
Hainge, Greg (2004), 'The Sound of Time is Not *Tick Tock*: The Loop as a Direct Image of Time in Noto's *Endless Loop Edition* (2) and the Drone Music of Phill Niblock', in *Invisible Culture: An Electronic Journal for Visual Culture*, Issue 8.
Hutchings, Peter (2014), *The Horror Film*, London: Routledge.
Labelle, Brandon (2010), *Acoustic Territories: Sound Culture and Everyday Life*, New York: Bloomsbury.
Menaker Michael and Arnold Eskin (1996), 'Entrainment of Circadian Rhythms by Sound in Passer Domesticus', *Science*, 154, no. 3756 (December), pp. 1579–81.
Morley, David (2002), *Home Territories: Media, Mobility and Identity*, London: Routledge.
Nobre, Kia (2010), *Attention and Time*, Oxford: Oxford University Press.
Norberg-Schulz, Christian (1971), *Existence, Space and Architecture*, Santa Barbara: Praeger Publishers.
Norberg-Schulz, Christian (1980), *Genius Loci: Toward a Phenomenology of Architecture*, New York: Rizzoli International Publications.
Rushdie, Salman (1992), *The Wizard of Oz*, London: BFI.
Wrightson, Kendall (2000), 'An Introduction to Acoustic Ecology', *Soundscape, The Journal of Acoustic Ecology*, 1, no. 1, pp. 10–13.

CHAPTER 7

Our House Now: Flat and Reversible Home Spaces in Post-war Film and Television
Adrian Martin

'A home – isn't that an optical thing?' (Émile Rousseau [Jean-Pierre Léaud] in *Le gai savoir*, Jean-Luc Godard, 1969)

Preamble

The essay that follows is a hybrid of academic research and poetic or creative research. In fact, it is less a bounded essay than a fragment of a thread of work that I have been tracing for over thirty years. Poetic research begins not from a thesis or intuition to be argued and proven, but from a figure or trope – necessarily shadowy, multiple in its social meanings and uses, perhaps somewhat 'mythic' (see Schwartz 2014 for one model of this type of research and writing). This figure is then (as it were) placed at the centre of an empty field, a mental screen. Gradually, over time, examples arrive to associate or constellate themselves around the central figure; it is a work of accumulation, and also serendipity. Different 'families', subgroups, variations and metamorphoses of the figure form across the board. A rhizomatic logic may appear, connecting some of the zones or layers bunched on the field/screen. One discovers what the diagram is about by following its paths, meditating upon it. In a very real sense, the subsequent narration of these research endings can begin or end anywhere, since the entire process is *in media res*, always happening in the midst of things; no linear chronology, no rhetoric of 'overview' is possible.

Nonetheless, for the sake of an initial orientation to this sliced fragment, I shall point to the schema that formed here around the initially chosen figure of 'home' and its spaces. A history of sorts is inaugurated in the post-Second World War period with John Ford's iconic images of a home in his classic Western *The Searchers* (1956). It is here, I have come to believe, that a first true 'haunting' or evacuation of home space –

outside of the generic confines of horror and fantasy cinema – begins. But a slightly earlier work little seen in its time, Josef von Sternberg's *The Saga of Anatahan* (1953), has revealed itself, across a cultural 'delay', as an even more radical instigation of what I call the boomerang effect of reversible space: once domestic space is flattened and emptied out so thoroughly, it sends us, the spectators, back to our own resources and origins.

Cinema has lived – and struggled – with this legacy ever since. For every sentimentally redemptive drama or comedy of a home repaired and reunited (a conventional history I do not survey here), there is a countertendency, in the modern period, toward flight, wandering, melancholia. This becomes particularly acute in the 1970s and 1980s with the emergence of filmmakers including Wim Wenders, Chantal Akerman, Terrence Malick and Olivier Assayas. Others, such as Lynne Ramsay and David Cronenberg, return, in a doubting, ironic, ultra-critical or even violent way, to the iconic homestead of Ford's 1950s imagery.

The figure of home – like any prominent figure in culture – cannot be confined to cinema. Once placed in the centre of an empty frame for inspection and meditation, it attracts scraps and phenomena from all over: poems, advertisements, theoretical, philosophical and essayistic writings, TV series, fiction of many sorts. There is yet no end in sight – hence the most recent sightings of the flat or reversible home gathered here, in Jane Campion's *Top of the Lake: China Girl* and David Lynch's *Twin Peaks: The Return* (both 2017).

Haven

> He has a secret place where no one can find him
> and worlds to explore in his own backyard.
> (Geoffrey Hayes, *Bear by Himself*, 1998: 4)

How many memories of childhood are bound up with the dream – whether manufactured as artefacts by the culture industries (children's books, songs, films), or as the souvenirs of an individual's mental and emotional history – of the secret place? And this spot as a refuge, a haven – often part of a home, but also somehow set apart from it. Frances Hodgson Burnett's beloved novel *The Secret Garden* (1911), for example, has given rise to (at least) three film adaptations, three TV series, two Western animations, plus a Japanese anime. But the secret place need not even be something as localisable as a patch of garden. 'I have a soft spot for secret passageways, bookshelves that open onto silence, staircases that go down into the void and hidden safes', wrote

Luis Buñuel in his autobiography. 'I even have one myself, but I won't tell you where' (Buñuel 1984: 225).

In Nicholas Ray's *The Lusty Men* (1952), Jeff (Robert Mitchum), the once and now broken king of the rodeo, returns to his childhood home, which is abandoned, desolate, dishevelled. What is he doing, climbing underneath the house, below its front steps? First the oddness and then the poignancy of this moment derive from the sight of this great man no longer on his feet but flat on his stomach, hemmed in, made docile and feminine by the rotting beams and cobwebs that press in on him. He has, in fact, returned to his own secret place: to the silly little box of tokens (a coin, a stamp, a lock of hair) kept hidden under the stairs. But this is no longer a home, and Jeff is no longer a child – and so, after this moment of haven, he must haul himself up and along to a future which contains only the certain prospect of death.

It is a scene to conjure with: in Wim Wenders's *Lightning Over Water* (1980), Ray himself shows precisely that same moment from *The Lusty Men* to a campus audience at Vassar College in the USA: 'That's me', he remarks, pointing at the screen. The rodeo star and the film director: two public lives, and two public deaths (Jeff in the rodeo arena, Ray in Wenders's film) – with, for a fleeting second in between, in a place that no one else really knows or shares and that can never perish whilst consciousness still flickers, a haven. What did Ray say to the student about this old film of his? 'It's really about people who want nothing more than a home of their own. That was actually the great American dream at the time.'

Childhood is that time when children (for reasons good and bad, or simply pragmatic) are often left alone to their own resources. What films and books celebrating the secret place express is an awestruck respect for the privacy and autonomy of the individual – something that is (in general) allowed to children but denied to adults. The imagery of the secret place relates to all manner of strategies of hiding. In her autobiography *A Little House of Your Own* (1954), children's picture book author Beatrice Schenk de Regniers pleaded: 'This is the important thing to remember. Everyone has to have a little house of his own. Every boy has to have his own little house. Every girl should have a little house to herself' (de Regniers 1954: 10).

'He has a secret place where no one can find him / and worlds to explore in his own backyard.' The double movement in the fantasy of the secret place is, in the first instance, a shrinking of time-space co-ordinates, a drawing in of the world and oneself; and then, as if magically, the explosion of space into a new realm, a new world. We are in the realm of cinematic intensification here, of that precious 'phantasmagoria of the interior' (as Walter Benjamin [2003: 25–6] dubbed the poetics of Charles Baudelaire) that shines in the extreme, close-up inserts of weird, bric-a-brac objects in the films of Walerian Borowczyk, or the ring that spins the plot of a delirious Hollywood romantic fantasy, Henry Hathaway's *Peter Ibbetson* (1935):

> It looks like a ring, but it isn't. It's the walls of the world. Inside it is the magic of all desire. Inside it is where she lives. And everything inside leads to her – every street, every path, and the eighth sea. It's a world. It's our world.

The problematic of the haven is not that of the elsewhere (Utopia) but that of the within. Havens are always inside, at the secret heart of things – inside one's head, off in a corner, tucked away downstairs in a shopping mall, even behind a makeshift mask; they are secreted. The haven is the break, the relief, the island amidst the duty and terror of everyday, public life. But what is the fate of such havens in contemporary film and television?

The Boomerang Effect

It is a unique film, and among the strangest in all cinema. It is also, on many levels, profoundly prophetic – especially when it comes to the screen figuration of home. Based on a true Second World War story, set on a tropical island but shot entirely inside a studio in Japan, Josef von Sternberg's *The Saga of Anatahan* (initially 1953, then re-edited by the director in 1958) takes the lush, baroque style for which the director is most famous and deliberately flattens it. Literally every frame is a clotted, spatially indecipherable tangle of artificial tree branches, leaves, veils, nets, planks. Pictorial depth is cancelled, brutally telescoped; Sternberg's lighting schemas no longer enhance the beauty of a face or a figure, but hide or obscure it, even blot it out. Jonathan Rosenbaum gives an accurate summation:

> The cornerstone of Sternberg's reputation, his visual obsessions (from [Marlene] Dietrich to nets to bric-à-brac to textures of fog and smoke) are denied their Hollywood upholsteries and either flattened to the point of parody, or, a formula that seems more accurate, x-rayed into a diagram that emphasizes their limitations while reducing their more seductive illusionist aspects. (Rosenbaum 1995: 89)

The space of *The Saga of Anatahan* – understanding space, in cinematic terms, as the complex concatenation of visible place, the spatial relations staged within the image, and the ever-shifting, variable distances established by the camera and montage – is, appropriately, unusual. It is singular both in its eccentricity and its monotonality: every portion of this space looks almost exactly the same. Referring to the characteristic 'closeted Sternbergian space' married, on this occasion, to a 'dull procession of compositions with dead-center framing' resulting in 'a formalism run amok, whose overall texture has become so flat, hard, and consistent that one is finally able to walk on it like a floor', Rosenbaum concludes with a striking simile: 'the diverse areas on Anatahan resemble the interchangeable parts of a pipe organ' (all quotes Rosenbaum 1995: 89).

The celebrated *nouveau roman* writer Claude Ollier (1922–2014), among the earliest, in-depth champions of Sternberg's testament film (although it was not, strictly, to be his last, it was avowedly his most cherished and personal production), grasps the aesthetics and ethics of *The Saga of Anatahan* in a somewhat different way. All of Sternberg's works, in his view, follow a roughly similar spatial itinerary: they journey from the macrocosm (often signified by the animation of a cartographic map) into the microcosm; their diegetic worlds progressively shrink in scale, often landing, finally, within a home space. This film follows the general model:

> A series of concentric circles is tightened from the beginning: a circle which is the Pacific (general theatre of war), another being the island where the shipwrecked characters are cast ashore (another, but derisory, theatre of war); a circle of the jungle (a homogenous, abstract ambience), a circle of the hut on piles (a sanctuary presided over by the woman who 'animates' this space). (Ollier 1980: 958)

However, when we reach the innermost point of the progressively focalised trajectory of *The Saga of Anatahan* – that home which is a 'hut on piles' – we hardly feel, as spectators, that we have arrived inside anything or anywhere. (Curiously, the Japanese title of a 1998 novel by Kaoru Ohno that dramatises the same real-life tale translates as *Distant Seas, Locked Room*.) Ollier stresses the centrality of the woman-figure, Keiko (Akemi Negishi), in this distilled, Sternbergian scenario:

> At the centre of this planetary microcosm, drawing back a curtain of sea shells, Keiko appears, the last stake in these struggles. Through a blinding narrowing of frontiers, an exemplary transfer – once again – from the field of history to that of eroticism. (Ollier 1980: 958)

Yet this erotic component – doubtless essential to the story and its logic – does not inflame anything in *Anatahan*, neither the film nor its spectator. We are no longer in the realm of 'havenly' intensification or ecstatic concentration, that affective explosion from within a secret space. Things remain flat and distant; the pipe organ parts remain interchangeable, indistinguishable. Sternberg transforms the interior of the solitary home in the story into a stage set, via his wide, frontal framing and lateral *mise en scène*. Views of spying faces at its makeshift window, throughout the tale, only increase the artifice of theatricality, rather than intensifying the sanctified interiority of this (quasi-marital) space.

But this is not quite a dead end, or a disappointment. The effect of Sternberg's stylistic choices here is to hurl us outside, beyond the enclosed family circle of the home. It works as a sudden turning inside-out of the space, in a boomerang effect. Once this porous home is penetrated, after the inexorably inward-twisting drama in which 'the signs of war are inverted' and 'the weapons turned around' (Ollier 1980: 958), then there is another turn of the baroque spiral (or screw): we, like the characters, begin the journey once more to the outside, back to the wider world of Japan – to re-join history, to rendezvous with a welcoming party, the airport of another ghostly homeland, turned into a reflexively cinematic flicker-show by the paparazzi's flashbulbs.

Unspeaking Night

Petr Král's *In Search of the Essence of Place* – a less self-consciously Proustian rendering of its title into English would be *Investigation of Places* – is an unusual autobiographical memoir, in that the normal, expected traces of the author's 'human story' are almost entirely absent from it. It is a recording, an evocation, of places that the narrator – he dubs himself 'the explorer' – has passed through, across at least six decades and as many nations. But a place, here, is rarely a city or country; it can be something as banal, as unexceptional, as a field, a wall, a shop front or a street corner.

A surrealist in his early adult life, Král at first sets out to discover mysteries and wonders in the seemingly banal scraps of the everyday cityscape; he entertains reveries about the marvellous acts of theatre that likely take place between objects in abandoned department stores at night, empty classrooms, or unused, makeshift offices perched at the edge of construction sites. Underpinning all his work is a deep feeling of being flung from his home (and homeland) of origin, and thereby adopting the role of an eternal exile or wanderer. 'What he seems to be clinging to', he writes reflexively, 'is an idea of an *impossible sanctuary*' (Král 2012: 148).

But can you go home again, or find even the trace that long-lost haven? What will it mean once one adopts Rainer Maria Rilke's injunction to 'step out in to the evening' (Rilke 2012)? Král lives for the poetic experience of intensification; yet, as he travels on, this type of incandescent, surrealistic illumination eludes him more and more. 'By confronting these objects and insisting that they let him into their secret', he pines, 'all the explorer manages to do is persuade them to edge open the door of the unspeaking night whose gatekeepers they are' (Král 2012: 166).

The unspeaking night turns out to be merciless; in a manner that recalls the philosophy of Martin Heidegger in *The Essence of Reasons* (translated into English by a young Terrence Malick) and, in his wake, Stanley Cavell in *The World Viewed*, the world that Král strides out to encounter rebuffs him, keeps him at a distance. What he once optimistically called, apropos the final, breathtaking scene of Malick's *Days of Heaven* (1978), the 'temporary reopening of the world' – 'we are in the wings of the universe, but it's the stage as well' – finally 'does not clear a way for anything other than its own void' (all quotes Král 1985: 23). Elsewhere he declares with flair: 'A summer landscape – open in every sense – is an inaccessible room *par excellence*' (Král 2008: 102). Nearing the end of his lifelong investigation of places, Král wonders about the 'ultimate secret':

> Can he really have done all this only to find that he has been searching for something that doesn't exist, that the only thing of substance that can be grasped about places – and objects – is that they can never be grasped? (Král 2012: 193)

It is another version of the inside-out, boomerang effect in the experience of space: 'All that is waiting for him on the other side of the doorway is the place that exists inside him already' (Král 2012: 195). Yet there is nothing terribly comforting about this self-revelation: 'the greatest mystery that places possess is that by going inside we remain on the outside; that the explorers, too, are inevitably and forever *external*, never containing anything' (Král 2012: 206).

Král is also a dedicated writer on cinema, associated for many years with *Positif* magazine, and the author of two important books on silent, burlesque comedy. As a film connoisseur he is, as it happens, another Josef von Sternberg obsessive, finding (like Rosenbaum) a disconcerting flatness hidden within the seeming illusion of depth in all the director's work: their 'scenographic over-charge' ends up constituting a 'nostalgia for bodies', where the elements of the *mise en scène* 'appeal to a density elsewhere lacking in the image', and also inside the characters/actors/people themselves. 'Finery, and the illusion it creates, is in this sense the sole reality of the body, the only thing that gives it a substance and, by virtue of this fact, constituting it' (all quotes Král 2000: 157–8).

And this, in a nutshell, is Král's theory of most things in cinema, from bodies to homes.

In his book on place, he devotes a section to cinema – his other, replacement home, wherever he may travel:

> The presence of impenetrable layers which he finds so fascinating about certain scenes or images derives [...] from the way the director creates links between everything, how the editing, the camera angle manages to connect the vague, dark shape of a corpse with the brightly lit doorway of a cellar in a single bold stroke. Passing shudders that freeze the moment they are born, the only striking aspect of films is their shifting constellation. (Král 2012: 221)

Spirits

One of the most celebrated images of home in world cinema is the oft-cited, oft-remade tableau in the opening scene and the very ending of John Ford's classic Western, *The Searchers* (1956). The eternal loner, Ethan Edwards (John Wayne), stands just beyond the threshold of a family home, seemingly set in a desert. The image of the domestic threshold is itself a charged one, with a complicated cultural history: in his poem 'Entrance', for example, Rilke declared 'Your house stands as the last thing before great space' and that we need to 'step out in to the evening/out of your living room, where everything is known' (Rilke 2012) – an open evening which is decidedly not Král's 'unspeaking night'.

In *The Searchers*, although Ethan has staked his life on saving the honour and integrity of the family unit that dwells inside the home, he ultimately can find no secure, lasting place within it. His pose cuts a melancholic figure as the door, almost magically, either opens to reveal his presence, or shuts to obliterate him altogether from the narrative and its world. Ethan is left to – as is said in the film of the unfulfilled spirit of a dead person – 'wander between the winds', another exile.

Ford's cinema, as all sympathetic critics testify, is all about the sanctity of home and family. It is also about the dangers and threats (both internal and external) that menace this iconic home, and about everything that must done, sometimes *in extremis*, in order to preserve or rebuild it in its ideal state. In a brilliant, visionary essay titled '*The Searchers* – Dismantled', Ross Gibson looks closely at the first scene and discerns:

> The whole film is given to us, not as a set of themes or meanings, but as a system of power-oscillations back and forth between the incursive and the indigenous, the built and the given, the imposed and the impounded. (Gibson 2005)

As Gibson persuasively argues, the beginning of Ford's film is built on a powerful identification of the spectator, not with any character, but with the vital spirit of a house itself, its beams and corners and fixtures, its accumulated energy as a dwelling, soaking up all the experience that has occurred within itself. Ford imagined such a domestic place many times on film, as for instance in *How Green Was My Valley* (1941) (Martin 2014: 147–54). This is the kind of emotionally rich home once evoked by Arthur Symons (author of the short tale *Esther Kahn* upon which Arnaud Desplechin built a movie), albeit as a dream of a life (his text is titled *A Prelude to Life*) that he had not lived, and could only imagine:

> I have never known what it was to have a home, as most children know it; a home that has been lived in so long that it has got into the ways, the bodily creases, of its inhabitants, like an old, comfortable garment, warmed through and through by the same flesh. (Symons 1905)

In slightly more conventional dramatic terms than those that Gibson proposes, we could say that what Ford plays upon is a sense of a home – and specifically its entrance way – as a dynamic threshold, a place where representatives of good and evil, threat and restoration, will face off. It is in this mode that, for instance, David Cronenberg quotes (consciously or unconsciously) the Western iconography of *The Searchers* at the start of his dark, contemporary fable, *A History of Violence* (2005): we discover, moment by moment during the opening scene's choreography, which figures (the ordinary home-owners or the vicious villains) have entered through that front door, and which will never leave by it again (Martin 2014: 24–6).

The domestic threshold thus rests on a type of sudden, instant reversibility – another boomerang effect, like a swinging door – that the philosopher of design Vilém Flusser once described so well, with a drollness strictly opposed to Ford's teary, Irish American sentimentality:

> Doors are holes in walls for going in and out. One goes out to experience the world, and there one loses oneself, and one returns home in order to find oneself again, and in so doing one loses the world one set out to conquer. [...] Home and homeland are favourite places for con-tricks. [...] Doors are devices that do not provide happiness, nor are they to be trusted. (Flusser 1999: 82)

Something in the Kitchen

Personally, I have always found something odd, something less than rich, in the famous image of John Wayne inside the door frame. Namely, the absolute, jet-black darkness of the surrounding walls. Yes, I realise that this is deployed primarily as a powerfully pictorial effect, with reference to the painting tradition of Frederic Remington (1861–1909) and others. But its effect is stark, stripping out (for me, at least) that homely spirit of which Gibson speaks, or what Ollier called, in traditional fiction, 'a concordance between man and space' (Lindsay 1988). This affect seems to banish the realm of the human altogether as it comes out of, and makes way for, the total darkness of the cinema screen.

Contemporary American cinema, from Martin Scorsese's *Taxi Driver* (1976) and Paul Schrader's *Hardcore* (1979) through to Abel Ferrara's *Dangerous Game* (1993) and Mike Newell's *Donnie Brasco* (1997), has often played on the ambiguity of the 'rescue from captivity' narrative immortalised by *The Searchers*, complete with its immortal line spoken by Ethan: 'Let's go home.' Movie after movie has hinted at the soullessness of this home to which the wanderer (male or, more rarely in these films, female) finally returns, the likely crushing banality of security after the wildness of adventure – like the final, 'all in the family' shot of John Cassavetes's *Husbands* (1970), where the errant husband, Gus (Cassavetes), walks slowly down the driveway to the back door of his suburban home, to immediately be confronted with his small, crying daughter (Xan Cassavetes), while his boy (Nick Cassavetes) yells mockingly: 'Oh boy, you're in trouble!'

In these films, even if home and domestic life remain an 'off space' for most of the narrative, at least we are never led to doubt that it has the solidity of objective reality, the weight of accumulated time and experience. Even when homes were depicted at their most hellish and imprisoning – as in a classic Hollywood 'woman's melodrama' such as Max Ophüls's *The Reckless Moment* (1949) – they still vibrated with life. More recent cinema and television series have taken a different turn, intensifying the boomerang effect that Sternberg triggered on his artificial island of Anatahan.

More and more, the domestic home becomes a flat facade – or, at best, a faded icon, the memory-token of an ideal place that can no longer exist. In either case, it tends in the direction of becoming a purely two-dimensional image. Greg Yaitanes' eight-part series *Quarry* (2016), based on novels by Max Allan Collins, makes explicit iconographic reference to *The Searchers* when, in the pilot episode, Mac (Logan Marshall-Green) returns home a day early from marine service in Vietnam (it's 1972) and stands in the back door frame, gazing at his wife Joni (Jodi Balfour) in their swimming pool; and the corresponding switch-around, after much violent plot action, when Joni stares uncomprehendingly at Mac from the same vantage point. Now the darkness that surrounded the door in Ford's composition speaks heavily of social and personal distance, alienation.

Often, pining characters in contemporary narratives scarcely set a foot inside the lost homes they gaze at. That is the case for Detective Robin Griffin (Elisabeth Moss) in the second season of Jane Campion's *Top of the Lake: China Girl* (2017), as she compulsively drives past the house where dwells her teenage daughter, Mary (Alice Englert), whom she gave up for adoption seventeen years previously. And, although we see many scenes staged inside this abode, it scarcely registers as a warm, rich, lived-in space: truly a house divided, it is marked by incessant splits, evacuations, escape routes.

A transitional figure in the schema I am sketching here is Olivier Assayas. In the mid 1990s, Assayas was part of a trend in cosmopolitan, border-crossing cinema that included works by Edward Yang, Claire Denis, Wim Wenders and especially Wong Kar-wai. They portrayed postmodern existences pursued at a restless, speedy blur in the air or on the highways, in cars or on motorcycles, always between hotels in temporary locations, always 'connected' (via mobile phone and Internet communication) but never 'grounded' in a stable, domestic, home environment. It was the period in which, in the domains of cultural studies and hip journalism, McKenzie Wark's slogan caught fire: 'We no longer have roots, we have aerials. We no longer have origins, we have terminals' (Wark 1996: 8). Assayas's *Irma Vep* (1996) is among the most vivid films of that mid '90s cultural moment; with its scenes of characters unfussily fleeing difficult situations through open windows, it recalls Jean Douchet's reverie on domestic architecture in the work of Jean Renoir, a sunnier complement to Flusser's theoretical picture:

> The window has as its natural mission to open onto the landscape, toward the outside, finally to open onto the entire world. While the door obliges us to film a physical movement, the window invites a mental movement. It implies an aspiration toward something; it evokes release, escape, self-blossoming. It expresses the force of desire, the irresistible need for freedom. In Renoir, there is no freedom without a window. (Douchet 1997: 111, my translation)

Later works, such as *Summer Hours* (2008), show Assayas's sensibility tuning into a mellower, home and family, lived-in mood. *Personal Shopper* (2016) sits exactly midway between these two poles of his cinema. On the one hand, Maureen (Kristen Stewart) is the classic, zipping-around Assayas heroine, on a motorcycle and in trains, atomised and seemingly in permanent, self-imposed exile from any stable notion of home base. On the other hand, the film is literally about homes and their spirits in the horror/*fantastique*/haunted house sense, equating dwelling spaces with the 'unfinished business' of interpersonal attachments that imbue them with a spooky, disquieting life. While it artfully hesitates between purely rational, supernatural and psychoanalytical explanations of the mystery plot that it unfolds, *Personal Shopper* undeniably 'homes in' on domestic space as a locus of intersubjective experience.

No film or TV series, however, has gone so far into the complete and utter evacuation of the home icon than David Lynch and Mark Frost's *Twin Peaks: The Return* (2017) – and let's not forget that an original actor in the series, Hank Worden (as 'The Elderly Room Service Waiter'), literally rocked on the front porch of *The Searchers'* homestead in 1956. A central site in this third season is (as it was in the first two seasons, twenty-six years ago) the home of the Palmer family. It is truly, by this point in the saga, a haunted house, in which (as it transpires), the ultimate evil spirit code named Judy probably dwells, mainly inside the household's tormented, alcoholic mother Sarah (Grace Zabriskie), but also in odd, secret places everywhere within it – including the TV set, locked into an eerie, unstable, audiovisual loop during a wrestling program. As *The Fireman* (Carel Struycken) gnomically says to Dale Cooper (Kyle MacLachlan) in the White Lodge: 'It is in our house now.'

The very final shot of the third season shows the entire facade of the Palmer house in wide shot at night, its lights blowing out to give us the ultimate closed-curtain of screen darkness. But, throughout the season, Lynch is careful to never map this domestic space in anything like a conventional way. All we are get are fragments, cold, cut-off islands of house-bits: a staircase and ceiling fan fixture glimpsed in an alternate-world vision of Gordon Cole (Lynch); the dank lounge room where Sarah seems to spend most of her existence. In a chilling moment of the twelfth episode, Sheriff Hawk (Michael Horse) calls at the front door to check on Sarah's state of ill-being – and overhears an enigmatic, clanking sound from somewhere inside ('something in the kitchen', she says), unseen. In fact, the cinematic category of 'off space' comes to entirely define this house by the time of the ghostly, deliberately hyper-slowed-down final episode: even its real owner in another historic timeline, Mary Reber, communes (as Sarah did) with off-screen voices, more secrets beyond the door … and that door will again never fully open to let any visitor (or spectator) in.

The Glass House

It may be a mere coincidence that several key shots of *The Saga of Anatahan* seem to be closely mimicked in Terrence Malick's war movie, *The Thin Red Line* (1998). But there can be no doubt that Malick has, right from his own contributions to 1970s American cinema up to his most recent experiments, contributed enormously to the poetic creation of a new kind of haunted house in cinema – one that has never been possessed by spirits, whether good or bad.

Already in *Badlands* (1973) – a film whose bloody odyssey is almost entirely set outdoors, with makeshift, temporary dwellings dotted along the trail – the initial flight into the wilderness of nature is signalled by the striking montage of a house, and inside that a doll's house, burning up (Martin 2006). Like *Top of the Lake*, *Song to Song* (2017) offers us fleeting, tantalising glimpses of the outer facade of a home – a home both lost in the past and haunted in a turbulent, emotional, traumatic sense – connected to the character of Rhonda (Natalie Portman) and her mother. It is a space we never enter.

Malick's most elaborated work on the figuration of home takes place first in *Days of Heaven* and then, in a modern vein, in *Knight of Cups* (2015). The former, a story of itinerant workers on the eve of the First World War, initially gives us home – a single house, standing alone in a vast field, belonging to a wealthy farmer (Sam Shepard) – as a pure image or icon, unapproachable and impenetrable, clearly modelled on Andrew Wyeth's classic Americana painting *Christina's World* (1948). The film is devoted to (appropriating Gibson's description of *The Searchers*) the tensions between 'the incursive and the indigenous, the built and the given, the imposed and the impounded' – nature and culture intertwining in paradoxical ways at every point.

However, once the tragic, triangular romance of the plot kicks in, Malick and his cinematographers Néstor Almendros and Haskell Wexler do everything in their considerable power to both enter this house while also turning it inside-out: every interaction and movement is rendered in terms of spatial lines-of-flight leading from interior to exterior (thanks to the extraordinary Steadicam set-ups), and the domestic space is rendered completely porous to elements of light and wind. This home, just as Král described the dawn scene that closes *Days of Heaven*, equally 'does not clear a way for anything other than its own void' (Král 1985: 23).

In *Knight of Cups*, Malick continues the exploration of contemporary living spaces that he began (with cinematographer Emmanuel Lubezki) in *To the Wonder* (2012), with its eerie, deserted supermarket aisles and suburban vistas. Here, the boomerang effect of reversible space is total: the home of Rick (Christian Bale) is all glass windows (exaggerating further a motif already mined by Michelangelo Antonioni in *Zabriskie Point* [1970]), sight-lines proceeding, everywhere he turns, into the deep-focus infinity of landscape and sky. This melancholic view of urban existence even turns to comedy, when our anti-hero no longer notices, in this obscenely all-visible world, burglars fleeing in the distance – and anyhow, how would he or anyone else even be able to recognise what is missing from his featureless pad, or remember what was there in the first place?

Among current filmmakers, only Lynne Ramsay in *Ratcatcher* (1999) has equalled Malick's intensity in showing and exploring the flimsy, reversible, modern home. In a manner resembling David Lynch, she raises the representation of this architectural fixture to a veritable ontological problem, a probing question of its very reality-status. In a key moment late in *Ratcatcher*, its central child protagonist, James (William Eadie), enjoys himself playing in a new home – once again, a sole structure set within a field. But it is an oddly sterile haven, and it seems to vanish from the plane of reality almost as soon as it has appeared. Ramsay deliberately suspends the clarification of whether this is truly the new house into which his whole family is relocating at the behest of the local council, or just James's dream, his reverie. If it is a dream, it has no clear beginning or ending. The idea of home becomes the universal trigger for poignant, tearing fantasy – a fantasy that faces off against the grimness of domestic and suburban interactions, as in Ramsay's subsequent *We Need to Talk About Kevin* (2011). Intriguingly, her most recent feature is titled *You Were Never Really Here* (2017).

The entire history of film and TV could no doubt be rewritten today from the sole vantage point of how emotionally and spiritually full or empty – for better or for worse – the home is made to appear. Looking back today at Alfred Hitchcock's *Vertigo* (1958), for instance, we can struck by how utterly rootless its anti-hero (James Stewart as Scottie) appears to be: even the place that briefly functions as his home seems, for all the world, like a transitory hotel apartment. Scottie is another 1950s presentiment (like the soldiers of *Anatahan*) of what Gilberto Perez described as the prevailing 'sentimental homelessness of our time' (Perez 1998: 394). Wandering between the winds, once again and forever.

Two quotations to conclude, in the hope of provisionally pinpointing the ambivalence of 'our house now'. First, Rainer Maria Rilke, in a fragment composed two years before his death:

> After such long experience let 'house,'
> 'tree,' or 'bridge' be dared differently.
> [...]
> To untangle daily creation,
> which all differently endure,
> we make ourselves a constellation
> out of the known figure. (Rilke 1975: 75)

And second, Petr Král, who indeed 'dares differently' with concept of 'house' and makes his own, unknown constellations from known pieces, but still comes to a sad and sticky end:

> He wavers between speaking and saying nothing; the language he uses while walking, the words and phrases that his mind scatters over the surface are a way of transforming them into a mobile house, yet this alone isn't enough to build one. (Král 2012: 228)

Works Cited

Benjamin, Walter (2003), *Selected Writings Volume 4: 1938–1940*, Cambridge, MA: Harvard University Press.
Buñuel, Luis (1984), *My Last Sigh*, New York: Vintage Books.
Cavell, Stanley (1979), *The World Viewed: Reflections on the Ontology of Film*, Cambridge, MA: Harvard University Press.
de Regniers, Beatrice Schenk (1954), *A Little House of Your Own*, San Diego: Harcourt, Brace.
Douchet, Jean (1997), 'Les fenêtres de chez Renoir', *Trafic*, 24 (Winter), pp. 111–18.
Flusser, Vilém (1999), *The Shape of Things: A Philosophy of Design*, London: Reaktion Books.
Gibson, Ross (2005), 'The Searchers – Dismantled', *Rouge*, 7, <http://www.rouge.com.au/7/searchers.html> (last accessed 26 June 2019).
Hayes, Geoffrey (1998), *Bear by Himself*, New York: Random House.
Heidegger, Martin (1969), *The Essence of Reasons*, Evanston, IL: Northwestern University Press.
Král, Peter (1985), *Private Screening*, London: Frisson.
Král, Peter (2000), 'Josef von Sternberg et les personnages de Marlene', in J. Aumont (ed.), *La mise en scène*, Brussels: De Boeck Université, pp. 155–65.
Král, Peter (2008), *Working Knowledge*, London: Pushkin Press.
Král, Peter (2012), *In Search of the Essence of Place*, London: Pushkin Press.
Lindsay, Cécile (1988), 'A Conversation with Claude Ollier', Dalkey Archive Press, <http://www.dalkeyarchive.com/a-conversation-with-claude-ollier-by-cecile-lindsay> (last accessed 26 June 2019).
Martin, Adrian (2006), 'Things to Look Into: The Cinema of Terrence Malick', *Rouge*, 10, <http://www.rouge.com.au/10/malick.html> (last accessed 26 June 2019).
Martin, Adrian (2014), *Mise en scène and Film Style: From Classical Hollywood to New Media Art*, London: Palgrave.
Ollier, Claude (1980), 'Josef von Sternberg', in R. Roud (ed.), *Cinema: A Critical Dictionary*, London: Secker and Warburg, pp. 949–59.

Perez, Gilberto (1998), *The Material Ghost: Films and Their Medium*, Baltimore, MD: Johns Hopkins University Press.

Rilke, Rainer Maria (1975), *Rilke on Love and Other Difficulties*, New York: W. W. Norton and Company.

Rilke, Rainer Maria (2012), 'Selected Rilke Poems in English', rainer-rilke. blogspot.com (last accessed 26 June 2019).

Rosenbaum, Jonathan (1995), *Placing Movies: The Practice of Film Criticism*, Berkeley: University of California Press.

Schwartz, Hillel (2014), *The Culture of the Copy: Striking Likenesses, Unreasonable Facsimiles*, Brooklyn: Zone Books.

Symons, Arthur (1905), *Spiritual Adventures*, Project Gutenberg, <http://www.gutenberg.org/ebooks/38893> (last accessed 26 June 2019).

Wark, McKenzie (1996), *Virtual Geography: Living with Global Media Events*, Bloomington: Indiana University Press.

CHAPTER 8

From Myth to Reality: Images of Domestic Space in Post-Soviet Baltic Films

Lukas Brašiškis and Nerijus Milerius

Introduction

Domestic space, and its varying functions in Soviet and post-Soviet societies, has recently been discussed in a number of scholarly works. This interest in domestic space echoes more general tendencies in recent works by Eastern European film scholars. In the twenty-first century, according to Ewa Mazierska, the field of post-Soviet film studies started to witness a growing interest in the spatial aspect of films and a shift from temporal to spatial analysis took place. Theoretical insights on the importance of space have formed what Mazierska (2017) terms a 'space wave', in her article 'Squeezing Space, Releasing Space: Spatial Research in the Study of Eastern European Cinema'.[1] Mazierska suggests that a spatial approach offers a very different perspective to narrative-centred film analysis. According to the Polish scholar, the latter method overlooks the fact that films can be analysed by looking at a cinematic vision of space: a vision that might provide new insights into the historical events represented in these films. By choosing to study the representation of domestic space in post-Soviet Baltic cinema, we aim to situate this chapter in the light of this new wave of film analysis that prioritises the spatial constituent in cinematic chronotopes.

The domestic space in post-communist films has been analysed in various ways: some studies emphasise the importance of the role of domestic space in the construction and dissemination of Soviet ideology, and how this role is reflected in socialist and post-socialist films (see Boym 1994; Hirt 2012; Milerius and Cope 2008; Siegelbaum 2011). Other scholarly work focuses on the significance of this space in terms of understanding changes to everyday life in post-socialist countries.[2] In agreement with the majority of these works, we maintain in this chapter that the Soviet past inevitably informs the current conditions of post-Soviet domestic space. As David Crowley and Susan E. Reid point out, in Soviet times 'domestic space became an important site for ideological intervention' (2002: 11). The idea of using a residential area for political goals was notably prevalent during the Khrushchev era, when the intensive union-wide apartment building programme began. In order to homogenise Soviet space, gigantic housing projects were carried out in every republic of the USSR, including the Baltic states. Although this Soviet housing no longer performs its ideological function, architecturally similar apartment buildings still accommodate millions of people due to high demand for housing in the post-Soviet region. It is not surprising that filmmakers find prolific grounds for their metaphorical and documentary narratives in the concrete jungles erected in the communist past. Stripped of its ideological content, it nevertheless retains its influence on the geographic, social and cultural landscape of post-Soviet everyday life. In this chapter, we will build on the studies by Ewa Mazierska (1999) and Eva Näripea (2010), who have focused on the images of apartment buildings in films by post-socialist Polish and Estonian directors respectively. To better understand the role of domestic residential spaces built in the socialist period in post-Soviet Baltic cinema, we choose to analyse the development of their representation in Baltic films produced after the fall of the Soviet Union. As we explore the dynamics of the cinematic representation of domestic space in our chosen films, we consider both its interior and exterior manifestations. In the first instance we pay attention to the social trajectories of characters inside the homogenised dwellings built during the Soviet era, whereas in the second we are interested in the outside spaces – the ex-socialist neighbourhood areas that, as Michel de Certeau (1998: 5–7) has shown, connect and mediate between the private and social spaces of everyday life. In the first two parts of this chapter, we discuss the history of Soviet domestic space and its portrayal in several Lithuanian films which belong to the transitional Baltic cinema of the 1990s. In these sections, we emphasise the notable mythologisation of private domestic space by way of transforming it into a space for reflection on eternal, existential questions. In the third part of the chapter, we analyse the works of a new generation of filmmakers that return the everyday space to the big screen, whilst keeping its quotidian features and highlighting its realist dramas. We argue that, in contrast to the transitional Baltic cinema, the new role of domestic space in films made in the 2000s and the early 2010s reveals itself through realistic development of characters and their stories set in the spaces of the ex-Soviet apartment buildings.

All in all, in this chapter we contend that the radical change in the portrayal of passivity and resistance becomes visible through the comparison of the representation of domestic space in Soviet films to that in post-Soviet Baltic cinema. Representation of (in)activities in domestic space, which in the Soviet cinema were treated as acts of systemic resistance, acquires a completely different meaning in post-Soviet cinema. We suggest that urban domestic space is mythologised in the films of the 1990s, but serves as an instrument to critique contemporary social reality in the films of the twenty-first century.

Domestic Space in the Soviet Era: Ideological Instrument and Potential for Resistance

In order to understand why the housing project in the Soviet era took on such a conspicuous political dimension, we have to consider the history of the relationship between Soviet ideology and industrialisation. Following the 1917 October Revolution and the Bolshevik establishment in Russia, industrialisation became a symbol of economic and technological progress. Moreover, it signified the superiority of Soviet ideology over all reactionary ones. Gigantic industrial projects such as factories, power plants and bridges were portrayed as a battlefield where natural resources and the elements were conquered, and began working towards the goals of the revolution. Following the victory in the Second World War, the battle within the Soviet Union continued on the ideological and industrial front – enormous masses of people were mobilised to rebuild the destroyed country. Only when Khrushchev came to power after Stalin's death in 1953 was it acknowledged that previous victories had been achieved largely through inhumane repression in Stalin's Gulags.

However, the famous Twentieth Assembly of the Communist Party in 1956, where Khrushchev condemned Stalin's repressions, did not permanently reject the military rhetoric, but only changed its direction. The practice of dividing the economic rhythm into five-year plans (so-called *piatiletkas*) in the Soviet states was constantly forcing them to fight for the realisation of their plans. The previous military mobilisation continued as a permanent mobilisation of the workforce. After the rebuilding of the country's economic infrastructure, the problem of housing for the proponents of working classes was eventually addressed. It is not surprising that after aggressive industrialisation the intensive programme of housing provision took on an equivalent revolutionary rhetoric.

In 1927 the Swiss modernist architect Charles-Édouard Jeanneret, better known as Le Corbusier, in his manifesto *Towards A New Architecture* stated that 'a house is a machine for living in' (1986: 4). Le Corbusier meant that a dwelling unit should be as effective and pragmatic as a machine, while aesthetic features such as ornaments and decorations are absolutely unnecessary for realising the machine's essential function. By modifying the modernist inclination towards functionality and pragmatism in its own distinctive way, Soviet urbanisation launched the mass production of standard houses where standardised Soviet people were to be settled. Secluded by the Iron Curtain, the Soviet Union was creating its own version of the modern individual. Michel Foucault (1995) has demonstrated how disciplinary institutions (schools, barracks, hospitals and so on) transformed society into a laboratory for the construction of useful individuals. The Soviet system, however, turned strict military discipline into a visible, permanent and continuous process of building communism.

Everyday life in the ideology of the Soviet Union was treated as a site where the new structure of the unified social reality fully revealed itself. As Franco Berardi states, one of the most important modernist ideas was the belief in a better future (2011: 14–15). The bright future was always one of the most, if not the most, important products of the ideological laboratories of the Soviet regime. According to Russian cultural theorist Evgenii Dobrenko, Soviet authorities were the first to introduce a new collective temporality, which he calls 'the concluded future'. In describing it, Dobrenko writes: 'In order to free the ground for this new future, the present was shifted into the past, and the future-directed future was transformed into the present, as a result of which the present itself underwent complete de-realisation' (2008: 6). The construction of this particular temporality was implemented by the standardisation of everyday life. Every individual in the Soviet system was oppressed by the gigantic machine of Soviet ideology. No individual interest could be more important than public interest, no wasting of time and energy for personal reflections, explorations or passions was allowed. Soviet ideology publicly championed the development of every human characteristic potentially useful to the system, and, if necessary, the sacrifice of the present in favour of a brighter tomorrow.

Wide-scale urbanisation was one of the most common practices of a transformation towards the homogenisation of socialist everyday life. As architecture theorist Florian Urban points out, political, ideological, social, economic and even technological aspects of urban architecture were standardised across the Soviet Union in the 1950s. With the advent of large panel prefabricated blockhouse building technology, the colossal housing projects were gradually implemented in all Soviet republics and thus the unification of Soviet everyday life reached enormous proportions (see Urban 2008). By means of a uniformity of socialist architecture, the utopian residential districts aimed to synchronise the daily lives of the New Soviet individual.

This Soviet model of urbanistic modernity generated consequences that were completely antithetical to those of the capitalist model. The diametrically opposed vectors of the capitalist and socialist worlds were stipulated by a different treatment of the relationship between macrostructures (history) and microstructures (everyday life). In 1961, Guy Debord stated:

> Just as the accelerated history of our time is the history of accumulation and industrialisation, so the backwardness and conservative tendency of everyday life are products of the laws and interests that have presided over this industrialisation. Everyday life has until now resisted the historical. (Debord, cited in Highmore 2002: 240)

Debord believed that depoliticising and historically sidelining everyday life was an intentional act which allowed new forms of enslavement and repression to hide within it. Thus, Debord's entire resistance programme, as we know it, is simply an agenda to return everyday life to the historical arena. If a dwelling actually functions as a 'machine for living in', then this machine must drive on historical highways rather than on back streets or into dead ends. In the Soviet realm, however, the agenda of returning everyday life to the historical arena would have been meaningless since there was no essential difference or break between macrostructures (history) and microstructures (everyday life) within the conditions of a totalitarian ideology. Official Soviet doctrine turned urban domestic space inside out as the private milieu came to occupy the very epicentre of social space. In other words, it blurred the separation between the territories of everyday life as distinguished by Michel de Certeau: the private, the neighbouring and the social (1998: 7). The Soviet doctrine claimed that there was nothing private that could not potentially become public. Therefore, the unofficial position of the Soviet individual was often diverted in the opposing direction – towards the quiet bay of everyday domestic life. It would be presumptuous to state that this drive from the public towards the private space had intrinsic anti-Soviet charge. However, the public-to-private vector was marked by resistance potential in the sense defined by de Certeau. Paradoxically, if we adhere to de Certeau and identify the ability to engineer one's own meaning as an act of resistance, even passive disruption of the ideology of the 'useful individual' and the cultivation of 'useless' characteristics can be regarded as resistance.

The system does not necessarily strive to directly suppress anti-systemic struggle. It often tolerates a level of resistance that is enough to compensate for the need for rebellion, but not sufficient to seriously threaten the stability of the system. Measured anti-systemic manifestations are thus often incorporated into the system and reinforce its stability rather than destroy it.[3] This specific relationship between systemic and non-systemic resistance eventually left a notable mark on the existence of Soviet individuals inhabiting homogeneous Soviet apartment buildings. The oppression of Soviet ideology became less direct after the first wave of housing unification and operating through individuals. Next to the dominating ideological narratives, other, minor narratives were introduced in 'homeopathic' portions tailored to contemplate the niche, small-scale experiences of apartment block inhabitants; and to be harmless to the system itself. It is symptomatic that Sartrean existentialism was one of the minor narratives installed into the consciousness of Soviet citizens. Although Jean-Paul Sartre's landmark text *Existentialism is a Humanism* was not entirely in accordance with Marxist-Leninist teaching, it was translated into Russian in the year of Stalin's death in 1953 and it was seen as perfectly consistent, even complementary to the official doctrine. On the one hand, by stating that the meaning of existence is discovered neither within the self (*en soi*) nor at home (*chez soi*), but rather in the world – the street – in existential terms, Sartre justified the priority of the public world above the private, as underlined by Marxism-Leninism as well. On the other hand, Sartre's existentialism does not negate private experiences. On the contrary, it expresses them by finding an adequate language. Despite the global popularity of existentialist philosophy and literature, existentialist terminology was probably nowhere as widespread as in the Soviet Union. Organically it became fashionable to raise questions about the meaning and meaninglessness of existence within the tight spaces of Soviet blockhouse apartment buildings. Existentialist vocabulary was integrated into the Soviet urban consciousness, often losing sight of its French origins and becoming infused with authentic Soviet meanings.

While Sartre's type of existentialism was subordinated to the Soviet doctrine, Albert Camus's existentialism remained taboo. The official reason is, of course, Camus's complicated relationship with the French Communist Party. However, the clearer distinction between the existentialism of Sartre and that of Camus lies in the very concept of existentialism. The Soviet system dissected Sartrean existentialism and transplanted a humanist face onto socialist doctrine. In comparison to the humanist version, Camus's existentialism was far more destructive and dramatic, thus less compatible with the concept of the useful Soviet individual.

That which could not be transmitted through the official channels of existing literary translations developed naturally by deciphering the meanings encoded in existential questions on the meaning and meaninglessness of life. Existentialism became the lingua franca of niche experiences in Soviet apartment buildings, naturally drifting along the direction highlighted by Camus rather than Sartre. The incongruence between individual expectations and the world was called an absurdity by Camus, meaninglessness which has only two honest solutions – suicide or radical rebellion. By entering the world – the street – the Soviet citizen regularly experienced the phenomenon of incongruence. The experience of the absurdity of Soviet reality was particularly permanent. It forced the majority to collaborate, to adapt while in the outside, in the world, but at the same time to raise existential questions inside, at home. The resistance potential of this ambivalent attitude was not contained in the active position, but in the experience of alienation that was pushing from the street towards the space of home.

As the archives became available, in the last years of the Soviet Union and after its collapse, the harsh and systematic fight of Soviet censorship against the cinematic versions of the Camuesque 'stranger' became apparent. Many films featuring the stranger in crisis have never seen the daylight. Many more films were censored and featured rather reduced and withdrawn figures of the outsider raising existential questions.[4] It is questionable whether or not the system defeated the cinema of the Camuesque stranger. However, it is much more important to register the tendencies of escapism and withdrawal from the world that took various forms and left a significant mark, even in the aftermath of the collapse of the USSR. One of the most peculiar ways of retreating from the social and political worlds into domestic space can be observed in the early post-Soviet Lithuanian cinema.

The Mythologisation of Domestic Space in Lithuanian Films of the 1990s

The standardisation of urban space and the housing programme functioned as a basis for the uniformity of the Soviet life. In IT terms, it was a hardware with software installed that ensured the synchronicity of life in the Soviet domain. Identical houses furnished with identical furniture, identical TVs and radios transmitting identical or nearly identical TV and radio programmes – this was the everyday life of the Soviet individual, floating synchronically in a broad sense as well as through dozens of micro-segments on the farthest shores of the Soviet Union, from Moscow to Ashgabat.

Nonetheless, the synchronicity of individual Soviet lives was not a given phenomenon, but rather an aspiration of Soviet ideology. In fact, the homogeneous Soviet society never existed. Different nations in the

USSR had different histories, and different experiential capacity with regard to their existence within the union. For some time, the repressive mechanisms and unifying everyday practices functioned as if all differences were non-existent, or at least completely insignificant. Shortly, however, these differences became more notable, until eventually, and inevitably, they came to the fore. Since the 1980s everyday life practices began to disconnect from the socialist temporality initially intended to regulate it. The breakdown of the Soviet temporality of 'concluded-future' was particularly noticeable in the western part of the Soviet Union – especially in the Baltic countries. It was on these outskirts of the Soviet Empire that it became clear in the mid-1980s that the ideological background of the Soviet Union had already been practically disintegrated, and the illusion of a linear progress towards communism was no longer present. As a result of this process, the recent past was seen in a new and often traumatic light, the collective future abandoned its foregone communist conclusion and, eventually, with the breakup of the Soviet Union, opened up to the unknown.

Seemingly these transformations should have stimulated political activism and caused a return of everyday life to the political arena. Indeed, political activism moved towards the micro-levels that previously would have seemed too private or too mundane. On the grand scale cinema in post-Soviet countries turned towards themes that were previously considered restricted, unofficial, petty, trivial or even dirty. However, a certain type of cinema did not use its new freedom to depict whatever it wanted to strike a balance between the festive street and the regular home. Instead it used that freedom to penetrate further into the spaces of privacy. Recurrent rhythms of situations and events are typical for domestic monotony and routine. Moreover, they are quintessential in the mythical flow of time that maximises and universalises human passions whilst at the same time radically minimising the details of social and political issues. If the fragments of social and political space do appear in this kind of cinema, their status is transformed into particular, shifting and vanishing elements of the universal domestic space.

The turn towards this universalised domestic space resulted in a number of films set in abstract, non-urban, deterritorialised, imaginary places. According to official statistics published by Latvian and Lithuanian national cinema institutions, only a small percentage of all listed feature films produced before the turn of the millennium were set in a recognisable urban environment. Instead of presenting recognisable everyday spaces, many films directed in the 1990s mythologise and transform the urban domestic spaces into a universal mythic space.

The Corridor (*Koridorius*, 1994), *The House* (*Namai*, 1997), both directed by Sarunas Bartas, and *The Yard* (*Kiemas*, 1999), directed by Valdas Navasaitis, to name just a few Baltic films of the 1990s, propose an image of domestic space detached from both the Soviet past and the everyday realities of the post-Soviet present. Abstract images of ruined household places with passive characters in these films acquire narrative autonomy, as if diegesis was not their responsibility. A conceptual corridor–house–yard sequence designates the universal axis of the world where the eternal return of omnipresent existential dramas take place. Hence, in these films, the domestic space is portrayed in a circular, mythic time that reproduces itself in a repetitive rhythm and does not coincide with progressive linear history.

As it has been noted, the strategy of turning domestic space into the universal axis of the world in the mythic cinema was provoked by resistance to the norms of Soviet ideology, so it is unsurprising that this mythic cinema could appear as an inverted form of Soviet ideological cinema. Soviet ideology treats any empty time as parasitic or openly dangerous, as opposing the global goals of socialism. The development of the essential, existential dramas in mythic cinema takes place specifically in that empty time: liberated from political goals, social initiatives or pragmatic interests. Progress and loyalty to the system in Soviet cinema are reinforced by narrative and voice, whereas in mythic cinema the voice loses its importance and the privilege of meaning is given to all-encompassing silence. In Soviet cinema useless qualities are stigmatised, whilst in mythic cinema even debauched drinking is turned into an expression of authentic existence. The inhabitants of block apartment buildings in Bartas's *The Corridor* and *The House* carouse as if they were ancient demigods, or even gods.

It should not be surprising that this mythic cinema also seems totally detached from the realities of the post-Soviet world, although this detachment was qualitatively different in regards to that of Soviet cinema. As has been mentioned, an individual submerged into the existential domestic space was perceived as the Camuesque 'stranger' in the Soviet system, which therefore aimed to subdue and control the scale and form of withdrawal. The individual in mythic cinema is not withdrawn from his or her own present realities, but looks down on them, as if from the top of Mount Olympus. The corridor–house–yard axis in the block apartment building marks a certain centre of the world with regard to which any political or social realities seem constantly shifting. This is therefore less meaningful than the existential 'divine debauchery' in the dirty apartment kitchens. *The Corridor* is a particularly good representation in this respect. The film makes use of documentary scenes from anti-Soviet resistance footage in Lithuania – funerals of ordinary citizens shot or crushed by tanks in the defence of the TV tower, common people gathered to guard the first democratically elected parliament, bonfires in the square in freezing temperatures in the middle of winter, flags of an independent Lithuania floating over a bridge. These scenes would undoubtedly have a clear political charge in any other type of cinema. In mythic cinema, however, they lose direct political meaning and function as externalised existential projections that are subordinate to the inner existential passions of apartment block dwellers.

To paraphrase Sartre's famous assertion, even the most active street battles did not draw the characters outwards, but pushed them even more towards focusing on the mythical domestic space. On one hand, the optical enlargement of inner states and the prevention of their expression on the street undoubtedly indicates a deep existential crisis. On the other, this crisis surely appears as a sign of authentic existence that manifests a liberation from the false or transitory, and therefore less valuable, events on the street. In this sense the crisis, accompanied by empty time, silence and useless actions, is a positive response that provides meaning to the standardised block apartment housing generation on the threshold of the Soviet and post-Soviet eras. Therefore, in these films of the 1990s we observe a notable mythologisation of domestic space and its transformation into a space for reflecting on eternal existential questions. As the characters in these films live in a solipsistic world which operates cyclically, the everyday actions, and even the historical changes, outside their homes are either not depicted at all, or play a secondary role; while the existential questions remain the focus of the films.

Domestic and Neighbourhood Space as a Reflection of Social Reality in New Generation Films

At the beginning of the twenty-first century, at a time when social reality in the Baltic countries took on clearer neoliberal contours, urban domestic space has regained attention in the films of the second generation of Baltic filmmakers, who, as illustrated by recently made films, have started to explicitly portray realist stories centred on current inhabitants of the ex-socialist domestic space.[5] Andrius Blaževicius's short *Ten Reasons* (*Dešimt priežasčių*, 2012), Aik Karapetian's *People Out There* (*Cilveki Tur*, 2012), and Juris Kursietis's *Modris* (*Modris*, 2014) exemplify a shift from the mythologisation of the domestic space to its narrativisation. The films are characterised as distinctive portrayals of the current inhabitants of the ex-socialist residential districts. These works, along with a few other recent films, such as *Autumn Ball* (*Sügisball*, 2007), the Estonian drama directed by Veiko Õunpuu, or *Together Forever* (*Amžinai kartu*, 2016), the Lithuanian family drama directed by Lina Lužytė, are based on strikingly similar plot patterns.

Ten Reasons tells the story of twenty-year-old Vytas, who lives with his retired parents in a poor, ex-socialist residential area in Vilnius, Lithuania. Paranoid about an affair between his girlfriend and another man residing in the city centre, Vytas arranges a revenge plan which he attempts to implement in his native jungle of blockhouses. *People out There* tells the bleak story of a young man called Janis, who lives with his grandfather in Liepaja, Latvia. In contrast to his depressed grandfather, a retired Soviet academic who stares apathetically at his TV screen day after day, Janis tries to escape his imprisoning situation. He actively attempts to establish a connection with his sister (it is implied in the film that Janis's parents have emigrated), whose existence was kept secret by his grandfather. Out of despair Janis even joins a religious sect. But everything is in vain. At the end of the film Janis organises a mass robbery together with his neighbourhood friends, and subsequently becomes involved in a gang rape attempt. In a similar vein, *Modris* (Kursietis 2014), another depressing film by a Latvian director, portrays the drama of a seventeen-year-old boy residing in the maze of an ex-socialist blockhouse residential area in Riga, Latvia. Raised by a poor single mother and bored by his monotonous everyday life, the reticent boy develops a habit of playing slot machines in the neighbourhood bars. Modris starts borrowing money from his classmates, drops out of school and eventually, after losing all his money, steals and pawns the electric heater from his own apartment in one of surrounding blockhouses. Modris's misfortunes have just begun when his mother reports her own son to the police. Seeking help, he tries to find his father but before he does so, becomes entrapped in a sequence of unfortunate events that happen in his neighbourhood, and finally ends up in jail.

It is symptomatic that all of the aforementioned dreary stories of young people trapped in hopeless situations begin with panoramic establishing shots revealing the setting of the action. These opening shots depict a vast, grim and apparently unsafe space occupied by ex-socialist apartment buildings. The blockhouses typical of these areas frame almost every move of each of the main characters. Therefore, bringing these recent films together helps to conceptualise the cinematic image of the current inhabitants of these domestic residential areas. By inquiring generally as to how these films represent domestic space, it is possible to reveal a spatial trace of the social abjection of which all three films are characteristic.

Although the dull images of ex-socialist blockhouses could be endowed with metaphorical meanings, in contrast to the above-mentioned slow, abstract and contemplative transitional films made in the 1990s, the overall style of the films by the new generation of filmmakers is realistic. Having chosen to employ natural lighting, as well as long, mobile and unsteady takes that were shot on location, all three directors try to keep their films both narratively convincing and authentic. An overwhelming impression of spatial and social imprisonment in each of the films is conveyed through the use of depth of field and framing that foregrounds the exteriors and the interiors of the obsolete domestic environment. Trapped in the small, homogenous apartments of their immense blockhouse buildings, in elevators, on staircases, on concrete pavements and sidewalks, the main characters of these films are cut off from the outside urban world – the contemporary centres of economy and entertainment. Apart from occasional excitement of bodily pleasures, the young protagonists look passive and indifferent as they wander through their ex-socialist residential areas with typically identical gloomy streets surrounded by grey blocks. Despite the fact that these areas seem to be densely populated, social interaction by the local characters in the streets, yards and playgrounds – neighbourhood spaces in de Certeau's terms – appears to be very limited. Moreover, although the ex-socialist apartment buildings were supposed to play the role of a shelter for individual privacy in communist times; the young boys in all three post-Soviet films are portrayed as incurably alienated while living there with older relatives. All their attempts to establish closer relationships typically end up in frustration and disappointment on both sides. Inside their cubicle socialist-style apartments the young protagonists therefore feel confined by the despair of their depressed families who belong to the lost generation – the generation that was incapable of adapting to a neo-liberal present.

In their attempts to overcome the claustrophobic pressure of the ex-socialist cubicle apartments and alleviate the feelings of worthlessness common to their parents, the young protagonists of these three films adopt different strategies. They are portrayed as killing their time by habitually consuming lowbrow television shows (Vytas in *Ten Reasons*), regularly watching internet porn (Janis in *People out There*) or dispassionately gambling in the local bars (Modris in *Modris*). These virtual activities help the characters to survive their monotonous everyday life, and create the illusion of their engagement in the dominant consumerist regime. Given this illusionary participation in a consumerist life, it is not surprising that the real physical attempts to escape their environment – leave their home or start independent lives – are unsuccessful. In the scenes where they physically cross the borders of their neighbourhood areas, the young characters appear to be extremely vulnerable. Every time they reach the city centre they find themselves unable to communicate with this different kind of environment. Furthermore, these journeys threaten their freedom – both Modris and Janis are sought by the police even before they commit actual crimes. Thus, it appears that whenever Janis, Vytas or Modris leave their domestic space, they carry a feeling of entrapment within them. It hinders them from public contact with people who do not belong to their neighbourhood, and limits them to the stereotypical role of outsiders, who belong only to the ex-socialist concrete jungle.

At the first glance this representation of a tendency towards a hermit lifestyle might be reminiscent of the resistance potential in the Soviet era which was characterised by ignoring the public and rejecting the ordinariness of everyday life. However, after neoliberalism has replaced communism and the pressure of Soviet ideology stopped existing, the passive position in these post-Soviet films assumes different nuances and connotations. The useless young individual is not a threat to the capitalist system, but is actually beneficial.

The ambivalence of capitalist consumerism with regards to the inhabitants of these residential districts is more or less emphasised in all three films. Newly built upscale apartment buildings, department stores, shopping malls, fast-food restaurants and slot machine salons wake a desire in the young characters to experiment with their identity. The setting lures them in with colourful contrast and produces the illusion of a possibility for refuge from the entrapment of the bleak housing projects. The inaccessibility and unaffordability of all these capitalist places and objects proves that the neoliberal everyday lifestyle is unattainable for the young characters. And yet, unable to resist the allure of capitalism, the youngsters break the law in despair and commit crimes: both Janis and Vytas are shown stealing clothes from the glamorous department stores or shopping malls located in city centres. As the title of Karapetian's film implies, the inhabitants of post-socialist space are 'out there' not only in terms of being physically stuck in their ex-socialist apartment buildings and residential districts, but also in terms of being excluded by inclusion. As has been stressed by many, social reality is not inclined to be transformed by the erasure of the past in emerging neoliberal states (as was common in the USSR). On the contrary, neoliberalism accommodates itself to this past. Meanwhile the young hostages of socialist urban environment have been deprived of both the past and the future, which is confiscated from them by the neoliberal present. As Fredric Jameson suggests (2003), it is precisely capitalist logic that tries to prove the halt of temporality. According to Jameson, the emphasis on the present as the end of temporality is a fantasy masking a number of forms of capitalist suppression, and helping to cut off the otherness, strangeness and alterity (2003: 712–17). Thus, even if ex-socialist residential apartment block districts in these films are portrayed as a place of malaise, anger, scarcity and despair, it is particularly important that a second generation of Baltic filmmakers inverts the common de-temporalisation or mythologisation ascribed to this domestic space and the people 'out there'.

The realist impulse that drives all three films represents the complexities of the everyday life of their inhabitants. Therefore, it can be said that the films by the directors of the post-memory generation expose the results of the collapse of the socialist chronotope that has left a certain 'jetlagged' group of young people behind. Their confinement in the old domestic environment abjects them physically, while the neoliberal drive attempts to eliminate this jetlag. It creates the illusion that the de-temporalisation of their daily life is somewhat bearable, and, though they barely live, their lives are not bare of meaning.

To sum up, from the analysis of twenty-first-century cinema it becomes evident that in the films of the new generation filmmakers the neighbourhood – residential district space – extends the private domestic space and becomes the field of activity for the post-Soviet individuals, whilst at the same time demarcating their potential in the neoliberal environment. The younger generation of filmmakers in the Baltic countries tracks down and inspects the ex-socialist domestic places now bereft of both their ideological aura and their hypersensitivity, which they used to stir up in communist generations. They reflect communal histories and articulate current social problems emanating from the material substances charged with the failed content of past time. By calling into question the synchronicity of the capitalist system, these young filmmakers highlight the ghostly domestic spaces otherwise lost in neoliberal temporality. The past of socialist domestic space in their films, to paraphrase Svetlana Boym (2001: 76), suggests other dimensions of the lived experience and haunts these places like a ghost. This ghost, for the new generation of Baltic filmmakers, is not just a product of the traumatic past, it is also an active participant of the present. In other words, although the recent Baltic films clearly recognise that ex-Soviet residential districts function as the remnant of Soviet domestic space, we argue that these works touch

Figure 8.1 Andrius Blaževičius's *The Saint* (2017). Film still. Courtesy of the producer.

not only upon a historical rupture, but also upon a spatial continuity. The aforementioned films of the twenty-first century manifest an interest in approaching ex-socialist domestic spaces anew, that is, not only as a trigger of collective trauma and coping with the failed social utopia, but also as a suppressed part of the political and social realities of present-day Baltic countries.

In Lieu of Conclusion

The Saint, the first feature film by Andrius Blaževičius, director of *Ten Reasons*, came out in 2017 (Figure 8.1). When presenting the film at the International Vilnius Film Festival *Kino Pavasaris* the director mentioned that the working title of the film was *Crisis*. As he said, crisis in this case expresses not only the state of the characters, but also that of the director's own generation. Therefore, the film is not just a duplicate or a mechanical sequel to the aforementioned new generation of Baltic filmmakers' cinema, but a certain manifesto of a whole generation, capturing the experiences of the post-Soviet milieu in the same way that the experiences of the transitional generation were captured by Bartas, Navasaitis and other directors.

The Saint is set in a Lithuanian provincial town. The main character gets fired from the factory he worked at before the economic crisis of 2008. Pushed by his wife, he immediately starts looking for a new job,

Figure 8.2 Andrius Blaževičius's *The Saint* (2017). Film still.
Courtesy of the producer.

but with no luck. Without a job, Vytas is stuck in his block apartment house, for the first time having free time to do as he pleases. He exercises every day, and browses the Internet together with his unemployed friend; simultaneously, after getting a new haircut, he starts a secret love affair with his hairdresser. After a series of disappointing occurrences, encouraged by his buddy, Vytas gets involved in searching for a local guy living in a similar block house who posted a video on YouTube claiming that he has seen Jesus Christ in front of the wall of one of the standard ex-socialist blockhouse buildings of their town.[6]

The film was shot in several ex-socialist residential areas of small Lithuanian towns (Figure 8.2). Instead of big city neighbourhoods Blaževičius chooses provincial urban spaces that even Lithuanians would not be able to recognise and with this achieves a specific effect. On one hand, the filming locations do not register a specific area, but they portray *any* space that could basically function in the entire habitat of the post-Soviet territory. In this respect one might even draw certain parallels between the *any* space and the mythic space, which also cannot be fixed to a particular site. On the other hand, in contrast to the mythic space that is located in the opposite of the centre and manifests a certain axis of the world, the *any* space of *The Saint* is fundamentally peripheral and marginal. In defining the processes of globalisation, Zygmunt Bauman (1998) makes a distinction between free mobility and forced localisation. What Bauman applies to people essentially can also be applied to spaces. In the process of globalisation certain spaces were forcibly localised, turned into almost isolated social ghettos, segregated from the grand processes of globalisation and doomed to circulate in the meaningless monotonous rhythm of repetitive, identical everyday practices.

As stated above, the localisation in private domestic space was not forced in the conditions of Soviet reality, but voluntary, at least partially rescued from the false ideologised realities of the street. This is how the Soviet everyday resistance form was significantly different from the Western, capitalist one which, as mentioned before, attempted to return the private everyday domestic space into the historical arena. The characters of *The Saint* do not see any meaning either at home or in the street. Apartments in the blockhouse buildings function like pockets, caves or appendices which, instead of performing any positive functions, may cause sickness or even death (Figure 8.3). Alternatively, the street only offers a temporary relief that evaporates with the remains of alcohol or the charms of forbidden love. The streets of provincial block apartment neighbourhoods are basically the same kind of appendices as provincial apartment homes – their removal would not affect the globalised world or historical processes in any way.

This precisely is the fundamental position of the protagonist of *The Saint*. Camus's choice between suicide and rebellion, formerly problematic and even censored by the Soviet ideology, seemingly loses its meaning as the clear boundaries between these alternatives are broken down. Existential crisis and suffering lose their privileged status and can no longer serve as a sign of authentic existence. Crisis does not dignify

Figure 8.3 Andrius Blaževičius's *The Saint* (2017). Film still. Courtesy of the producer.

and suffering does not purify. Empty time does not liberate, but instead highlights the tight, smothering spaces of the household and the street.

And what about the idea of Jesus Christ encountered on the wall of a dilapidated Soviet apartment building? On the one hand, it indeed manifests the need for the *sacrum* emerging from empty time. On the other, it is difficult to resist the suspicion that it is the product of insanity, or at least an innocent joke in the *profanum* context of apartment blocks. If crisis no longer liberates or offers any authenticity, it can at least offer some ambiguity that brings a little bit of meaning into the meaningless world of standard ex-socialist blockhouse apartment buildings and streets.

Notes

1 See Andis Cinis et al. (2008), 'Perfect Representations of Soviet Planned Space', *Scandinavian Journal of History*, 3, no. 3, pp. 226–46, and Evgeny Dobrenko and Eric Naiman (2011), *The Landscape of Stalinism: The Art and Ideology of Soviet Space*, Washington, DC: University of Washington Press, among others.
2 Ewa Mazierska (2017), 'Squeezing Space, Releasing Space: Spatial Research in the Study of Eastern European Cinema', in Sanja Bahun and John Haynes (eds), *Cinema, State Socialism and Society in the Soviet Union and Eastern Europe, 1917–1989: Re-Visions*, London: Routledge, pp. 8–9.
3 In the description of Dina Iordanova's and Pavle Levi's course 'Eastern European Cinema', Iordanova links the issue of the censorship in the Soviet states with the Marcusean notion of 'repressive tolerance' permitting politically non-dangerous forms of social criticism (Iordanova 1999: 60).
4 For more about censorship that Baltic cinema underwent during the Soviet era see Lina Kaminskaitė-Jančorienė and Anna Mikonis-Railienė (2016). Almost the same strategy to depict Polish urban space as 'any space, and any town' is described by Ewa Mazierska (1999). Nevertheless, she explains such strategy to screen the post-soviet Polish urban space as a means to avoid the parochialism and to compete with commercial American cinema, which is not the case in the mythological trend of Lithuanian films we are discussing here.
5 As Maruta Zane Vitols argues, the turn towards the everyday spaces has also been characteristic of films by Laila Pakalnina, one of the best known contemporary Latvian film directors. However, Pakalnina's attitude to the everyday is that of poetisation and beautifying, and not of realistic depiction. See Maruta Zane Vitols (2010), 'Alternative Spaces, Alternative Voices, The Art of Laila Pakalnina', *Acta Academiae Artium Vilnensis*, 56, p. 38.
6 One could rightly argue that Vytas's character represents a crisis of masculinity in post-Socialist countries, cinematic representations of which are described in Mazierska (2003).

Works Cited

Agamben, Giorgio (1998), *Homo Sacer: Sovereignity and Bare Life*, Stanford: Stanford University Press.
Bahun, Sanja and John Haynes (eds) (2017), *Cinema, State Socialism and Society in the Soviet Union and Eastern Europe, 1917–1989: Re-Visions*, London and New York: Routledge.
Bartas, Sarunas (1994), *The Corridor* (*Koridorius*), Hubert Bals Fund, Why Not Productions, Ministry of Culture Lithuania, Studio Kinema, TV-Ventures: Lithuania.
Bartas, Sarunas (1997), *The House* (*Namai*), Gemini Films, La Sept Cinéma, Madragoa Filmes, Studio Kinema: Lithuania,
Bauman, Zygmunt (1998), *Globalization: The Human Consequences*, New York: Columbia University Press.
Berardi, Franco (2011), *After the Future*, Edinburgh, Oakland and Baltimore: AK Press.
Blaževičius, Andrius (2012), *Ten Reasons* (*Dešimt priežasčių*), prod: Lithuania.
Blaževičius, Andrius (2017), *The Saint* (*Sventasis*), M-Films and No Sugar Films: Lithuania.
Boym, Svetlana (1994), *Common Places: Mythologies of Everyday Life in Russia*, Cambridge, MA: Harvard University Press.
Boym, Svetlana (2001), *The Future of Nostalgia*, New York: Basic Books.
Cinis, Andis et al. (2008), 'Perfect Representations of Soviet Planned Space', *Scandinavian Journal of History*, 3, no. 3, pp. 226–46.
Crowley, David and S. E. Reid (eds) (2002), *Socialist Spaces. Sites of Everyday Life in the Eastern Bloc*, Oxford: Berg.
Debord, Guy ([1961] 2002), 'Perspectives for Conscious Alteration of Everyday Life', in B. Highmore (ed.), *The Everyday Life Reader*, London and New York: Routledge, pp. 237–45.
de Certeau, Michel (1998), *The Practice of Everyday Life*, Minneapolis: University of Minnesota Press.
Dobrenko, Evgenii (2008), *Stalinist Cinema and The Production of History. Museum of Revolution*, Edinburgh: Edinburgh University Press.
Dobrenko, Evgeny, and Eric Naiman (2011), *The Landscape of Stalinism: The Art and Ideology of Soviet Space*, Washington, DC: University of Washington Press.
Eliade, Mircea (1991), *The Myth of Eternal Return*, Princeton, NJ: Princeton University Press.
Foucault, Michel (1995), *Discipline and Punish: The Birth of the Prison*, New York: Vintage Books.
Hirt, Sonia (2012), *Iron Curtains: Gates, Suburbs and Privatization of Space in the Post Socialist City*, Oxford: Wiley-Blackwell.
Jameson, Frederic (2003), 'The End of Temporality', *Critical Inquiry*, 29, no. 4, pp. 695–718.

Kaminskaitė-Jančorienė Lina and Anna Mikonis-Railienė (2016), *Cinema in Soviet Lithuania: System, Films, Directors*, Vilnius: Vilnius University Press.
Karapetian, Aik (2012), *People Out There* (*Cilveki Tur*), Locomotive Productions: Latvia.
Kursietis, Juris (2014), *Modris*, Red Dot Media: Latvia.
Iordanova, Dina (1999), 'Eastern European Cinema', *Journal of Film and Video*, 51, no. 1, pp. 56–76.
Le Corbusier [1923; first English translation 1927] (1986), *Towards A New Architecture*, Mineola, NY: Dover Publications.
Lužytė, Lina (2016), *Together Forever* (*Amžinai kartu*), Alinen Film and Just a moment: Lithuania.
Mazierska, Ewa (1999), 'Any Town? Post-Communist Warsaw in Juliusz Machulski's *Girl Guide* (1995) and *Kiler* (1997)', *Historical Journal of Film, Radio and Television*, 19, no. 4, pp. 515–30.
Mazierska, Ewa (2003), 'The Redundant Male: Representations of Masculinity in Polish Postcommunist Cinema', *Journal of Film and Video*, 55, no. 2/3, pp. 29–43.
Milerius, Nerijus and Benjamin Cope (eds) (2008), *P-S Landshafty: Optiky gorodskich issledovanij*, Vilnius: EHU International Press.
Näripea, Eva (2010), 'From Nation-Scape to Nation-State: Reconfiguring Filmic Space in Post-Soviet Estonian Cinema', *Acta Academiae Artium Vilnensis*, 56, pp. 65–75.
Navasaitis, Valdas (1999), *The Yard* (*Kiemas*), Arte France Cinéma, Les Films de L'Observatoire and Studio Uljana Kim: France and Lithuania.
Õunpuu, Veiko (2007), *Autumn Ball* (*Sügisball*, 2007), Homeless Bob Production, Kuukulgur Film and Tugev Tuul Films: Estonia.
Siegelbaum, Lewis H. (2011), *Borders of Socialism: Private Spheres of Soviet Russia*, Basingstoke: Palgrave Macmillan.
Urban, Florian (2008), 'Prefab Russia', *Docomomo Journal*, 39, pp. 18–22.

CHAPTER 9

No | Home | Movie: Essay Film, Architecture as Framing and the Non-house
Laura Rascaroli

The House and the Real

Placing the accent on the pervasiveness of the migratory experience in our times, and on its production of a ubiquitous condition of homelessness, John Berger (1991) – drawing on Mircea Eliade – describes the original meaning of home as the ontological centre of the world, positioned at the heart of the real:

> In traditional societies, everything that made sense of the world was real; the surrounding chaos existed and was threatening, but it was threatening because it was *unreal*. Without a home at the centre of the real, one was not only shelterless, but also lost in non-being, in unreality. Without a home everything was fragmentation. (56; emphasis in the original)

The home, for Berger, was at the centre of two ideal lines, one vertical, with the sky and the underworld at its two extremities, and one horizontal, representing 'the traffic of the world, all the possible roads leading across the earth to other places' (56). At the reassuring intersection of the two lines, the home was 'nearest to the gods in the sky and the dead in the underworld [and] at the starting point and, hopefully, the returning point of all terrestrial journeys' (56). The loss of the home that characterises emigration as the emblematic condition of our times, therefore, implies a profound deprivation of meaning for which one can go as far as 'abandoning oneself to the unreal which is the absurd' (56).

The home, in this conception, is what used to make sense of the world. For Berger, this ancient meaning of home having been lost, it has been replaced with that of the house as temporary shelter, in which habits involving gestures and objects strive to create a sense of protection. As Gaston Bachelard (1994) writes, whenever humans find the slightest shelter they make a home of it with their imagination, and can 'build "walls" of impalpable shadows', comforting themselves with the illusion and memory of protection (5). Yet, it is the unbridgeable gap between the values of the modern house and the ontological centredness of the traditional home, 'the original fullness of the house's being' (Bachelard 1994: 8), that I want to bear in mind as the backdrop of my discussion, which will deal with the real insofar as it concerns itself with nonfictional filmic houses – as distinct at once from constructed sets and from fictional homes. At the same time, I am interested here in the conception of a surrounding chaos that the home attempts to fence off and, thus, in the structuring function of the house in the cosmos – the latter seen as a 'non-house in the same way that metaphysicians speak of a non-I' (Bachelard 1994: 40). For Bachelard, 'it is easy to establish all sorts of contradictions' (40) between the house and the non-house, such as intimacy versus exposure, or order versus chaos. The purpose of my discussion is to reflect on specific forms of nonfiction that place the house at their heart, with a view to reaching a better understanding not just of how they comment on the house and its structuring function, but also, more specifically, of how film as a medium thinks, produces, and frames images of the house/home.

Framing Homes

This chapter concerns itself with essayistic films that directly engage with houses to make sense of them and of their relationship with the cosmos, the non-house surrounding them. Two types, if not genres, of films will be at the centre of my attention: the architectural essay film and the authorial home movie. On account of their reflective engagement with the house as a building and as space of the 'I' both genres are ideally positioned to support the aims of my discussion in this chapter.

Penelope Haralambidou (2015), drawing on the noteworthy corpus of essay films that 'specifically focus on urban or architectural design subject matter' (237) – from *Man with a Movie Camera* (1929) by Dziga Vertov to *Toute la mémoire du monde* (1957) by Alain Resnais, from *London* (1994) by Patrick Keiller to *Los Angeles Plays Itself* (2003) by Thom Andersen – has proposed to treat what she calls the architectural essay film as a distinct subgenre, in which 'the reflective and introspective attitude of the director is reflected on the architecture, revealing a link between our perception of the built environment and the structure of intellectual processes' (238). Film, in other words, can help 'reveal architecture's relationship with memory, in symbolic, affective, and structural terms' (236). By the addition of the dimension of time, Haralambidou asserts, film creates an 'amplified sense of identification with architecture' (247) and allows for the exploration of its 'storytelling potential' (237).

Equally attracted to the house, although starting from different, more quotidian premises, the home movie, as its name suggests, is often based in the family home, which is at once its main setting and the place where the film is produced and consumed. Scholars have theorised and investigated social, class and gender aspects of the construction of the family in amateur cinema, and have demonstrated the centrality of the home to the genre's glorification of private life, in particular at the height of the ideology of familialism in the 1950s, when 'home movie-making ... synchronized with the elevation of the nuclear family as the ideological centre of all meaningful activities' (Zimmerman 1995: 134).

Whereas my first case study in this chapter, Ila Bêka and Louise Lemoine's *Barbicania* (2014), is an uncontested example of the architectural essay film, my second example, Chantal Akerman's *No Home Movie* (2015), is not a fitting example of its genre, as its title seems to suggest. Akerman's is an authorial home movie, a director's experimental, reflective family film. This is by no means an isolated case, for *No Home Movie* sits comfortably within a history of avant-garde diary/ amateur films mixing some of the generic underpinnings of the home movie (the intimate focus, the artisanal approach) with a marked reflectiveness and an authorial style – famous examples include the work of Jonas Mekas, Maria Menken and Stan Brakhage, among many others.

In spite of their widely different generic contexts and cultural and artistic points of reference, *Barbicania* and *No Home Movie* are both related to the essay film, for they may be read as essays on homes and how we inhabit them. Essay films are texts in the tradition of the literary essay, which engage intellectually with an object; their overt reflective and self-reflexive stance implies that issues of framing, both textual and contextual, are at the centre of their critical practice (Rascaroli 2017: 165–86). Framing is here to be intended at once as the literal operation of *mise en cadre* and as discursive practice; in other words, as narrative, ideological and cultural framing.

In writings on film, the frame is usually understood as an element at once of the image, of the apparatus of the cinema, and of filmic language, which participates in, supports and structures meaning-making in multiple ways; these, in turn, have to do with diverse spheres including technology, perception, psychology, aesthetics, narrative, ideology and culture (Branigan 2003). Here, I am particularly interested in the practical act of framing, either through a lens or through postproduction devices, and in its critical dimension. It seems to me that a reflection on framing is essential to reach an understanding of how the cinema films homes and constructs their meanings. Framing is, in fact, an operation that film shares with architecture. As Kim Dovey (2008) has written:

> Architecture and urban design 'frames' space, both literally and discursively. In the literal sense everyday life 'takes place' within the clusters of rooms, buildings, streets and cities that we inhabit. Action is structured and shaped by walls, doors and windows, framed by the decisions of designers. As a form of discourse, built form constructs and frames meanings. (1)

Other authors have recognised the affinity between art and architecture, and specifically cinema and architecture, as rooted precisely in the frame. In particular, Bernard Cache (1995) draws on Gilles Deleuze to suggest that architecture may be defined as the 'manipulation of ... the frame' (1) and that, as such, it is the prime structuring impulse behind all the arts of the image that rest on framing: 'Architecture, the art of the frame, would then not only concern those specific objects that are buildings, but would refer to any image involving any element of framing, which is to say painting as well as cinema' (1). Framing is, therefore, a compelling point of convergence of film and architecture. This is not simply an aesthetic similarity, however; as Dovey (2008) claims, the act of architectural framing amounts to an intervention within a historical and social context: 'Because architecture and urban design involve transformations in the ways we frame life, because design is the imagination and production of the future, the field cannot claim autonomy from the politics of social change' (1).

Every time it engages with an architectural structure, then, a film not only frames but it reframes. The *mise en cadre* of a building or, in other words, the setting of the building to a filmic frame is necessarily duplication, not only of the building's structure, but also of its act of framing – seen at once as ordering of everyday life and intervention into a sociocultural context. The relationship between these two acts of framing – architectural and filmic – is, I claim, at the empirical and conceptual core of cinema's association with the house.

The Architectural Essay Film: Ila Bêka and Louise Lemoine's *Barbicania*

In this section, I will be concerned with films that self-consciously address the house with an essayistic gesture of reframing. Through this gesture, they comment on architecture as a framing activity – which, according to Elizabeth Grosz (2008), is the primary territorialising force.

Figure 9.1 Forming again the already hyperformed: hyperframing in Alexander Kluge's and Peter Schamoni's *Brutality in Stone* (*Brutalität in Stein*, 1961). Film still.

The argument of the architectural essay film is, indeed, an argument concerning the built environment in its many impacts – variously historical, cultural, aesthetic, economic, ideological, affective, and experiential. Reframing is, furthermore, a rhetorical strategy that directs attention to the epistemology of seeing and, thus, to the historicity of images. The architectural essay film, in other words, always works at a metadiscursive level.

Architectural essay films, I argue, are often split between offering an aesthetic re-presentation of their architectural object and putting forward a critique of it. Commenting on Alexander Kluge and Peter Schamoni's *Brutality in Stone* (*Brutalität in Stein*, 1961), an eleven-minute essay film on Nazi architecture and urban planning (Figure 9.1), Eric Rentschler (1990), for instance, observed that 'the film's dominant strategies involve contrast, counterpoint, and parody. Its schematic and patterned editing rhythms underline and overstate the object of investigation, forming again the already hyperformed, exaggerating the regularity of spaces, shapes, and surfaces' (35). The architectural essay film is, indeed, an act of repetition, a reframing of the already framed, which tends to produce 'hyperframing' – as is evident in other essayistic nonfictions like Jean Vigo's *À propos de Nice* (1930), Alain Resnais's *Toute la mémoire du monde* (1957), Heinz Emigholz's series *Architecture as Autobiography* (1986–), Lotte Schreiber's *Borgate* (2008) and *Quadro* (2002), and Thom Andersen's *Reconversion* (*Reconversão*, 2012), to mention but a few, but also in fictions incorporating a study of architecture, such as Peter Greenaway's *The Belly of an Architect* (1987). Its conundrum is, therefore, how to avoid being confined to a pleonastic, reiterative formal discourse, how to escape the 'demarcation, enframement, containment' (Grosz 2008: 16) of architectural framing to unlock its multiform subconscious – at once narrative, political, and philosophical. This is the point I wish to explore here, which I will do through the discussion of a representative case study, with a view to contributing to a general understanding of strategies employed by filmic work that engages reflectively with homes as architectures.

Ila Bêka and Louise Lemoine's architectural films are examples of successful negotiation of the above-described conundrum. Trained in architecture and art history respectively, their films are not entirely lacking in hyperframing, symmetrical emphasis and aestheticising reiteration; however, these are just one element of a complex focus, which privileges the everyday usages and less visible features of buildings, the fragment, the detail and the moment. Their films, therefore, resist conveying wholeness and closure, as can be seen in *Barbicania* and other works by the two authors, such as *Koolhaas Houselife* (2013), which from the start immerse the spectator in the detail of the houses and relegate the customary imposing views of the buildings to a later point, if not to the very end of the films.

Barbicania is a ninety-minute exploration of the brutalist Barbican Estate in the City of London, an iconic development built between 1965 and 1976 in an area devastated by Second World War bombings. It comprises, among other structures, three tower blocks, thirteen terrace blocks, and two mews, and it hosts a series of cultural institutions including the arts venue the Barbican Centre, a public library, and the Museum of London.

The film is divided into thirty-one chapters differing in length and contents, each identified by a title that emphasises an idea or element of the episode, while also corresponding to one of the thirty-one days of shooting – although the episodes are not spliced together in chronological order, as is evidenced by a calendar featured at the start of each episode. Filming an estate such as the Barbican, which extends over a thirty-five-acre site, and conveying a sense of both its overall character and its diverse features obviously presented significant challenges; the episodic structure of the film provides flexibility, allowing for the progressive build-up of notations, stories and images of the buildings and their inhabitants and users. Rather than a house, the Barbican is almost like a town, and can even lend itself to becoming a metaphor of the world, as suggested by the distorted drawing of the estate in the shape of a globe that both opens and closes the film. Yet, it is its aspect of private abode that the film ultimately privileges, while also paying attention to its public spaces and to the city outside it. It is precisely the presence of the latter – of the non-house, the space where we are not at home – that emphasises the idea of the home. It is to this idea that I now wish to pay attention.

The Barbican in Bêka and Lemoine's film is a true home of our times – a home for the homeless and the rootless. As David, the first resident interviewed by the filmmakers, explains, there is an obvious spatial hierarchy in the Barbican: the higher up one lives, the closest one is to being a god, or a king. This is confirmed by other residents, and becomes explicit in the episode 'The Sky Above', set in the penthouse of the forty-three-storeys-high Cromwell Tower, from which the views of the city below are breathtaking. John Berger's description of the ancient house's function of connecting its inhabitants to the gods springs to mind. Equally, the film invokes the dead below them: not least because the Barbican was built over the site of devastating bombings. As long-term resident Rita recalls in the 'Burial-Playground' episode, 'all this was all holes; quite deep'. She also tells of how, during the war, the tombs in the burial ground became uncovered by the explosions, and so she used to play with her friends underground, inside the graves. Long-forgotten graves also appear in another episode, 'The Impossible Picture'. In 'The Salvage Store', then, Cynthia shows the filmmakers the underground storage area, where the original fittings of the Barbican are still kept.

Although the sky and the underground are two key reference points for the Barbican, the meanings of this scale in today's world has changed. Being close to the sky is mostly a matter of status, rather than of spirituality and order; and only the older residents like Rita, or like Lina and Tessa in 'War Memories', maintain a tenuous link with the dead. Residing in the Barbican is, for the many who have come to it in more recent times, a choice linked to the uniqueness of the place, to its iconicity and exclusiveness. It is not just a matter of status, however; residents refer, first and foremost, to the sense of protection and shelter that the Barbican grants them. The estate is presented by its dwellers as an enlarged home, which extends the shelter of the house's four walls, and which makes sense of the cosmos beyond its limits: the huge metropolis that we see in the distance, from the safety of the 'barbican', the fortified outpost. Such safety is, needless to say, secured by money: the higher the income, the more distant the threat of chaos implicit in the non-house.

Inside the fortress, many residents like to restore the austere 'Barbican look', seeking the original fittings in the underground store, when these have been replaced by previous owners. This also seems a choice dictated by the need for security, by the nostalgic pleasure that comes with inhabiting the past, seen as the place that is known and familiar and, therefore, stable and safe, unlike the chaotic present and the imponderable future. Each home visited by the filmmakers, then, reveals its owners' dwelling strategies, which, while personal, overlap in essence: daily gestures and habits, invisible demarcation lines, closely guarded private spaces, the familiar objects surrounded by which one feels at home. One of the dwellers, a psychologist, speaks of the unconscious of the Barbican as something that keeps its residents there, in some cases with more than a hint of pathological attachment to the fortress. The filmmakers tell her that they would like to be let into the Barbican's unconscious, and ask for the 'magic key' that opens its doors (the theme of the 'key to the Barbican' runs throughout the film, demarcating insiders and outsiders, those who are at home and those who are strangers); but the psychologist warns them that it is out of their reach, and that finding it would require much longer than the one month of shooting.

If Bêka and Lemoine cannot find the magic key, they still construct a portrait of the Barbican that successfully eludes the demarcation and containment of the brutalist enframement of spaces to provide an insightful and nuanced image of the estate. The film opens with the camera closely following a man who, sitting on a motorised chair, traverses a hall and arrives at the Barbican's public library. Instead of providing us with architectural establishing shots and imposing views of the estate to begin with, therefore, the filmmakers reveal their preferred strategy of shadowing its visitors and residents and observing their everyday gestures to uncover the Barbican seen as a form that generates a series of practices. A man who comes to play the piano each day at the same time, and who for twenty years has sat across from another man doing the same, having spoken to him only once; homeowners unveiling their apartments to the filmmakers, and revealing snippets of their lives; the postman who sorts envelops and parcels before walking through the Barbican to deliver them; a woman in red shoes joining an audience that gathers to attend a public concert; a gardener in charge of the conservatory, who every day feeds the koi fish in its ponds; an amateur photographer attracted to the buildings' shapes and colours: by observing, following and interacting with them, the film uncovers some of the many practices that the buildings produce, facilitate or obstruct, as well their views of the Barbican as a home and as a space. And it is not just human users: animals come to the Barbican too, and make of it their home, including a fox, a squirrel, snails and a falcon; their practices too are observed and discussed. The film, furthermore, catches moments in which inanimate objects assert their existence, like a vortex of wind that always affects a particular corner, or a tree that casts its shadow on a wall (Figure 9.2). All these encounters and idiosyncratic moments are completed by architectural shots of the facades, interiors, passageways and terraces, which 'hyperframe' the structures, but also interpret them, as in the 'Ballet Mécanique' episode, hinting at the 1924 Fernand Léger Dadaist film of the same title, as well as at the montage of *Man with a Movie Camera* (*Chelovek s kinoapparatom*, Dziga Vertov, 1929); or as in 'The Concrete Temple', in which shots of the building are accompanied by a chant that seems to originate from the walls themselves and to express their architectural subconscious.

Most importantly, each episode is a small, self-contained story, which progressively builds up a broader narrative through accumulation and a network of internal references. Even the moments that would seem

Figure 9.2 Inanimate objects assert their existence in Ila Bêka and Louise Lemoine's *Barbicania* (2014). Film still.

most observational are fragments of narrative development, such as the episode in which the camera stubbornly follows around a pair of red shoes among a crowd gathering for a concert; or the snails a dweller is puzzled to find on her elevated concrete terrace, and which are later lined up by the filmmakers and filmed as if they were on their way to the Barbican. The film overtly declares its narrativising approach by organising the material according to the calendar appearing at the start of each episode, and representing the thirty-one days of the shoot; the scrambled chronological order with which the episodes are spliced together reveals the contrived nature of storytelling. In combining these small stories of people, animals and cement, therefore, *Barbicania* explodes the constraint and aesthetic hegemony of the brutalist framing to reveal the practices it generates and, through them, explore its ability to protect, inspire, conceal, exalt and frustrate. The architectural framing is reframed through camera and sound and through narrative, so as to unlock its 'storytelling potential' (Haralambidou 2015: 237) and reveal its unconscious.

The Home Movie: Chantal Akerman's *No Home Movie*

The home movie genre is characterised by its domestic scope, intended at once in terms of production (the home is the origin, the studio and, often, the set of the film), of consumption (traditionally, amateur films were screened at home, to family and friends), and even of themes (the home is the direct or indirect focus of countless amateur films). For the purposes of this analysis, I am most interested in the traditional concept of the home movie as record of the family. By and large, these films presented an idyllic image of happy domesticity, often focusing on memorable, proud and cheerful moments of family life (birthdays, weddings, gatherings, religious ceremonies). In this sense, in the home movie the exceptional in family life is mixed with the banality of everydayness, most clearly encapsulated by the house itself, seen as the cradle of the family and its values, as the epitome of its concept of privacy (which the amateur filmmakers were nevertheless happy to film and show, albeit to their closed circles), and as a status symbol (a costly pastime, filmmaking was mostly confined to the bourgeoisie). As such, the house was displayed with pride, the focus being on its most public areas, such as the drawing room and the garden. Scholars, however, have deeply problematised the apparent idyll of the home as the set of the family film, revealing its fraught gender and class politics and its ideological constructedness (Zimmerman 1995).

Meanwhile, experimental filmmakers have often prided themselves on the title of amateurs. As Stan Brakhage (1982) has written, for instance:

> I have worked alone and at home, on films of seemingly *no* commercial value ... 'at home' with a medium I love, making films I care for as surely as I have as a father cared for my children. As these home movies have come to be valued, have grown into a public life, I, as the maker of them, have come to be called a 'professional,' an 'artist,' and an 'amateur.' Of those terms, the last one – 'amateur' – is the one I am truly most honored by. (162; emphasis in the original)

'Amateur' filmmakers such as Kenneth Anger, Stan Brakhage, George Kuchar, Jonas Mekas, Marie Menken, Michelle Citron and Joseph Morder have all made films at home and about the home, filming their families and friends, and turning the house into a place of radical creativity.

The title of Akerman's last film, *No Home Movie*, hints at both traditions of house-set 'family films', the amateur and the experimental, while also undermining its own generic belonging. The ambiguity of the title, with its negation of either 'home' or 'home movie', or both, raises questions at once on film's capacity to portray the home and on the existence of the home itself. *No Home Movie* is not a home movie in the traditional sense; the focus, indeed, is not on the typical memorable events that celebrate the family and its achievements, but on its daily life and on what is mundane, at least on the surface. As is typical of Akerman's work, the banality of the everyday is a powerful entry point into broad considerations that are at once autobiographical and universal. On the other hand, Akerman's film truly is a home movie. The handheld camera, the under- and over-exposed shots, the grainy images filmed with amateur equipment, and the preoccupation with the family record are typical of the genre. As Ivone Margulies (2016) has noted, 'As the director films in her mother's apartment, returning to the matrix of all of her films' interiors, she embraces the directness of the home movie form to redesign analogues for the intricate relationship of symbiosis and distance between herself and her mother' (62).

No Home Movie opens with an extended, still shot of a tree wildly shaken by the wind against the backdrop of a desert-like landscape. The wind is so strong that the camera also shakes. The violence of the weather and the barren landscape convey radical otherness, lack of protection and chaos. The film, thus, begins in the place of the non-house, the place of the metaphysician's non-I. The stark contrast with the following shot, taken in a verdant park on a calm, sunny day, where people are engaged in familiar, mundane and reassuring activities like strolling, tanning or walking the dog, only reinforces the opening shot's impression of threatening chaos. The following shot, of a private garden filmed from a window, conveys serenity, though the empty garden chair framed by Akerman may well hint to absence and abandonment and to the theme of human demise, which will be at the centre of the film.

With the fourth shot we find ourselves inside the home. An ageing woman stretches her arm to push a door open, and walks through it, slowly crossing a corridor and entering a dining room. She turns towards the camera touching her shoulder, complaining that it gets dislocated, and asking if her physiotherapy is today. The filmmaker answers from behind the camera that it is scheduled for tomorrow. This first exchange establishes the core modalities of Akerman's film. The woman is the filmmaker's mother, Natalia (Nelly). The film is a record of her last few months of life, and is made of everyday gestures; mostly, nothing happens, and the camera simply observes Nelly, who stands, eats or walks from one room to the next. Other times, meaningful conversations about the past take place between mother and daughter. Chantal probes her mother's memories in order to revisit the family history, confirm her recollections, or understand and adjudicate on past events and the choices made by her parents. Stories about Chantal's Hebrew upbringing, the hardship of war and its effect on her grandmother, her family's rejection of religion after her grandfather's death, and life for the Jews in occupied Belgium are at the core of the exchanges. These take place, meaningfully, in the kitchen, the room that traditionally was the very heart of the home and family, and the communal space of female life and solidarity – and an important room in Akerman's filmography, in particular in *Jeanne Dielman, 23, quai du Commerce, 1080 Bruxelles* (*Jeanne Dielman, 23 Commerce Quay, 1080 Brussels*, 1975). The kitchen in *No Home Movie* is also the setting of a key exchange between Chantal and Clara, Nelly's Mexican carer, who enquires about the family history. Chantal alludes to the emigration of her parents from Poland to Belgium to escape persecution and to their subsequent arrest in Brussels by the SS, who deported them to Auschwitz. However, Clara soon changes the topic of conversation – a chilling moment that confirms the unshareability of the memory of the Holocaust.

With some important exceptions that I will discuss below, the filmmaking is mostly patient, understated, at once deeply intimate with the setting and the subjects and tactful vis-à-vis the private life of the house. The camera is sometimes handheld, sometimes placed on a tripod or on furniture, and films in various parts of the house, most frequently the common areas of the kitchen, dining room and drawing room. Doorframes and windows are a recurrent feature, including computer windows: between Chantal's visits home, mother and daughter stay in touch via Skype.

Framing is, in fact, a prominent element of the film and its discourse on the house. Sometimes doors are left fully open, with their frames clearly visible in the composition of the shot; other times, they are only ajar, so that the effect of framing internal to the shot is even more noticeable, occupying as it does a large portion of the screen. This choice is not aestheticising; rather, it may be said to suggest at least three meanings. First, it conveys a sense of privacy, for it constantly reminds us that we are being allowed to peer into the intimacy of a real home. The noticeable framing of doors and windows, then, strengthens the material presence of the house – the real protagonist of *No Home Movie*, which is punctuated by shots of empty rooms, without human presence. The screen, then, is not only re-framed, but is also frequently split, as in a scene in which a large piece of furniture in the foreground visually cuts the screen in two, or a shot in which the space of action shrinks to a sliver of screen, most of which is occupied by walls and a doorframe. Similarly hyperframed are the images of the online calls between mother and daughter: the Skype window (itself containing the smaller window of the caller) is open against another, underlying window, further framed by the outer limits of the computer screen. All these hyperframing strategies are intensified by the extended duration of the shots and the sparse action, which invite us to study the composition of the image.

Yet another effect of the hyperframing is that it emphasises the entrapping power of architecture, the invisible barriers between family members, and the ultimate inaccessibility of the house intended as belonging, safety and wholeness. Frames are physical and metaphorical obstacles to 'the original fullness of the house's being' (Bachelard 1994: 8). During a Skype call home from Oklahoma, to her mother, who asks her why she's filming their conversation, Chantal responds: 'I want to show that there is no more distance in the world.' The point is reinforced by the seamless transition between this sequence and the next, filmed at home. The two rooms, the one in the States and the one in Brussels, are made to look like they are conjoined. Modern technology increases the accessibility of the home to the rootless emigrant, at least for the time of a call. Yet, Nelly's exclamation when she sees her faraway daughter online is a reminder of just how real the distance and separation are: 'My love! When I see you like that I want to squeeze you into my arms!'

Nelly is old and frail and her life is now mostly confined to the house. The bourgeois apartment, with its clearly demarcated spaces for day and night activities and its orderly and clean environment, at once lends protection to the displaced refugee and Auschwitz survivor and is entrapping, because of Nelly's limited mobility and waning control over her body and life. The entrapment is, of course, also the interiorised repetition of her former internment. The film's soundtrack is a constant reminder of the outside world, of the (un)reality the house attempts to fence off: the noises of the street filter in and compete with the domestic sounds. The non-house is all around, threatening to impinge on the fragile cocoon of the house – which in the past failed to protect the family from the horrors of Nazism.

The ultimate impossibility for the house to make sense of the non-house soon becomes evident. Right in its middle, the slow, quiet, banal home movie is torn apart by an extended travelling shot of a desert landscape filmed through an open car window. Berger's notion of the ideal horizontal line representing all the roads departing from and returning to the house springs to mind. At the same time, this landscape, possibly shot in Israel, represents another, equally lost homeland. No words are uttered, and the scene's rough sound lacerates the auditory space. As Barbara McBane has written,

> acoustic explosions are worked into *No Home Movie* (2015) by raising the volume on cuts to create sounds that, almost overmodulated, have an explosive effect, such as the shock of the sound of the desert windstorm that opens the film. The cut and the mix here suggest the acoustic violence of warfare; but it is also a very sustained sound, and as the volume gradually lowers – or as one's ears adjust to hear many frequencies – it is possible to hear the many 'voices' this wind actually contains ... Such sound cuts are engineered to detonate, the more so since no actual explosion takes place. Instead, the viewer/listener internalizes the violent effects, experiencing them as jolts that seem to remind one there is something else being represented, something not seen.

Later, the family film is ruptured again by similar shots of the desert, only this time much shakier and more overexposed, creating an impression of utter visual and auditory chaos. Both this and the next sequence are radically deframed; the clarity, control and order of the previous indoor sequences are replaced by deeply uncertain and confusing images. Next, we are plunged in total darkness. It takes us some time to understand that we are back at the mother's house, so hard is it to make out the by-now familiar rooms, on account of a deliberately incorrect exposure. The camera is handheld and the images convey displacement, anxiety, and threat. These radically different shots are associated with the worsening of the mother's health: when the exposure changes again, allowing us to decipher what we see, Nelly is heard prolongedly coughing at the dinner table, nearly choking on her food. The recurrent image of the

Figure 9.3 Fragile order: hyperframing of the family home in Chantal Akerman's *No Home Movie* (2015). Film still.

empty garden chair acquires a clearer meaning as we watch Nelly losing consciousness while lying in an armchair in her drawing room.

The very last section of the film is introduced by more (but clearer) images of the same barren landscape as before. The outline of a faraway town can be made out on the horizon, almost a mirage, conveying the impression of the remote, untouchable wholeness of a lost home – or a home never had. Back at her mother's house, Chantal closes the curtains of her bedroom and leaves, possibly for the last time. The film's last shot is of the empty house. It is a fixed, hyperframed shot, in which the screen is symmetrically parcelled out by the regular outlines of doorways, furniture and paintings' frames (Figure 9.3). Order and containment are restored, but remain painfully fragile.

Conclusion

Like the Barbican in Bêka and Lemoine's film, Ackerman presents her mother's Brussels apartment as a house that has no connections with either the gods or the dead. Such connections have been severed by the family's loss of religion, of its home country and nationality, and then also of the country from which it had sought protection from Nazi persecution. The post-Holocaust homelessness of *No Home Movie* is more tragic than *Barbicania*'s modern rootlessness, but not radically dissimilar. In both films, dwellers seek to find protection and fence off the fragmentation and chaos of the non-house; however, in spite of the reassuring tidiness and order of their bourgeois apartments, the profound, solid values of the traditional home are out of their reach.

Both films, thus, mark the impossibility of home. It is significant that two genres that are devoted to representing and understanding real houses – the architectural essay film and the home movie – produced such a glaring absence. In both cases, framing is the key element of the filmic discourse on the house and on the non-house that surrounds it. Reframing and deframing are the strategies used by these films to explode the architectural enframement of space and let the subconscious of domestic rooms emerge. What we are given to see, in spite of the tidiness, pleasantness and even elegance of spaces, of the reassuring familiar objects, furniture and ornaments, is the substantive, irremediable homelessness that subtends the modern condition.

Works Cited

Bachelard, Gaston (1994), *The Poetics of Space*, trans. Maria Jolas, Boston, MA: Beacon Press.
Berger, John (1991), *And Our Faces, My Heart, Brief as Photos*, New York: Vintage International.
Brakhage, Stan (1982), 'In Defense of Amateur', in Robert A. Haller (ed.), *Brakhage Scrapbook: Stan Brakhage, Collected Writings 1964–1980*, New Paltz, NY: Documentext, pp. 162–8.
Branigan, Edward (2003), 'How Frame Lines (and Film Theory) Figure', in Lennard Højbjerg and Peter Schepelern (eds), *Film Style and Story: A Tribute to Torben Grodal*, Copenhagen: Museum Tusculanum Press, University of Copenhagen, pp. 59–86.
Cache, Bernard (1995), *Earth Moves: The Furnishing of Territories*, trans. Anne Boyman, Cambridge, MA: MIT Press.
Dovey, Kim (2008), *Framing Places: Mediating Power in Built Form*, New York and London: Routledge.
Grosz, Elizabeth A. (2008), *Chaos, Territory, Art: Deleuze and the Framing of the Earth*, New York: Columbia University Press.
Haralambidou, Penelope (2015), 'The Architectural Essay Film', *Arq: Architectural Research Quarterly*, 19, no. 3, pp. 234–48.
McBane, Barbara (2016), 'Walking, Talking, Singing, Exploding ... and Silence: Chantal Akerman's Soundtracks', *Film Quarterly*, 70, no. 1, pp. 39–47, <https://filmquarterly.org/2016/09/16/walking-talking-singing-exploding/> (last accessed 5 November 2019).
Margulies, Ivone (2016), 'Elemental Akerman: Inside and Outside No Home Movie', *Film Quarterly*, 70, no. 1, pp. 61–9.

Rascaroli, Laura (2017), *How the Essay Film Thinks*, New York and Oxford: Oxford University Press.
Rentschler, Eric (1990), 'Remembering Not to Forget: A Retrospective Reading of Kluge's *Brutality in Stone*', *New German Critique*, 49, pp. 23–41.
Zimmermann, Patricia Rodden (1995), *Reel Families: A Social History of Amateur Film*, Bloomington: Indiana University Press.

CHAPTER 10

At Home with the *Nouvelle Vague*: Apartment Plots and Domestic Urbanism in Godard's *Une femme est une femme* and Varda's *Cléo de 5 à 7*

Stefano Baschiera

In their groundbreaking move from the studio to the streets, embracing the idea of a 'camera-pen' (Astruc 1999) to tell personal stories and offer a personalised portray of urban geography, the directors of the French new wave not only challenged the established mode of production and the tradition of the *cinéma de papa* but also revealed new connections between characters, spaces and the camera itself. As James Tweedie (2013), among others, argues, it is in the attention given to the objects and spaces present in front of the camera, rather than the filmic style, that the innovative contribution of the *nouvelle vague* manifests itself. In particular, the representation of social space is considered one of the key features in the films of the young filmmakers, to the extent that it can be argued that the Lefebvrian 'urban revolution' found its manifestation in the early films of the *nouvelle vague*. The works of Louis Malle, Jacques Rivette, Eric Rohmer, Jean-Luc Godard, François Truffaut and Agnès Varda mapped the transformations, paradoxes, uncertainties and possibilities present in the 'critical phase' of the passage from an industrial to an urban society (see Lefebvre 2003). During this phase, the street acquired a double value: on the one hand, it became a meeting place, the crucial space of movement. On the other hand, the street gave rise to superficial interactions dictated by the commodification of the space. Since 'the street became a network organized for and by consumption' (Lefebvre 2003: 20), time changed as a function of the need to gaze at shop windows and to consume, or according to the modes of transportation associated with the street. The street, during this critical phase, is the demonstration of the power of the neocapitalistic organisation of consumption, and 'in this sense we can speak of a colonization of the urban space, which takes place in the street through the image, through publicity, through the spectacle of objects – a "system of objects" that has become symbol and spectacle' (Lefebvre 2003: 21). From this perspective, the constant interaction between fictional characters and real spaces present in early *nouvelle vague* films can be considered as part of this colonisation of urban space by the spectacle.

Jean-Sébastien Chauvin points out that the *nouvelle vague* is characterised by a representation of the city (Paris, in particular) built on a strong correlation between the room and the street (Chauvin 2005: 193–9). Such an association is based on a double movement:

> to step outside (outdoors, far from the studio) and to enter into one's self (the private chamber), far from the *cinéma de papa* which supposes a space external to the protagonists, from the vision of a 'totality' in which the characters are simply a mechanism. (Chauvin 2005: 193, my translation)

In this way, the room and the street lead to a personal cinema that is able to merge fictional heroes with 'real' people, cinematic plots with an autobiographical depiction of the urban space. The authors of the first period of the *nouvelle vague* appear, in fact, to be committed to tracing the real geography of the city while representing it within a fictional cinematic world; 'it's the geography of a place which, in some sense, determines how the story proceeds' (Chauvin 2005: 196, my translation). The characters' itineraries develop around the city, thus revealing its life, the crowds, the erasing of spatial distances, the new possibility of movement, and the presence (in the background) of an immutable history in the immediacy of the present. According to de Certeau (2002), this can be defined as the labyrinthine city that people experience (see also Tweedie 2013).

The 'urban' dimension of the Parisian films – which has been at the centre of several scholarly investigations – can be approached by considering Neil Smith's 'scaling of places' (Smith 1993), and by stressing the unavoidable connections between home, community and urban scales. The Parisian apartments portrayed in the new wave cinema are therefore understood (alongside the wider urban transformations) as the shifting locus of identity of the 1950s Parisian 'youth' and as a signifier of the emerging generational divide (see Neupert 2007). Considering also the mode of production of early low budget *nouvelle vague* films, we can grasp how the camera frames 'real' domestic spaces and objects, within a performative moment. The Lefebvrian system of objects, in fact, did not stop at the colonisation of the streets but penetrated the intimacy of the domestic space. Commodification and spectacle permeate the dwelling in the Parisian apartments of the *nouvelle vague*, compromising the borders between domestic walls and the busy streets of commerce and casual encounters.

In my contribution, I aim to draw attention to the representation of the domestic space in two 'urban films' of the early *nouvelle vague* shot by two key figures of French cinema, namely Godard's *Une femme est une femme* (*A Woman is a Woman*, 1961) and Varda's *Cléo de 5 à 7* (*Cléo from 5 to 7*, 1962), in order to examine the relationship between the Parisian streets, the compromised intimacy of the characters' rooms, and the system of objects that define them. The goal is to analyse the links between the street and the home or, better, the experience of 'domestic urbanism' (Wojcik 2010) emerging from these films, and to highlight the central role played by domesticity in framing social spaces in the Paris of the *nouvelle vague*.

Dans la chambre

While the close relationship between the *nouvelle vague* and the Parisian urban space has been consistently at the centre of scholarly work – and further supported by a well-established interdisciplinary relationship between urban studies and film studies – the representation of domestic space has been generally overlooked. Recently, a contribution by Hilary Radner and Alistair Fox drawing attention to the role played by the apartment in the cinema of the *nouvelle vague*, and in particular that of Truffaut, can be considered one of the first much-needed interventions in this area of investigation (2018).[1] Radner and Fox remind us how the domestic spaces portrayed in the early phase of the French new wave were actually 'real' spaces, usually apartments owned or rented by the directors themselves, or by their friends and colleagues. For instance, Rivette's *Le Coup du berger* (*Checkmate*, 1956) was shot in Claude Chabrol's apartment and Truffaut's first short film, *Une Visite* (1955), used Jacques Doniol-Valcroze's apartment as its main location. This allowed the young directors to shoot films as cheaply as possible, as well as to bring their quest for the 'real' and location shooting from the street into the domestic space.

The use of these apartments in the early films of the *nouvelle vague* is evidence of the low budget of those productions, as well as of a desire to create greater distance between the 'truth' of the location and the 'fakeness' of the film studio. Radner and Fox maintain that

> the relationship between what is shown about the apartment when used as a setting in these New Wave films and the emotional, psychological and sociological issues presented by the characters-in-action who inhabit them served a crucial function in defining these works. (Radner and Fox 2018: 56)

Their analysis of the apartments shot by Truffaut at different stages of his career reveal a sort of itinerary through the director's work, by linking his filmography to his personal life, involving questions of class belonging and taste. In fact, a look at the domestic spaces used in his films shows the evolution in the dwelling habits of the youth in 1950s Paris and how they related to the question of modernity as emerging through a different approach to interior design, privileging flexibility and multi-purpose objects and spaces.

What I would like to stress here is that the same Lefebvrian urban revolution, which seems to be embodied in the early films of the *nouvelle vague*, does not stop at the street, but affects domestic spaces and their constant renegotiation in the films. Generally speaking, as we will see in greater detail in the course of my discussion, the *nouvelle vague* apartments tend to defy the traditional space of patriarchy, reshuffling rules and the tensions between real spaces and fictional characters, often by focusing on the theatrical element of the space in question.

Pamela Roberts Wojcik introduces the concept of 'apartment plot' to refer to 'any narrative in which the apartment figures as a central device. This means that the apartment is more than setting; it motivates or shapes the narrative in some way' (Wojcik 2010: 3). While not necessarily belonging to the 'apartment plot', films of the *nouvelle vague* — such as *Cléo de 5 à 7* and *Une femme est une femme* — allow us to redefine certain elements of dwelling, stressing the role of this domestic space in the *nouvelle vague* storylines, and denoting a useful way to look at the relationship between urban and domestic space. In fact, the apartment 'conveys ideologies of urbanism'; different from the traditional family home, and from suburban dwellings, the apartment is deeply connected to the dynamic of the urban space and its typically modern features. Wojcik argues that '[t]he apartment plot can also serve as focal point for a host of other city spaces — bars, taxis, offices, hotels — that highlight the way in which the apartment plot blurs distinctions between public and private, work and home, masculine and feminine, inside and outside' (2010: 5). While Wojcik's work engages exclusively with the American context, we can see how, across the Atlantic, the same distinctions have been blurred and how the apartment presents itself as the dwelling of choice of a new 'urban' generation.

The cinema of the *nouvelle vague* succeeded in creating a new series of connections between characters and space, and between the actor and film styles (Testa 1990). Among the strategies employed to forge such connections, Bart Testa lists how 'New Wave films often tend more radically to disrupt the way the "human presence" is conventionally constituted in film' (Testa 1990: 95). The human presence mentioned by Testa challenges not only filmic conventions centred on depicting an idealised home as a space for identity building and family self-portraiture and perpetuation, but also the material culture of the time, which inevitably moves inwards from the street to the weakened boundaries of the domestic environment. In fact, the movement is as much inwards as it is outwards. While the characters are invited to leave their domestic space, favouring a 'life out' engaging with the urban space and the consumption offered by the city's social geography of the time, from cafes to cinema theatres, the apartments cannot keep the street out. They become an ideal extension of urban life. A clear example can be seen if we focus for a moment on a material culture approach, a theory of things 'that will give theoretical shape to the idea that objects make us, as part of the very same process by which we make them' (Miller 2010: 60). The objects featuring in the characters' apartments (often having the same 'aura' of reality as those in urban and domestic spaces) are revealing of the characters' identity and identity-building process. *Nouvelle vague* characters, for instance, tend to privilege more cultural/political mementos than familial ones in their domestic spaces: movie posters, instead of family photos, while the furniture arrangement in these modern open spaces constantly challenges the organisation of the traditional home. The identity of the characters, then, is built and constructed through objects which are increasingly mediated, in the sense that photographs of actors and film posters take on the walls the place usually reserved to family photos.

From another perspective, the permeability of domestic boundaries invites us to consider also some of the features of the *nouvelle vague* characters – such as the mimicking of films (Testa 1990) – as revealing of an identity that is not fully established and formed through the domestic walls, but that strongly relies on popular culture.

Une femme est une femme: Renegotiating the Home

The representation of the movement between the room and the street develops further in *Une femme est une femme*. In fact, if in an early film by Godard, such as *À bout de souffle* the itinerary followed proceeded mostly from the street to the room, in *Une femme est une femme* it takes the opposite direction: it is Paris that is depicted as an extension of the private space.

The 'musical-like' love story between the stripper Angéla and the newsagent Émile, centred on their divergence about having a child, is realised in the renegotiation of the spaces of their house.[2] The home, with its rituals and its gender-based organisation, is the scene of a constant struggle between the corroboration of its traditional uses and spatial coordinates, and their instant subversion. The house is a small but open space in which the camera often pans around every centimetre of every wall and in which the characters' bodies perform almost restlessly, showing all their dynamism and their physical presence. They perform a feat, they ride around the living room with a bicycle, they sweep the floor as if they were playing football, they dance and, of course, they act. Sellier, in her recent work on the representation of women through the masculine first-person singular gaze of the *nouvelle vague* filmmakers, wrote that

> The first 'couple sequence' between Emile and Angela lasts ten minutes and links together a series of gags that highlights each of the actors, using as pretext the most conventional of gender divisions: Angela invents a comedy because she has burned the roast; Emile imitates a soccer match with the broom instead of sweeping; Angela wants a child, but Emile refuses under various pretexts, all the while riding around the apartment on his bicycle (...). The astonishing choreography of the scene uses the entire space of the cinemascopic screen to develop the characters inside the apartment, but it is noticeable that the camera highlights the inventive mobility of Emile, who uses the apartment space as a game field, while Angela goes from the table to the kitchen and then to bed, as if determined by her domestic functions. (Sellier 2008: 161)

I certainly agree with Sellier when, writing about Angéla's desire for a child and the lack of interest on the part of her partner, she argues that the film 'stages sexual difference and inscribes as natural, outside of any possible discussion, the contradiction of their desire' (Sellier 2008: 161). However, Sellier does not acknowledge some important aspects of the dinner sequence. Firstly, the gender divisions and the characters' actions are staged in an 'untraditional' domestic space, where the living room is transformed into a bedroom (and vice versa) by moving around a lamp. Angéla's itinerary, 'determined by her domestic functions' develops, in fact, in a space that renegotiates the organisation of the traditional bourgeois home, typically built around the dining-room and the bedroom, hence in a space which can be considered as 'generationally' determined – a space of the present time, in conflict with the past. Baudrillard, in 1968, described this modern domestic space, remembering how

> the organization of space changes, too, as beds become day-beds and sideboards and wardrobes give way to built-in storage. Things fold and unfold, are concealed, appear only when needed. Naturally such innovations are not due to free experiment: for the most part the greater mobility, flexibility and convenience they afford are the result of an involuntary adaptation to a shortage of space – a case of necessity being the mother of invention. Whereas the old-fashioned dining-room was heavy freighted with moral convention, 'modern' interiors, in their ingeniousness, often give the impression of being mere functional experiments. (Baudrillard 2005: 15)

This description perfectly matches the apartment of Émile and Angéla (which, moreover, was Godard's residence at the time), a flat completely devoted to representing this idea of modernity. The irruption of the fictional cinematic world, the functionality and flexibility of the spaces, and the characters' actions subvert the conventional use and representation of private spaces and family rituals. The bicycle ride around the dining table and the dance performances are not part of the everyday use of the domestic space; furthermore, despite the organisation of activities based on domestic functions, there is a clear shift with respect to the conventions. Godard begins the dining sequence (a crucial ritual for the traditional patriarchal family) by depicting the most stereotypical and gendered organisation of the house: the woman is in the kitchen taking care of the food, while the man waits in the living room, listening to a football game on the radio and reading the newspaper. However, the situation completely changes because of the absence of food, the external intrusion (on the part of two policemen) and, in particular, the exaggerated and 'inappropriate' physical activity of the characters. In this modern organisation of the house, in fact,

> the function is no longer obscured by the moral theatricality of the old furniture; it is emancipated now from the ritual, from ceremonial, from the entire ideology which used to make our surroundings into an opaque mirror of a reified human structure. (Baudrillard 2005: 16)

The domestic space does not preclude any physical activities, it no longer offers a chronology of actions by reference to the furniture; all of the barriers, the internal organisation and the forced itineraries, are dismissed in order to merge private and urban spaces. Inside the house, the bathroom is, on different occasions, the centre of attention and a place for meetings and discussions, and, as we have seen, the bedroom (the most intimate and protective space in the house) and the living room (which at the opposite end is the most social space) are merged together. Therefore, considering that the presence of domestic spaces devoted exclusively to man's privacy (the studio, for instance) was at the basis of the patriarchal private space (Cieraad 1999: 7; Wigley 1992: 346–8), *Une femme est une femme* presents a clear renegotiation of gender relationships (which is part of the plot of the film) and of the idea of family altogether. What Munro and Madigan point out as being a characteristic of modern domestic space is portrayed here, where

> the family home is centered on the one room that is necessarily a shared and communal space. It not only symbolizes the family together, but as an important pathway to the front door, to the kitchen and to the stairs ... it cannot be closed off from any members of the household for private use. (Munro and Madigan 1999: 109)

Furthermore, the apartment – and the building that hosts it – lives in a symbiosis with the city; it is part of the street life. There is, in fact, a constant dialectical exchange between the house and the street. The home is shot from the road several times and vice versa; between the house's windows/balcony and the street there is a mutual exchange of gazes and verbal communication that give to the house the same value as a cafe, as a meeting point in the urban environment. The neon lights of the city are always visible from the windows, making the borders between inside and outside thinner from every point of view (aural, visual and physical). The building itself constitutes a minimal but active neighbourhood community: the stairs are a shared space in which people meet and where the relationship with the prostitute who lives next door to Angéla, and who shares with her the use of the telephone and some food, unfolds. The protagonists' jobs are connected to the threads of urban life, from entertainment (the stripper) to consumption (the newsagent's stand), and to the 'organisation' of space (the parking assistant); 'the result is the transcendence of the closed and the open, the immediate and the mediate, near and far orders, within a differential reality in which these terms are no longer separated but become immanent differences' (Lefebvre 2003: 39–40).

The house, having lost its role as a shelter where family history is perpetuated, favours a renegotiation of its inhabitants' identities elsewhere – in the city, in the world of commodities, in the cultural landscape. Considering that the

> home is a projection and basis of identity, not only of an individual but also of the family. But homes, the mere secrecy of private lives concealed from the public eye, also structure social life. Homes delineate the realms of intimacy and public life. It is frustrating to be forced to live in a space that we cannot recognize or mark as our personal territory. (Pallasmaa 1992)

This is perfectly exemplified by the objects and images present in the house. Whereas in traditional homes the family photos framed on the wall had the 'moral' task of re-presenting the family history, in this modern apartment the images on the walls and the objects around the home refer instead to a shared cultural background present in the film: films, books, newspapers, music and magazines that defined the identity of that generation. According to Rutherford, 'identity marks the conjuncture of our past with the social, cultural and economic relations we live within' (Rutherford 1990: 19). Certainly, this cultural horizon is still dominated by divisions between men (*Sport Events*, the poster from *L'Équipe* dedicated to the Tour de France) and women (*Marie Claire*). For the women, this affects in particular the level of the body; a constant confrontation with the representation of women in consumerist society is evident. As Loshitzky writes:

> Godard's films are concerned mainly with the image of woman as a libidinal cathected commodity, and with the image of the woman/consumer obsessed with the imperfection of her real/private body as opposed to the imaginary/public body of advertisement. (Loshitzky 1995: 160)

The characters acknowledge the existence of the fictional world of spectacle, live in an urban space dominated by the display of products and images of bodies, and construct their identities through the common background of the society of the spectacle. In brief, they mimic appearances and gestures in order to be part of the show – of the film.

Cléo: The Apartment and the Performer's Identity

Cléo is one of the films of the *nouvelle vague* that best represents the relationship with and the rediscovery of the urban space, in particular with regard to the questions of theatricality and performativity within the reality of the social space portrayed. In doing so, it follows a particular approach towards representation of urban space which characterised Varda's early works, and in particular her documentary *Daguerréotypes* (1976), set in her own neighbourhood in Paris. As James Tweedie points out,

> from her earliest films, Varda conceives of space, and especially urban space as *théâtre du quotidien*, and *Cléo*, with its windows and mirrors, its spectators and people on display, is one of her most thoughtful meditations on the interaction between theatricality and the real. (Tweedie 2013: 123)

The previously discussed features of the Lefebvrian urban revolution abound in *Cléo*, as the film maps space and time coordinates of the urban experience from a well-defined point of view, while at the same time offering a sort of nostalgic view of the Parisian landscape.

The key role played by Paris and the protagonist's itinerary has been at the centre of several academic investigations, focusing in particular on the gendered gaze of the protagonist (and the camera), with many references to the *flânerie* of the urban wanderer and the documentary nature of the film. Jill Forbes, for instance, develops her work from the feminist analysis of the film made by Flitterman-Lewis, by looking in detail at Cléo's itinerary across the city and the series of *topoi* it mobilises, underlining at the same time the documentary quality of the film and its ability to offer an ethnographic/anthropological view of the city and the ways in which it is experienced. The blending of fiction and reality, in fact, characterises the snapshots of the Parisian everyday life within the modern cinema trope of the 'woman walking the streets' (Forbes 2002: 86) and its gendering implications for the understanding of urban space.

Cléo's wandering through Paris has also been defined as a voyage of self-discovery (Morrissey 2008), stressing how our understanding of the character's identity is shaped by her experiencing of the urban space. Different analyses of the film from a spatial perspective have not failed to notice its depiction of the problematic relationship between public and private, interior and exterior. Varda's use of mirrors, frames, shop windows in order to delineate the agency of the protagonist within the spatial coordinates problematises, as I shall discuss later, the locus of identity and reveals her transition from object to subject of the gaze (Forbes 2002). As Tweedie argues, 'Cléo, like her contemporaries from *Cahiers du cinéma*, and like Varda herself, assumes the role of filmmaker rather that remain an object of the gaze (Tweedie 2013: 124).

This is another example of how fictional characters wandering in the urban locations convey the cinematic relationship between the directors of the *nouvelle vague* and the Parisian cityscape, in this case with all the implications imaginable for the gendering of space. Furthermore, such a visual appropriation of the urban experience shared by filmmaker and character is fundamental in order to reveal and define the character's identity.

I would argue that to better grasp such construction of a character's identity, we need to go beyond the urban experience in order to look at the sphere of domesticity, and to do that by considering the materiality of this space and the objects it contains. In fact, by considering a material culture approach – and specifically, as already indicated, how our objects 'make us' and contribute to the construction of our identity (see Miller 2010) – the interactions with the elements of the profilmic become particularly relevant, first of all, in order to underline the question of filmic performance within real settings; secondly, in order to have an overview of the material culture of Parisian youth of the 1950s; and finally, in order to grasp the narrative development of the characters.

As previously mentioned, the role played by mirrors, shop windows and masks has already been addressed by scholars, arguing how their presence in the film (often as framing devices) contributes to Cléo's process of self-discovery. Those analyses are also strongly intertwined with the different places featured in the protagonist's wandering progress through the city, as well as the different forms of transportation used. In this context, the apartment plays an interesting role among the other stages in Cléo's itinerary. I would argue that its depiction reveals the new approach towards domesticity and modernity portrayed by the films of the *nouvelle vague*. From a narrative perspective, the scenes at the apartment represent the shift in Cléo's agency and a key passage in her journey of self-discovery. Forbes, for instance, argues that even the name of the street where the apartment is located (6 rue Huygens, near Montparnasse) represents a clear indication that it is a key feature for Cléo's identity. In her analysis of Cléo's itinerary and the location of the apartment, Forbes maintains that 'the conjunction of time, place and optics are united in Cléo's home' (Forbes 2002: 88). The street number underlines the midpoint of the film, as a 'point of stasis before the pendulum begins to swing in the other direction' (Forbes 2002: 88), the street being named after astronomer Christiaan Huygens (1629–95) who worked on the use of pendulum in the movement of the clock. For Forbes, the stop at the apartment marks the point of stasis of the pendulum before the story shifts: after that, Cléo (a stage name) becomes Florence, and her self-discovery begins (see also Flitterman-Lewis 1996).

From a narrative perspective, the short period Cléo spends in the apartment undoubtedly represents a clear turning point, mirrored by the change in her appearance (her attire, in particular) and attitude. While the thirteen minutes spent in the domestic space coincide with the highest moment of performance for the protagonist and of display of a 'performative' identity, they also introduce a key moment of self-awareness that will define the protagonist's self-discovery in the second part of the film. Overall, as Neroni argues, in *Cléo* the private world is 'the place of a primordial self-deception' (Neroni 2016: 104). However, I argue that it is also the place where the character achieves an awareness of such self-deception, thus realising she needs to go into the urban space in order to understand her true self.[3]

As different scholars have pointed out, if in the first part of the film (set in the cafe) Cléo is defined as a child, in the apartment her association is with the several kittens spread around the domestic space, underlining an attitude of playfulness. Flitterman-Lewis defines Cléo's domestic space as 'a veritable panoply of masquerade, vanity, narcissism and femininity' (1996: 272). Far from being a personal haven, however, for Cléo the apartment is a place of encounters and of work. The scenes within the domestic walls are characterised by the introduction of three new male characters, for each of whom Cléo performs in a different way. The first is Cléo's lover, José, who is also the one who pays for the apartment. In their encounter, Cléo abides by a series of unwritten rules (spelled out by the maid Angèle), in particular that of hiding her illness from her lover, as she needs just to look beautiful. The presence of José lets us know that the 'bohemian' lifestyle of the single woman which seems to be embodied in the apartment (see Wojcik 2010) is in fact the result of old-fashioned patronage on José's part, with Cléo performing a particular role in the domestic setting as a result. She does not leave the bed or reveal any fragility or uneasiness about her condition.

When José leaves, the two musicians come to the apartment, transforming the domestic space even more into a theatre. As soon as they walk in, they dress like doctors and pretend to visit the patient, in a brief comedy sketch around the bed. After this playful moment, they present Cléo with ideas for new songs (one is a musician, the other composes the lyrics), and not only do we discover that they are paid by José (meaning that it is her lover who finances her musical career) but we also witness the idea that the two musicians have of Cléo; or better, the kind of identity they would like to shape for her, through the tone of the music and the content of the lyrics. What looked like an amicable encounter quickly becomes framed as work and performance. Cléo lives in a place which is not really hers, where she works, performs and adapts to external expectations and demands.

It is during the performance of one of the new songs that we have a moment of diegetic detachment. The background turns black around Cléo, the 'documentary' depiction of the real place makes way for one of the stylistic features of the *mise en scène*: Cléo becomes isolated, outside place and time, and for the first time reveals her true emotions. The narrative pauses to leave space for the performance and, when we are summoned back into the diegetic continuum of time and space, Cléo has changed. She has taken her wig off, quickly changes into a black dress and leaves.

While the narrative dimension of the apartment scene is very revealing and central in the development of the film, it is from a material culture perspective that the domestic space is ultimately more interesting (Figure 10.1). It is an open space, as we often see in the *nouvelle vague* films: it is representative of the 'modern' idea of home (see Radner and Fox 2018); there is a little kitchen at the entrance, which Cléo never enters (it is the domain of Angèle), and then a big white, bright room, with no doors or internal partitions. The space is characterised by the 'retro' canopy bed clearly visible at the rear, where Cléo has the encounter with José.

Other key features of the open space are revealed by Varda's camerawork as they serve the narrative. I am thinking, for instance, of the swing in the middle of the room, or of the piano which comes into view only when the musicians enter the space. I would argue that this stresses the

Figure 10.1 Cléo's apartment in *Cléo de 5 à 7/Cléo from 5 to 7* (1962). Film still.

theatricality and the performativity of the domestic space, almost as part of a dispositif of spectacle. Whereas in theatre objects present on the stage appear thanks to a spotlight that suddenly switches on to reveal them, in Cléo's apartment, in the lack of an establishing shot at the beginning of the scene, most of the domestic space exists out of frame, and only the camera can draw it back into existence. A small room divider is where Cléo changes her dress and the only hiding place from the camera's gaze.

While in the traditional patriarchal home the bedroom is the innermost space, the bed in Cléo's apartment is where the visitors' encounters take place, and its proximity to the swing and the piano further underlines its playfulness and its 'opening' to the external world. The apartment is also characterised by objects displayed on the walls. All of them are aimed at the beautification of Cléo, and, like props, they contribute to the construction of her performance persona: necklaces, bracelets, dresses, a pair of wings. There are no family photos on display, or other features perpetuating the past and participating in the construction of identity, as happens in the traditional family home (see Baudrillard). Cléo's apartment, indeed, seems to exist in a persistent present.[4] If we consider the domestic space as a locus of identity, and the objects and furniture as 'makers' and signifiers of one's self, we can clearly grasp how this apartment really portrays the public figure of Cléo rather than her intimate self.

As Neroni points out, 'By locating Cléo's authentic self-recognition in public and by emphasizing the performance that occurs in private, Varda reverses our typical conception of public and private' (Neroni 2016: 103). This reversal furthermore underlines how the relationship between urban space and the apartment in *Cléo* emphasises the permeability of the latter, which is another key feature of the apartment plot. If we consider the 'apartment plot' approach, we can see how

> Rather than a 'shell' or a 'haven', the apartment is permeable and porous. Rather than a refuge from the modern, the apartment facilitates encounter, with an emphasis on chance and contingency. It is a transient space, dependent upon rent and not ownership. (Wojcik 2010: 147)

Although the big windows do not reveal a clear audiovisual connection with the busy streets, the domestic space does not seem different than other public spaces, from a privacy perspective. The apartment is the locus of the performance and of an identity built for the stage; its role is to underline once again its nature as a stage and for a performativity necessarily open to the outside world. The urban revolution present at the 'urban scale' extends to the domesticity, compromising its borders. The haven is not beyond closed doors.

Conclusions

In his work on global new wave cinemas, Tweedie mentioned that the critical approach to new wave cinemas needs necessarily go beyond the debates surrounding matter of style and authorship in order to embrace more prominently the analysis of the 'real' elements captured by the camera in the profilmic, stressing in particular the relationship between fictional characters and the everyday spaces they inhabit. While the busy streets of Paris have been a recurrent and crucial feature in the *nouvelle vague* and have consistently attracted scholarly attention, the role played by the spatial scale of the house and its material culture is still significantly understudied. However, I would argue that the depiction of the domesticity, on the one hand, further underlines the important role of the urban space of modernity, while on the other hand, it helps to disclose key sociological features associated with the emergence of new wave cinema and in particular the generational shift embodied in such cinematic experience.

The characters' performativity on the commodified streets moves seamlessly to the domestic space, in a constant renegotiation between public and private which is based on a consistent challenge to spaces, objects and values of the traditional family home. In fact, if the American 'apartment plot offers a vision of home – centred on values of community, visibility, contact, density, friendship, mobility, impermanence, and porousness – in sharp contrast to more traditional views of home as private, stable, and family based' (Wojcik 2010: 5), the *nouvelle vague* apartments are notable for similar contrasts to the *cinéma* and the *maison de papa*.

Because the *nouvelle vague* is intrinsically urban and a materialisation of the Lefebvrean urban revolution, the dwelling is mainly characterised by small city apartments where elements of material culture dominating the streets (posters, etc.) assume the place of objects embodying family history in the apartment. The movement between the room and the street is far from following a one-way path but represents a constant movement between the two correlated spaces, each influencing the other. The result is that the locus of identity for 1950s youth is no longer traced back to domestic spaces, but shifts to the quite different encounters and commodities of the urban space, and brings back to the apartment walls signs and references to films, popular culture, fashion, public histories and so on, all fictional and social features that are key in the construction of new – albeit constantly shifting – identities.

The certainties and the rules of the patriarchal bourgeois home are reshaped in the attempt to produce new manifestations of class and gender, which are, however, outward-looking, rather than reflecting inwardly on the values of the family. The 'reality' of several domestic spaces portrayed by the cameras of the young directors of the *nouvelle vague* offer also a new display of the profilmic. What is interesting is that, as happened with the use of real urban spaces, it is the theatricality of the domestic space that comes to the fore. Fiction takes over the real spaces, performance takes over the depiction of everyday life, stressing once again the creation of an identity strongly linked with cinema and culture. The apartment thus becomes part of a *dispositif* for the filmmaking performance; it is a set, it is real, it is fiction, and it is, once again, fully representative of the characters' identity.

Notes

1 Another example of a recent analysis of domesticity is Mani Sharpe's (2017) engagement with the depoliticisation of the domestic space in Jacques Rozier's *Adieu Philippine* (1962) and Robert Enrico's *La Belle Vie* (1963).
2 The film also presents several references to melodrama, a genre deeply rooted in representations of families and domestic spaces. On the role that the home plays in melodrama films see Richard Dyer (1987).

3 Arguably, the sequences in the apartment bring to a conclusion an itinerary of self-deception which began in another particular domestic space, the card reader's apartment.
4 The other apartment shown in the film (the one belonging to the card reader) present instead a series of features of traditional domesticity, embodying a past. However, also in that case, the space is a space of performance, open to the public and with a problematic intimacy.

Works Cited

Astruc, Alexandre (1999), 'The Birth of a New Avant-Garde: La Caméra-Stylo', in Timothy Corrigan (ed.), *Film and Literature: An Introduction and Reader*, Upper Saddle River, NJ: Prentice-Hall, pp. 158–62.

Baudrillard, Jean (2005), *The System of Objects*, London and New York: Verso.

Bronfen, Elizabeth (2004), *Home in Hollywood: The Imaginary Geography of Cinema*, New York: Columbia University Press.

Chauvin, Jean-Sébastien (2005), 'Nouvelle vague', in Thierry Jousse and Thierry Paquot (eds), *Encyclopédie: la ville au cinéma*, Paris: Éditions Cahiers du cinéma, 193–9.

Cieraad, Irene (1999), 'Anthropology at Home', in Irene Cieraad (ed.), *At Home: An Anthropology of Domestic Space*, New York: Syracuse University Press, pp. 1–12.

de Certeau, Michel (2002), *The Practice of Everyday Life*, Berkeley, Los Angeles and London: University of California Press.

Dovey, Kim (2008), *Framing Places: Mediating Power in Built Form*, New York and London: Routledge.

Dyer, Richard (1987), 'Tales of Sound and Fury: Observation on the Family Melodrama', in Christine Gledhill (ed.), *Home is Where the Heart Is*, London: British Film Institute, pp. 43–69.

Flitterman-Lewis, Sandy (1996), *To Desire Differently: Feminism and the French Cinema*, New York: Columbia University Press.

Forbes Jill (2002), 'Gender and Space in Cléo de 5 à 7', *Studies in French Cinema*, 2, no. 2, pp. 83–9.

Lefebvre, Henry (2003), *The Urban Revolution*, Minneapolis: University of Minnesota Press.

Loshitzky, Yosefa (1995), *The Radical Faces of Godard and Bertolucci*, Detroit: Wayne State University Press.

Miller, Daniel (2010), *Stuff*, Cambridge: Polity Press.

Morrey, Douglas (2005), *Jean-Luc Godard*, Manchester: Manchester University Press.

Morrissey, Jim (2008), 'Paris and voyages of self-discovery in Cléo de 5 à 7 and Le Fabuleux destin d'Amélie Poulain', *Studies in French Cinema*, 8, no. 2, pp. 99–110.

Mouton, Janice (2001), 'From Feminine Masquerade to Flâneuse: Agnès Varda's Cléo in the City', *Cinema Journal*, 40, no. 2 (Winter), pp. 3–16.

Munro, Moira and Ruth Madigan (1999), 'Negotiating Space in the Family Home', in Irene Cieraad (ed.), *At Home: An Anthropology of Domestic Space*, New York: Syracuse University Press, pp. 107–17.

Neroni, Hilary (2016), *Feminist Film Theory and Cléo from 5 to 7*, New York, London, Oxford, New Delhi and Sydney: Bloomsbury Academic.

Neupert, Richard (2007), *A History of the French New Wave Cinema*, Madison: University of Wisconsin Press.

Pallasmaa, Juhani (1992), 'Identity, Intimacy and Domicile', <http://www.uiah.fi/studies/history2/e_ident.htm> (last accessed 12 December 2017).

Radner Hilary and Alistair Fox (2018), 'Truffaut's Apartments', in Alastair Phillips and Ginette Vincendeau (eds), *Paris in the Cinema*, London: British Film Institute, pp. 55–65.

Rhodes, John David (2017), *Spectacle of Property*, Minneapolis: University of Minnesota Press.

Rutherford, Jonathan (1990), 'A Place Called Home: Identity and the Cultural Politics of Difference', in Jonathan Rutherford (ed.), *Identity: Community, Culture, Difference*, London: Lawrence and Wishart, pp. 9–27.

Sellier, Geneviève (2008), *Masculine Singular: French New Wave Cinema*, Durham, NC: Duke University Press.

Sharpe, Mani (2017), 'Screening Decolonisation Through Privatisation in Two New Wave Films: Adieu Philippine and La Belle Vie, Studies', *Studies in French Cinema*, 17, no. 2, pp. 129–43.

Smith, Neil (1993), 'Homeless/Global: Scaling Places', in John Bird et al. (eds), *Mapping the Futures: Local Cultures, Global Change*, London and New York: Routledge, pp. 87–119.

Sorlin, Pierre (1991), *European Cinemas, European Societies 1939–1990*, London and New York: Routledge.

Testa, Bart (1990), 'Un Certain Regard: Characterization in the First Years of the French New Wave', in Carole Zucher (ed.), *Making Visible the Invisible: An Anthology of Original Essays on Film Acting*, Metuchen, NJ and London: Scarecrow Press, pp. 99–108.

Tuan, Yi-fu (1977), *Space and Place*, Minneapolis: University of Minnesota Press.

Tweedie, James (2013), *The Age of New Waves: Art Cinema and the Staging of Globalization*, Oxford: Oxford University Press.

Wigley, Mark (1992), 'Untitled: The Housing of Gender', in Beatriz Colomina (ed.), *Sexuality and Space*, New York: Princeton Architectural Press, pp. 327–89.

Wojcik, Pamela Robertson (2010), *The Apartment Plot*, Durham, NC: Duke University Press.

Wollen, Peter (1986), 'Godard and Counter-Cinema: Vent d'Est', in Philip Rosen, *Narrative, Apparatus, Ideology: A Film Theory Reader*, New York: Columbia University Press, pp. 121–9.

CHAPTER 11

Dwelling the Open: Amos Gitai and the Home of Cinema

Miriam De Rosa

For the past is the foundation,
And by destroying the foundation the building collapses. (Efratia Gitai)

Poetry is what really lets us dwell. (Martin Heidegger)

Landscape is a site of multiplicity, even when it is a domestic one. It is the result of a stratification of trajectories and stories simultaneously cutting across each other, which rearticulate the space containing them according to a set of complex relations. This chapter tries to unravel these complex relations by thinking domestic space with the help of an interdisciplinary approach based on film studies, philosophy and geography. It is in the encounter of these areas that I believe a number of interesting categories to approach domesticity lie, especially if we try to see the home not only as the on-screen stage of representation, a reconstructed or recorded set that is part of a diegetic discourse which cinema films, but also as an off-screen spatial dispositif where moving images are called to inhabit the environment as if that were their home. Whilst most of the existing scholarship feeds the discourse on domestic space as it is represented in films,[1] the latter approach seems less explored. In the following pages I embrace this twofold perspective on the home, in the conviction that a virtuous mutual benefit derives from an analysis that pairs on- and off-screen dimensions. To test such idea and put it into practice, my reflection will be centred on the latter approach, but I will develop my argument by looking at the films by Israeli director Amos Gitai, which portray the home in a variety of ways.

Gitai's interest in domestic space is very clear in films such as *House* (1980), *A House in Jerusalem* (1998) and *News from Home/News from House* (2006), which compose a real 'home trilogy'. However, a wider and more diverse body of works better suit the twofold methodological perspective I am proposing and testing here. This is why my attention will focus instead on those films which, after a theatrical release, have been employed to build a multimedia multichannel video installation, presented with the title *Architectures of Memory* in late 2011 in Turin, Italy. I think this double use of Gitai's footage perfectly mirrors the two possibilities to attend to the narrative of domestic landscape which I have briefly outlined above, allowing for a broad reflection that not only moves from the on-screen space to the off-screen environment, but specifically binds them together through a dense system of interlaced symbols, images and meanings. In this sense, my study relates to the so-called spatial turn of moving images,[2] feeding the discourse derived from it and proposing at the same time a framework that offers new insights. The interesting circulation of Gitai's films is not the only reason why his work nicely lends itself to elicit a reflection on domesticity. Trained as an architect and son of one, his work represents a privileged platform to discuss the topic of the home, as it combines the filmmaker's and the builder's views at once. Each in its own way, films like *Berlin Jerusalem* (1989), *Kippur* (2000), *Free Zone* (2005), *Disengagement* (2007), *Plus tards, tu comprendras* (2008), *Roses à credit* (2010), and *Lullaby to My Father* (2011) that are included in *Architectures of Memory*, all depict figures of, or the quest for, a home. They work, in other words, as a catalogue showing the domestic landscape from diverse vantage points, historical contexts, geographical coordinates, and yet they feed into a unique narrative that sees the home as a site of belonging always traversed by multiple story lines, perceived as the heart of a web of ever-changing personal landscapes. Again, it is a site invested with a strong and multifaceted value, where the different facets coexist, mingle and sometimes clash among each other. It is an intimate and individual space, a place of the self, but it is also an environment connected to a larger history that transcends the subject, one that is generational, national, collective and, more broadly, cultural. As a site with a symbolical value built upon the more concretely spatial one, the home is informed by interrelations of various nature. Very often it is thought of as an intimate, safe, closed and therefore protected site. However, bringing together people, constituting their interacting spheres of action, and surviving time, the domestic landscape resembles more a platform for encounter and an event rather than a place with fixed features remaining untouched by time, the life and action of those inhabiting it. Gitai's production visualises this, puts it into practice and, in fact, disciplines such as the above-mentioned ones which will serve as a background for this study, also confirm the importance of this aspect.

For geographer Doreen Massey, space is to be understood as

> constituted through interactions [...], as the sphere of the possibility of the existence of multiplicity in the sense of contemporaneous plurality; as the sphere in which distinct trajectories coexist; as the sphere therefore of coexisting heterogeneity. [Also,] we recognise space as always under construction. Precisely because space on this reading is a product of relations-between, relations which are necessarily embedded material practices which have to be carried out, it is always in the process of being made. It is never finished; never closed. Perhaps we could imagine space as a simultaneity of stories-so-far. (Massey 2005: 9)

The conceptual linkage between an unfinished storytelling process as a way to portray space in relation to the subject, and the articulation of this spatial dimension brings to the forefront and reinforces the connection between the two perspectives that I intend to discuss here: space – and by extension *domestic* space – can be seen as an environment constituted by multiple threads unfolding within it, which shape it precisely according to the way they unfold. Film is of course an excellent language to tell a story that most often involves multiple storylines, that is, different threads developing throughout the story. When these threads concern domestic space, we can see how a conceptual and thematic respondence between Massey's idea of space and the way film works is created. Due to a widespread and now well-established tendency that sees cinema moving outside the movie theatre (Casetti 2012), this may take the form of an actual spatialisation, in that cinematic excerpts may literally bring the story they bear inside a plurality of different sites. The result is that this story feeds into the history of the actual physical environment where the moving image is installed. This determines a conjunction or linkage between the on- and off-screen dimensions creating some room for re-consideration and experiment with the film as well as with the gallery space (Fowler 2008; Butler 2010). If such physical environment, as we saw, is 'the sphere of the possibility of the existence of multiplicity', then when *disposed* in a certain space (De Rosa 2016), moving images and the diegetic world they put forward contribute to the design of a new spatial dispositif, mingling the diegetic with an extra-diegetic, real – so to say – world. To reiterate, it is this dimension of encounter I am interested in.

Massey's approach, however, does not simply echo the importance of the storytelling element, it offers instead a clear sense of how spatiality is a complex dimension, defined by constant imbrications, multiplicity and openness. A key text in philosophy of space addresses the same issues and frames them within a reflection on dwelling. In his famous lecture *Building, Dwelling, Thinking* Martin Heidegger provides a definition of space and distinguishes it from place. According to him, space is 'pure extension' (1993: 357); it is a dimension potentially open to the subject, that is, an environment which is there to become the stage of one's life. As such, space is for him a neutral dimension, while place is instead a practised, effectively lived, experienced space that is marked by this action. In this perspective, space would be an environment available for things and subjects to enter and inform around them, around their history or the story and purpose that brought them there. Space is then the site where, through their presence, stay, action and movement, place can be built – 'gathered' around a 'locale' (1993: 356), an entity, as Heidegger argues. In his system of thought, the effects and the way in which such presence and action are expressed is what he terms 'dwelling'.

In what follows, I try to understand how film enters this dynamic, if it does at all, and apply it to a specific kind of space, the domestic one. Also, I address the question of what happens when the 'dwelling' at stake is not simply the on-screen depiction of someone's action on an environment that consequently becomes his place, his home, but coincides with those forms of inhabitation involving the subject off screen, that is, the spectator or visitor of an exhibited film installed in a space which he physically shares with the image. I look at how cinema and the subject similarly enter a space and 'dwell'. *Architectures of Memory* comes to our aid to answer these questions: in the first section of the chapter I focus on the structure of the show seeking for examples of how the articulation of space, the presence and unfolding of the moving image contribute to the construction of a place and the production of dwelling trajectories. To do so, I try to offer a combined reading that pairs the analysis of selected film sequences eventually installed in the exhibition space and the observation of the space itself, alongside the experience it favours. In section two I build upon the close analysis of *Architectures of Memory* to develop a concept of domestic space that takes further the geographical and philosophical notions I presented thus far. By way of an etymological route, I look in particular into the symbolic heritage of the term 'home', picking up from ancient hieroglyphics, up to the Greek term *oikos*, to finally relate it to cinema.

Architectures of Memory

Architectures of Memory is a multimedia piece comprising an eighteen-channel video installation and a collection of historical and family documents that premiered in November 2011 at the National Museum of Cinema in Turin.[3] The research informing and inspiring the piece stems from the work developed for the feature length film *Lullaby to My Father* (2012), which reconstructs the story of Gitai's father, Munio Weinraub, even if the installation comprises sequences excerpted from other films by the director, too. Thematically linked to *Lullaby*, however, *Architectures of Memory* is also centred on the figure of Weinraub, representing the final step of a trajectory started with a number of previous installations presented at the Kunstwerke Museum in Berlin (*News from Home/News from House*, 2006), at the Submarine Base in Bordeaux (*Citations*, 2009) and at the Palais de Tokyo in Paris (*Traces*, 2011).

Born into a Jewish family in a contested area of the Austro-Hungarian Empire at the beginning of the First World War, Weinraub moved to Dessau in 1928, and eventually to Berlin in 1932 where he lived until the Nazis came to power. In Dessau, he was admitted to the Bauhaus school of architecture led by Hannes Meyer and Walter Gropius, where he studied under the guidance of, and had the opportunity to meet, key artists and personalities of the Bauhaus movement, including Vassily Kandinsky and Mies van der Rohe. He collaborated with the latter until the racial laws prevented him from working and condemned him for treason against the German people due to his Jewish origins. Expelled from Germany, Munio first fled to Switzerland, eventually heading to Palestine, where he then became a pioneer in the construction of several buildings that contributed to the overall development of a specific architectural style conceived to ideologically represent the emerging Israeli state.

The installation builds upon this personal history and relates Munio's quest for a home to a broader multifaceted context that is well reflected in the multi-layered materials of both the set-up and the exhibited pieces composing the show. The spatial characteristics of the installation and the specific modalities in which the moving image materials are employed really reverberate this narrative, conveying a sense of journey, and translating the story told through the images into a three-dimensional path that is offered to the visitor as a space to physically enter and practise. The production of meaning results therefore from a mixture of the physical and the symbolic elements. Gitai is not new to this process of implication between cinematic and architectural materials, which also characterise his previous installations. For Gitai, the choice of the setting generally plays a crucial role in ensuring such a result and this particularly applies to Turin, where his choice was a rather extraordinary one.

Architectures of Memory was presented in a very peculiar setting, the basement of the Mole Antonelliana, a building now turned into the National Museum of Cinema, whose underground areas had never

Figure 11.1 Mole Antonelliana: basement. Courtesy National Museum of Cinema, Turin.

Figure 11.2 The Mole Antonelliana during Gitai's *Architectures of Memory* (2011): exterior. Courtesy National Museum of Cinema, Turin.

been opened to the public before (Figure 11.1). Approaching the Mole from the outside, the visitor is immediately presented with a gallery of selected film frames and family photographs that offer 'the surface of facts before diving into their representation' (Frodon and Gitai 2011: 31, my translation) (Figure 11.2). From the external space, the access to the internal one consists of a passage leading underground. This is a metal stair, gradually taking the visitor downwards into the depth of the building, inside an area that is generally prohibited to the eyes and thus symbolises the entrance into the recesses of memory, as well as into the inner space of the director's history. The impression of literally entering this dimension is strengthened by the act of walking down a stairway that, while it descends, leaves the visitor enough room to clearly see this descent through a central empty space that lets some light in from above and allows the eye to adapt to the increasingly darker surroundings. Additionally, the emptiness of the central part of the stairs amplifies the sound of the visitors' steps, adding an aural emphasis to their descent into the 'architectures of memory'. As in Gaston Bachelard (1994), this descent corresponds to a journey into a house – that is, towards an inner place, a place of comfort where memories are relived. The effect is strategically planned by the author who, from the very first approach to the piece, already shows the essential impossibility of separating the artistic and architectural aspects of his intervention, and the mutual importance of these two elements. Gitai efficiently accomplishes a first level of engagement of visitors to this place, dramatising their movements in order to involve them perceptively and affectively in the itinerary across Munio's and his own personal landscape and domestic memories. The choice of the specific building materials, such as the metal for the stairs, and their selected use in relation to the volumes of the exhibition space – another rather sensible architectural consideration – enhance the visual, sonic and symbolic construction, ultimately reinforcing the sense of respondence between the physical space and the reconstructed, imagined place.

The couple internal/external is not the only partition plotted by the director to model the exhibition space after the concept of his project: once downstairs, the installation unfolds into two separate rooms. The internal distribution of the piece across these two rooms is once again to be read in light of the mutual implication of the cinematic and the architectural components of the work: 'in Paris too [for the installation *Traces* – ed.] I have tried to play with two distinct spaces, different in dimension. Proportions and different scales represent an important challenge both in cinema and in architecture' (Frodon and Gitai 2011: 29, my translation). As they access the basement, the visitors first enter a small room that represents a sort of hallway offering materials that serve as basic coordinates to understand what the project is about, as if they were making their way into a house and looking at the entrance walls; showing family pictures, paintings, old photos of that house or even postcards or sticky notes hanging on a mirror would immediately provide an idea of who is living there (Figure 11.3). This access area is used as a very traditional exhibition space, gathering a documentation series featuring pictures, old certificates and letters, introductory texts about the author, his father and the Mole. However, the outlook and material characteristics of this room are not quite traditional, in that the surfaces where the pieces are placed are of plain concrete showing the lines of the casting process and plywood panels, a choice which somehow alludes to a construction in progress. This is not simply an aesthetic choice aligning with a temporary or fashionable taste for rough materials. It is a fact that hints at Massey's idea of space being never finished, as well as a conceptual indication of how the exhibition space in itself, its physical features, nature and history are woven into the artistic piece. These will both be key aspects of the rest of the project, too.

The second and bigger room is shaped like a path constellated by projected film sequences that mark a screening place unfolding through and across barriers and barbed wire. Darker and non-linear in its plan, this section of the exhibition space constitutes the centre of the show, the heart and home of the project. It also shows unpolished features, as in the previous area, if not more so. Certainly looking different from both a standard white cube and a classic screening room, everything here seems to underline that we are in a basement: the walls show the bricks, the mortar and plaster materials used to build them, the pillars and columns sustaining the entire building are very visible and not at all adorned or painted; on the contrary, they show the porosity and solidity of concrete without any embellishment to take the visitor's attention away from the structural details of the environment. The attention

Figure 11.3 The Mole Antonelliana during Gitai's *Architectures of Memory* (2011): interior. Courtesy National Museum of Cinema, Turin.

reserved to the materiality of the place is in other words quite apparent. Conceptually, it reminds once more of that unfinishedness of space as something that is always in the process of being made and never closed. At the same time, Gitai's intervention on the site feeds into this narrative of ongoingness by offering a room for experience and motion punctuated by film excerpts which lend themselves to a non-prescriptive, open interpretation from viewers. In the wake of this sense of dynamism, the installation presents itself as the trigger of a transformation process as well, because the space is changed by the presence of something entering it and re-informing it after its presence. Documents, photographs, footage and props enter the Mole and, consequently, the pure function of the basement is turned into something else – not an inaccessible space but a newly practised one, not a storage place or the site of technical machinery ensuring electricity, ventilation and the like to work properly on the storeys above, but an intricated gallery open for exploration, reflection and creativity. Not a 'forsaken spot' (Adorno 1967: 271) but a site for unexpected and redeeming forms of inhabitation, a 'place of hope'.[4] A place of memory due to the personal reconstruction of Munio's life exposed therein, a place of culture due to the historical documents on display, a place of cinema due to the presence of moving images, Gitai's home reconfigured due to the assemblage of all these components together. A particular aspect of this dynamics is the co-existence of the characters of the space and the peculiar identity of everything that enters it, with the effect of turning the extension – as Heidegger (1993) would say – into the place of that peculiar entity. In my view, the neutrality of the space as per the philosopher's view clashes here with the rich memory of the venue, which I do not think is switched into something completely novel but rather forms a fascinating and meaningful spatial background bringing its character into the piece it harbours. The nature of the space itself, in other words, plays an important role as it contributes to the unique *genius loci* Gitai plays with. Never obliterated, and conversely enhanced, this is what allows the author to create an echo between the venue and the storytelling he places in it. At times the latter partially covers the former, or reshapes it, complements it with a new set of meanings, functions, symbolical elements and opportunities for the visitors, ultimately introducing a slight variation, reinterpretation, enhancement, but never an erasure. It actually reminds the process of memory, which uses 'the traces of the past that remain in the present as raw material in the production of new stories about the past' (Kuhn 1995: 158). This has a direct impact on the design of *Architectures of Memory* (Figure 11.4):

DWELLING THE OPEN 197

Figure 11.4 *Architectures of Memory* (2011): a site-specific installation.
Photo by the author.

In Turin the basement of the Mole is an extraordinary place, with brick walls and concrete pillars. My projections are placed there, I don't want plasma screens, it's very important: in this work the image must be projected directly on the materials composing the wall. The screen is the building. The context here is essential: this is something true for the movies as well as for exhibitions. (Frodon and Gitai 2011: 30, my translation)

Besides its structural characteristics, the Mole is a place steeped in history, whose memory is reverberated and amplified by the project. Designed by architect Alessandro Antonelli in 1863, the Mole was founded as a Hebrew temple commissioned by the Jewish community of Turin. As some of the documents on display in the first small room show, the project was quite ambitious, very likely too ambitious, to the extent that the building never really became a synagogue due to the supervened lack of funds. Gitai's intervention on site revives the ancient vocation of the building, not necessarily on a religious basis, but rather celebrating his father, his family, his story as well as reconstructing the historical, cultural and ideological context surrounding and impacting on them. Alongside these, the bigger exhibition area evidences that the moving image – ever present in the exhibition space and uncontested protagonist to which the building is now dedicated – is celebrated as well. After being a monument for a long time, in 1996 the building was finally turned into the National Museum of Cinema, a fact that exposes the director's decision to have his installation here to a medium-specific oriented reading of the project: having

Architectures of Memory on display in this very place pairs the two big themes of Gitai's life and work side by side – architecture and cinema – giving him the opportunity to explore the linkage between the two, their capacity to activate memory, to articulate space and to offer the chance to dwell. Albeit coupled with this architectural suggestion, then, this location revamps the reflection upon cinema in relation to other arts and forms of expression, of which architecture is part. Also, it celebrates cinema itself, possibly taking us back to its very basics, for example projecting the image without even a screen but showing that a wall is indeed a screen. The choice of the basement, then, may be seen as a strategy to evoke a desire to come back to the essence of cinema, not in linguistic or aesthetic terms, but really in its simplest form, hence the absence of canonical conventions and formats such as the lack of elements typical of the classic apparatus, as well as of the film used in its entirety, in favour of more impressionistic sequences, shorter and interchangeable in their order, emotionally intense, abrupt and thought-provoking.

A brief focus on a couple of sequences will show this in closer detail. Placed behind a low barrier of displaced bricks and barbed wire is one of the bigger projections in the centre of the exhibition room, taken from *Free Zone* (Gitai 2005). The film is titled after a peculiar area across the border between Jordan and Israel where the neighbouring countries exchange and sell cars. This is a rather surreal area of freedom, politically unrecognised and disjointed from the diplomatic relationship between these countries. It is a zone of passage, liminality and encounter. Gitai follows the story of three women that, for various reasons, need to cross the border and arrange the journey taking advantage of a car that has to enter the free zone to be sold.

In the excerpt selected for *Architectures of Memory* we see one of them, Rebecca, depicted during the drive: she sits in the back of a car and as the vehicle exits the customs, she realises that the country she feels is hers has been just left behind. Along with her land, her childhood memories and failed love affair, both connected to that country, instantaneously enter the past. Caught in a tension between looking back and ahead, she seems to be very aware of what is happening: whilst the traces of the past will live within her, these memories are now projected onto something new to come, in a painful yet exciting game of back and forth from an imperfect but familiar past to an open and unknown future and the other way around. Gitai translates this process on-screen focusing on the relationship and exchange between the internal and external landscape, the self and the home. Picking this very sequence for the installation the author not only has the opportunity to underline how powerfully these two dimensions mutually impact one another, but also

DWELLING THE OPEN 199

reflects onto the physical externalisation of the diegesis: what Rebecca is going through is a very private and articulated mechanism, drawing on her life, which the viewer can only infer from the images of past experiences coming to her mind and rendered by Gitai through a superimposition of images fading one into the other. As if a rewind button has been pushed,[5] the fading technique creates a stratification of memories. If in the film mental images form a psychic material that becomes visible and temporarily covers the image of reality that is quickly passing outside the car window, the exhibited version of the sequence deeply enhances this effect, adding a physical dimension to it. Rebecca's emotional dynamics and mnestic activity are projected onto the bare walls, and the moving image activates the same off-screen space inhabited by the viewer. Her moving car and unfolding flow of thoughts find a counterbalance in the audience freedom to walk across the exhibition space. The result is that the Mole walls cease serving only as a support for the projection and become a further tangible layer of the narrative, as their rough, non-linear and porous nature speaks to the protagonist's story and confers a material quality to the image (see Lant 1995; Marks 2000) (Figure 11.5). Such a quality also characterises a sequence in *Lullaby to My Father* (2011) which reconstructs the events taking Munio

Figure 11.5 The material quality of the image in *Architectures of Memory* (2011). Photo by the author.

Weinraub from Dessau to Israel. Gitai selects for the Turin installation the re-enactment of the trial his father had to face once the Nazis came to power in 1933. Albeit very different in aesthetical terms from the previous one, this sequence also offers an interesting treatment of the diegetic space which is put in direct relation to the extradiegetic one. The explicit artificiality of the scene enhanced by the strong and saturated palette – the red, white and black of the flags, the room in the full light of the court – contrasts with the impressionistic, transparent strokes of light and colour of *Free Zone*; however, the neat material quality of the court walls is strengthened by that of the Mole walls. This physical overlap impression, alongside the loud sound and the authoritative tone of voice of the judge hook and involve the visitor, producing a direct access within the narration.

In both cases, then, the environmental characteristics of the on-screen image establish a dialogue with the off-screen space; this element and the practicability of the exhibition space are means to make Rebecca's and Munio's stories, thoughts and fantasies accessible to the public, to elicit the mechanisms of identification that are proper to the cinematic dispositif, and yet to dispose them in the threshold between intimate and public, internal and external space. Whilst the public literally moves across the protagonists' memories, these are indeed exteriorised but at the same time remain personal; they are projected as images acquiring a decoded visibility, they come to constitute a physical environment but somehow are guarded in a remote, hidden, 'internal' place, the basement, a site strongly connoted by the diegetic subject animating it, as well as by the viewers who reorganise the same space as they enter and dwell in there, too.

Both sequences offer in sum a place to walk through, where the moving image works precisely as the bricks and the concrete pillars building the Mole; where the cinematic component ceases to be an element that simply constellates the site but contributes to its articulation; where the set-up becomes an integral part of the dispositif in order to make an inhabitation of the space possible and to elicit dwelling. The viewing experience becomes an ambulatory, flexible, personalised experience modelled after Gitai's project and yet leaving the public free to design their own trajectory and architecture of space. Putting in practice the so-called spatial turn, *Architectures of Memory* positions Gitai within those directors who are explicitly experimenting new ways to expand, contaminate, or simply use the cinematographic language outside the movie theatre. Adding him to the long list of filmmakers who opened up their work to visual arts,[6] the installation allows for a classic viewing, as the public can potentially stop in front of each screen and watch the sequences for their entire duration. However, at the same time, the broader dispositif Gitai is putting into play here wraps the visitor in a texture that weaves textual and contextual elements, opening up multiple ways of experiencing the piece and betraying a tension typical of cinema to reinterpret its technological (production, transmission, distribution), and discursive (montage) aspects too.[7]

The Home as Site of Openness, Cinema as Site of Contamination

As discussed, *Architectures of Memory* is to Gitai a means to experiment on the different dispositifs that his artistic research requires, but what is at the heart of such production? Both the content, drawing from his family history, and the architectural modalities adopted to express it, taking advantage of his studies and background, show quite clearly that his artistic research represents an opportunity to reflect on his own work as an expressive necessity to produce new stories about the past. Not by chance then, as I have tried to explain, the installation primarily consists of the spatialisation of a microcosm, that is to say a sort of home entailing Gitai's exteriorised memory. At the same time, however, the current function of the building that he chose (which is now the National Museum of Cinema) makes it the home of cinema, ultimately creating a direct parallel between personal/domestic and cinematic landscape. In this sense, the exhibition space becomes the author's place, as much as the building represents the place of cinema. This makes the location unique and non-interchangeable and that is why the installation can be seen as a site-specific work. This time, in particular, the process of construction of space seems to be more explicit than in the previous installations, if anything because the title directly flags up what the objective of the piece is. There is an interest in building something peculiar and important to the author on the top of the actual building itself which requires a movement backwards, in the recesses of the family history, as if the past would serve as rough material to lay down the foundations of what is yet to come. Without that, without the foundations, as an evocative line excerpted from the correspondence between the author and his mother does not fail to mention, there cannot be a future – the building collapses (Gitai and Gitai 2012). Literally having the foundations of the Mole in front of us when visiting the show is then something endowed with a precise symbolic value. Pillar of his family, Munio is remembered, his story reconstructed, his heritage celebrated. It is within this narrative that the words of Keren Gitai, the author's daughter, featuring *Lullaby to My Father*, seem quite meaningful:

> I see Munio in you and in your memories [...] I think of you and I hear his voice, even if I feel your own way to pursue a result where he failed in accomplishing it [...] his texts and works are not the only heritage he left: there's something alive of him in your way of being father and in your work. Architecture is present, it manifests itself in a different form. [in you] It is visual, it's like a texture of fiction and film. It is a more visual and more literal redefinition of the concepts that were important to him. (Gitai 2011)

The disposition of the various pieces designed by the director, as well as his choice of projecting the selected excerpts from his films directly onto the surface of the building, render very well this texture of fiction, film and – I would suggest – reality. There is a clear sense that an architectural construction is achieved by means of the moving image: whilst Munio used wood, concrete and metal, a generation later and perhaps in a more poetic fashion, his son uses cinema, albeit 'by other means' (Levi 2012). Despite the adoption of a different language, the two share the same attitude, in the end, as one of the most evocative pages on dwelling recites, *poetically man dwells on this earth*, no matter the code employed to technically achieve that.[8]

In the bigger room, the transparency of the projected image unveils a textural work that is activated by the layers of image and text unfolding on the underlying physical one, in a seamless 'palimpsestic' process; that is, the building becomes a surface for inscription that combines new symbolic meanings with existing materials creating a set of 'associations at once residual, well-rehearsed and newly acquired' (Uricchio 2012: 45). This is one of the open-ended mechanisms taking place in the installation space: that cinema can be seen as an art and technology of inscription is a quite well-established concept (Astruc 1948; Rascaroli 2009), but the suggestion is pushed farther as the inscription becomes constant and continuous, producing a flawless re-inscription which is not simply made available on screen, but rather spatialised and reinforced by the ambulatory attitude of the visitors. They move throughout the show in search of a narrative to follow and yet designing their own trajectory across the space – 'songlines' that retrace step by step, intersect or divert from that offered by the author. It is precisely this freedom of creating one's own itinerary that represents what Gitai considers particularly important:

> Another relevant aspect is the visitors' freedom to move as they wish across the exhibition space. Compared to a film situation, where the spectator is constrained by the development of the story and a certain temporality, everything is all very different in an installation. There is a whole new set of opportunities, because one can go backwards, get back to see something again, linger a little longer on a detail. (Frodon and Gitai 2011: 3, my translation)

Munio's journey is articulated in the exhibition room through the eyes of a later generation, that of his son, and offered to further new eyes, those of the public. The viewers are given the opportunity to learn this composite, multilinear, multigenerational story adding on the top of it their own touches by hesitating on a passage, taking a little longer to observe the precious handwriting of a letter coming from the past, watching a sequence a couple of times, skipping another one, coming back to relate that one photograph seen at the very beginning of the show with the images of the last projection. Such open-ended structure allows for a fluid temporality: visiting the show I can go back and forth recombining and, so to say, editing the sequences on display at my leisure, taking time to dwell in front of the image. The implication between past and present is therefore literally spatialised in the installation, cleverly alluding to its title – *Architectures of Memory*, time made space. Whilst time is spatialised, space is designed after the shape of memory which reworks the remains of the past into new trajectories and paths to follow across the present and, from there, into the future. As mentioned, such agency is not something pertaining to the author alone. Differently from a theatrical situation, where the spectator is given a degree of freedom but has no chance to rework the sequences, temporality and mode of consumption, here the project offers itself to the visitors as an open place inviting to be inhabited. To the end of the analysis of our dispositif it is important to underscore once again that the visitors are those who reactivate the palimpsest articulated by the author by watching the selected and installed sequences. They are those who act upon the refashioned basement moving throughout the space, and thus rooting their experience in the physical and symbolic place they find themselves embedded in. If, on the one hand, the project leaves a good degree of freedom to the public to actually experience it, on the other hand, it does need the public to activate that memory, that story and that space to transform them into Weinraub/Gitai's place, that is, a place that is a home for architecture and a home for cinema together. In both cases, I would argue what is required is openness – openness toward the new possible iterations of a narrative which has been finding different forms over the years and potentially can therefore take new shapes in the years to come, but also, beyond the diegesis itself; openness toward the visitors who practise the exhibition space, literally entering the stories put on display, dwelling in front of the projected images and inhabiting that very space.

Let us try to see how the observation of the extradiegetic features of the installation proposed thus far help doing that, at the same time answering some of the questions I posed earlier. First, if the home is by definition the place eliciting dwelling, and if *Architectures of Memory* also favours a dwelling process in the visitors, then with good reason we can justify the claim that the installation turns the basement of the Mole into Gitai's home. Second, how to place the issue of openness in this frame? From what the project allows us to see, it looks like openness refers to a relational dimension that characterises the home as the place of a specific entity. Here, this specificity, this subject or entity certainly preserves its features, and in fact reverberates them onto its surroundings (which become its place, for instance). However, this process is validated in the encounter with another who acknowledges and reckons this specificity and, in turn, relates to it with its own. Openness represents in other terms the sphere of the possibility for interaction, for that multiplicity where – once again after Massey – distinct trajectories, each in the beauty of its specificity, coexist. Gitai's selected sequences also reinforce this concept: Rebecca is inserted in the project's narrative while in transit, that is, when overcoming a geopolitical separation – the border she crosses – which is represented in its permeable rather than impenetrable character. Similarly, Munio's trial is the event determining his movements throughout Europe and ultimately the reason why he would finally enter Israel and establish his home there. Nothing of this would have been possible without an underlying sense of openness of the context the protagonists of the two films live in. In sum, the diegetic level offers a representation of the home that is depicted as an open place. In continuation with this, openness is the modality to navigate *Architectures of Memory*, too. The 'design of the home' basically seems to revolve around openness. In fact, despite the most common (and rather simplistic) idea of what a home is – a closed, protected environment – the motif of openness has been characterising the concept of the home since ancient times.

According to historian Christian Cannuyer (2011), one of the first forms of description and inscription of the term 'home' is the Egyptian hieroglyphic ⌐ ¬. This is a sort of paddock but with an open access. This aperture, this door, seems quite key, as this symbol certainly alludes to a gathering place, but the one particular feature indicating the home as a building really seems the open way in, allowing one to come and go. Through this door, exchange is elicited and a process of coming into relation is constantly facilitated; one could in fact say that because of this structural opening, the home is a site of encounter, as if the basic condition to dwell were precisely this openness.

The Egyptian pictograms offer therefore a quite interesting background but it may seem they refer to a too distant system of thought, one in which language is not written with our alphabet. Still significantly back in time but closer in expressive and linguistic terms, the Greek etymology of the word home interestingly preserves the same suggestion I just discussed. When Aristotle refers to the primary form of community in his *Politics* (2013) he traces the first and most basic shape this can take to the *oikos*, that is, the household intended as gathering of woman and man who share the same rituals and food in that specific space. Rather than a simple material building, the emphasis is on the coming together, the gathering, the fact that this place is where two people meet and interact, better yet, meet *to* interact with each other. The dimension of an exchange is crucial – which explains the connection between *oikos* and the original meaning of the term economy (*oikos* + *nomos*; on the relation *oikonomia*/dispositif, notably see Agamben 2009), namely the measure and subsequent managing of the exchange between subjects happening within the home. In sum, the home is such if it alludes not to enclosure but to the liminality of a passage, to the space of an exchange, where the distinction between something and something-not – its opposite – are put in relation one another, the place of interrelations. It is precisely through the encounter and mingling that, by difference, the specific entities entering a space and calling it home can assess each other as such.

Applying this to *Architecture of Memory* in terms of the media involved in the project cannot but trigger a reflection about the use of moving images in the context selected by the author. As discussed, Gitai proposes his filmic work in a new fashion and some sequences of his feature-length films are basically relocated, installed, exhibited and inserted in a completely new relationship with a completely new space. The venue he selects to do this is an extraordinarily significant place, able to evoke a sense of history and memory, both personal and collective. But the Mole is also a very powerful symbol of cinema, hosting the National Museum and therefore providing an extra layer of connection to the director's activity. Arguing that the installation symbolically constructs Gitai's home is a way to emphasise precisely this linkage between the history of the building as such and the sensitivity for architecture characterising the director's artistic style, his familiar and personal architectural background, as well as his choice to employ the moving image as his main working and construction material. Pairing the concept of the home and cinema means to focus on a specific entity – Heidegger's 'locale' – reflecting its shape around and, in so doing, informing the surroundings after itself. When it comes to the home this is a personal and physical specificity that reverberates the identity of the person inhabiting it – Gitai reverberating Weinraub's story, his family heritage, memory and his work as a filmmaker. Relating the same logic to cinema opens instead the question of medium specificity that obviously pertains to the moving image, adopted as the key element to elicit a more profound and evocative inhabitation. My suggestion is that in both cases what is described for the idea of the home applies: the multi-layered, variable, open quality of the home is what makes it what it is, as much as cinema can preserve itself by way of a radical openness to experimentation, an openness that takes the moving image in different contexts, revises the technical formats, the patterns of temporality and the consumption etiquette of the standardised film to introduce a set of variations (or even only the bare potentiality to *think* of some of those) in a well-established apparatus which sees its components being displaced and disposed in new ways so as to articulate a new dispositif.

Far from being disregarded as peripheral cinematic forms because of a structural lack of adherence to the classic cinematic apparatus, works such as *Architectures of Memory* offer to the public a possibility to dwell through the image, in the image, by way of the image. It does not matter if the ontological perspective ends up being questioned: as much as the domesticity of the home is constituted by its forsaken spots because they spark the imagination, open unconceived possibilities and, precisely for this reason are, according to Adorno, 'places of hope', so the magic that has been produced by the dream factory over the course of the centuries lies in the moving image in whatever way, shape or form it takes, freed from conventions and habits. Perhaps enlivening a forsaken spot and opening it up to people's dwelling is the best depiction of 'the home of cinema' and, in a nutshell, cinema's hope.

Notes

1 Please see Gledhill 1987; Bronfen 2004; Schleier 2009; Robertson Wojcik 2010; Andrews et al. 2015.
2 On the spatial turn in film studies, please see at least Hagener 2008; Butler 2010; Rhodes and Gorfinkel 2011; De Rosa 2013. On the navigation that the mobilisation of the cinematic dispositif elicited, especially in the context of the museum, please refer to Bruno 2002 and to the recent updated iteration of the author's argument in Bruno 2018.
3 The installation appeared from 4 November 2011 to 8 January 2012 as part of a wider initiative comprising a retrospective of more than eighty films by Amos Gitai, all screened at the National Museum of Cinema.
4 The idea of 'forsaken spots' is included in an interesting reflection by Matt Waggoner who offers a reading of Adorno's philosophy of housing and dwelling. Indicating the spaces of the house which have no real function and thus become overlooked sites in the economy of the house plan, the concept

is employed, clearly by opposition, in the discussion of exteriors: 'While they may be incomprehensible to the mature realities of the home's formal arrangement, in these dark and forsaken spaces obsolescence becomes a habitable scene for which it was never intended' (2018: 83). Despite this, or perhaps because of it, Adorno sees these spots 'used as storage for unwanted things' as 'places of hope' – I am stressing this aspect as it will be key for the conclusion of this study.

5 An interesting result of a similar process, albeit played as a fast forward rather than a rewind action, can be found in Kevin L. Ferguson's video work (2016) on John Ford's classic *The Searchers* (1956). If Ferguson activates a sequential summing (https://vimeo.com/170473567), Gitai aims instead to retrieve and possibly slow the course of time. The aesthetic effect is quite different and yet it would be rather interesting to consider the procedures adopted by the two authors side by side as I would argue they stem from the same procedural work on the temporality of film even if they are part of two diverging traditions, one more experimental and exquisitely digital, the other more classic in its relation to the narrative and gallery film.

6 In the past decade or so, film studies have been increasingly reflecting upon this: among the most recent works, see at least Aitken and Daniel 2006; Brougher et al. 2008; Connolly 2009; Mondloch 2013, 2018; Marks 2012; Balsom 2013; Uroskie 2014.

7 On this aspect, please see at least Janine Marchessault and Susan Lord 2007; André Parente and Victa de Carvalho 2008; and more recently Casetti 2015.

8 I am taking this verse from the famous poem by Friedrich Hölderlin, from which Martin Heidegger (1971) draws part of his philosophy of space.

Works Cited

Adorno, Theodor (1967), *Prisms*, Cambridge MA: MIT Press.

Agamben, Giorgio (2009), *What is an Apparatus?*, Stanford: Stanford University Press.

Aitken, Doug and Noel Daniel (eds) (2006), *Broken Screen: 26 Conversations with Doug Aitken: Expanding the Image, Breaking the Narrative*, New York: d.a.p.

Andrews, Eleanor et al. (2015), *Spaces of the Cinematic Home: Behind the Screen Door*, New York: Routledge.

Aristotle ([1984] 2013), *Politics*, Chicago and London: University of Chicago Press.

Astruc, Alexandre ([1948] 2009), 'The Birth of a New Avant-Garde: La Caméra-Stylo', in Peter Graham and Ginette Vincendeau (eds), *The New Wave*, London: BFI, pp. 17–23.

Bachelard, Gaston (1994), *The Poetics of Space*, Boston, MA: Beacon Press.

Balsom, Erika (2013), *Exhibiting Cinema in Contemporary Art*, Amsterdam: Amsterdam University Press.

Bronfen, Elisabeth (2004), *Home in Hollywood: The Imaginary Geography of Cinema*, New York: Columbia University Press.
Brougher Kerry et al. (2008), *The Cinema Effect: Illusion, Reality, and the Moving Image*, Washington, DC: Hirshhorn Museum and Sculpture Garden.
Bruno, Giuliana (2002), *Atlas of Emotions: Journeys in Art, Architecture and Film*, New York: Verso.
Bruno, Giuliana (2018), 'Architecture and the Moving Image: A Haptic Journey from Pre- to Post-Cinema', *LFU*, 34, <http://www.lafuriaumana.it/index.php/67-lfu-34/781-giuliana-bruno-architecture-and-the-moving-image-a-haptic-journey-from-pre-to-post-cinema> (last accessed 20 April 2018).
Butler, Alison (2010), 'A Deictic Turn: Space and Location In Contemporary Gallery Film and Video Installation', *Screen*, 51, no. 4, pp. 305–23.
Cannuyer, Christian (2011), 'Il geroglifico della casa come classificatore in egiziano antico: spazio abitabile o liminale?', in Silvano Petrosino (ed.), *Monumentum. L'abitare, il politico, il sacro*, Milan: Jaca Book, pp. 79–98.
Casetti, Francesco (2012), 'The Relocation of Cinema', *NECSUS*, 1, no. 2, pp. 5–34.
Casetti, Francesco (2015), *The Lumière Galaxy: Seven Keywords for the Cinema to Come*, New York: Columbia University Press.
Connolly, Maeve (2009), *The Place of Artists' Cinema*, Bristol: Intellect.
De Rosa, Miriam (2013), *Cinema e postmedia. I territori del filmico nel contemporaneo*, Milan: Postmedia Books.
De Rosa, Miriam (2016), 'Disposition and Duality: Notes on Marie-Claire Blais and Pascal Grandmaison's *La Vie Abstraite*', *Aniki*, 3, no. 2, pp. 385–91.
Fowler, Catherine (2008), 'Into the Light: Re-considering off-frame and off-screen Space in Gallery Films', *New Review of Film and Television Studies*, 6, no. 3, pp. 253–67.
Frodon, Jean-Michel and Amos Gitai (2011), 'L'installazione *Architetture della Memoria*', in *Amos Gitai. Architetture della memoria*, exhibition catalogue, Turin: Museo Nazionale del Cinema, pp. 27–31.
Gitai, Amos (2005), *Free Zone*, France, Spain, Israel, Belgium: Agav Films, Agat Films & Cie, Golem, Artémis Productions, Agav Hafakot, Hammon Hafakot, Arte France Cinéma, Cinéart.
Gitai, Amos (2011), *Lullaby to My Father*, France: Agav Film.
Gitai, Efratia and Amos Gitai (2012), *Storia di una famiglia ebrea*, Milan: Bompiani.
Gledhill, Christine (1987), *Home is Where the Heart is: Studies in Melodrama and the Woman's Film*, London: BFI.
Hagener, Malte (2008), 'Where is Cinema (Today)? The Cinema in the Age of Media Immanence', *Cinéma et Cie.*, 11, pp. 15–22.
Heidegger, Martin (1971), '... Poetically Man Dwells ...', in M. Heidegger, *Poetry, Language, Thought*, New York: Harper and Row, pp. 221–39.
Heidegger, Martin (1993), 'Building, Dwelling, Thinking', in M. Heidegger, *Basic Writings*, New York: HarperCollins, pp. 343–63.

Kuhn, Annette (1995), *Family Secrets: Acts of Memory and Imagination*, London and New York: Verso.
Lant, Antonia (1995), 'Haptical Cinema', *October*, 74, pp. 45–73.
Levi, Pavle (2012), *Cinema by Other Means*, Oxford: Oxford University Press.
Marchessault, Janine and Susan Lord (eds) (2007), *Fluid Screens, Expanded Cinema*, Toronto, Buffalo and London: University of Toronto Press.
Marks, Laura U. (2000), *The Skin of the Film. Intercultural Cinema, Embodiment, and the Senses*, Durham, NC and London: Duke University Press.
Marks, Laura U. (2012), 'Immersed in the Single Channel: Experimental Media from Theater to Gallery', *Millennium Film Journal, Structures and Spaces: Cine-Installations*, 55, pp. 14–23.
Massey, Doreen (2005), *For Space*, London, Thousand Oaks and New Delhi: Sage.
Mondloch, Kate (2013), *Screens: Viewing Media Installation Art*, Minneapolis: University of Minnesota Press.
Mondloch, Kate (2018), *A Capsule Aesthetic: Feminist Materialisms in New Media Art*, Minneapolis: University of Minnesota Press.
Rascaroli, Laura (2009), *The Personal Camera: Subjective Cinema and the Essay Film*, London: Wallflower.
Rhodes, John David and Gorfinkel, Elena (eds) (2001), *Taking Place: Location and the Moving Image*, Minneapolis: University of Minnesota Press, 2011.
Robertson Wojcik, Pamela (2010), *The Apartment Plot: Urban Living in American Film and Popular Culture, 1945 to 1975*, Durham, NC and London: Duke University Press.
Schleier, Merrill (2009), *Skyscraper Cinema Architecture and Gender in American Film*, Minneapolis: University of Minnesota Press.
Uricchio, William (2012), 'A Palimpsest of Place and Past', *Performance Research*, 17, no. 3, pp. 45–9.
Uroskie, Andrew (2014), *Between the Black Box and the White Cube: Expanded Cinema and Postwar Art*, Chicago: University of Chicago Press.
Waggoner, Matt (2018), *Unhoused: Adorno and the Problem of Dwelling*, New York: Columbia Books on Architecture and the City.

CHAPTER 12

What Is Cult When It's At Home? Reframing Cult Cinema in Relation to Domestic Space

Iain Robert Smith

> *To see a great film only on television isn't to have really seen that film. It's not only a question of the dimensions of the image: the disparity between a larger-than-you image in the theater and the little image on the box at home. The conditions of paying attention in a domestic space are radically disrespectful of film. Now that a film no longer has a standard size, home screens can be as big as living room or bedroom walls. But you are still in a living room or a bedroom. To be kidnapped, you have to be in a movie theater, seated in the dark among anonymous strangers.*
> (Sontag 1996: 60)

In her celebrated elegy to the bygone days of a dying form of cinephilia, Susan Sontag bemoans the shift from cinema being primarily experienced in a darkened movie theatre to an era in which films are being viewed at home in a living room or bedroom. While the rise of the 'new cinephilia' (Shambu 2014) has challenged this notion of cine-love being intimately tied to the communal space of the movie theatre, the terms of Sontag's critique nevertheless continue to resonate with much of the discourse surrounding cult cinema. From I. Q. Hunter's assertion that 'to some extent ... cult is a historical category' (Hunter 2016: xiii) to Jonathan Rosenbaum's claim that in the contemporary era 'cult films no longer exist' (Rosenbaum 2008), there is a recurrent emphasis upon a particular understanding of cult that is tied to the historical phenomenon of the midnight movie and the associated film theatres such as The Elgin in New York and The Scala in London. Even where there is acknowledgement that the concept of cult has undergone a semantic shift since its heyday in the 1970s and 1980s, there is nevertheless a continued nostalgic harking back to that earlier era in which cult films were primarily experienced in the communal environment of the movie theatre surrounded by a fellow group of cultists.

Given that we are nearing fifty years since *El Topo* (Alejandro Jodorowsky, 1970) first played as a midnight screening at The Elgin, it is evident that this limited conception of cult has been challenged by social and technological changes in the intervening years – not least of which was the introduction of cult films into the home through video, DVD and internet streaming. There is a growing body of scholarship on the impact of technological changes on cult cinema (Klinger 2010; Church 2015; Wroot and Willis 2017) that has helped challenge the notion that cult is necessarily tied to a particular exhibition context. From the introduction of VHS in the late 1970s through to the rise of Netflix and Amazon streaming services in the 2010s, the history of cult has been intimately tied to the history of home media technologies. In this chapter, however, I want to focus less on the technological dynamics of this process and instead pay more specific attention to the ways in which cult cinema functions within domestic space.

It is worth making clear at the outset that this will not be an analysis of representations of domestic space *within* cult cinema. Robin Wood famously described *The Texas Chain Saw Massacre* (Tobe Hooper, 1974) as a 'hideous parody of domesticity' (Wood 2003: 83) but cult cinema encompasses such an eclectic range of texts that I don't think that it has a particularly consistent relationship with depictions of domestic space. Rather, this will be an attempt to think through what happens to our understanding of cult cinema when we frame it through the domestic viewing context of the home. I will start by charting the ways in which domesticity functions within scholarly and critical discourses on cult cinema in order to establish the wider conceptual framework that underpins this phenomenon, and then I will relate these debates to the recently relaunched US television series *Mystery Science Theatre 3000* (1988–) in which there is an attempt to recreate the experience of being part of a participatory film screening for viewers watching at home. Applying these broader conceptual frameworks to a specific institution of cult viewing in the domestic context, therefore, I will investigate the ways in which this series helps us to think through the cultural politics of this shift from a communal cult film experience into the private space of the home.

Theorising Cult in the Domestic Sphere

In order to establish the specificity of cult cinema within the domestic sphere, it is important that we first discuss the communal cult cinema experience that helped define the concept and that is very much tied to the phenomenon of the midnight movie culture of the 1970s. Primarily associated with inner city cinemas and the latter years of the US countercultural movement, it was the midnight screenings of films such as

El Topo, Pink Flamingos (John Waters, 1972), and *Rocky Horror Picture Show* (Jim Sharman, 1975) that helped define the cult film experience as a particular model of ritualistic, communal film screening populated by audiences with some level of investment in countercultural politics. As Elena Gorfinkel has observed, the 'performative collectivity of the 1970s midnight movie made the experience of the cult film a spectacle of postcountercultural protest' (Gorfinkel 2008: 33). The cult film scene in the 1970s and early 1980s was therefore associated with a form of participatory audience engagement that was seen to subvert the notion of passive film viewing and to build a sense of collective identity amongst the attendees. The shift towards domestic film viewing, however, was to create a significant shift in the conception of cult viewing practices as the supposedly communal experience of theatrical viewing was replaced with the private space of the home.

Building on Tom Ryall's definition of 'public film culture' to describe an 'intermingling of ideas and institutions into recognisable formations' (Ryall 1986: 2), Barbara Klinger has proposed the concept of 'home film cultures' as a 'useful way of apprehending domestic space as an exhibition environment for cinema' (Klinger 2006: 241). Central to Klinger's approach is 'the consideration of the home as a discursively charged forum that generates taste formations and shapes film meaning' (Klinger 2006: 14). When we apply this approach to cult film viewing practices specifically, we can see the ways in which the taste formations that shape cult cinema discourse take on distinctive forms within the domestic sphere. As Matt Hills has argued,

> Cult 'films' can now be cultified by audiences not just via midnight movie screenings but also through consumption on home media such as DVD and Blu-Ray, or via downloading and streaming in the domestic space, whether this is legal (what's been dubbed 'formal distribution' via intermediaries such as DVD labels) or illicit, i.e. 'informal distribution' driven by fans. (Hills 2017: 49)

The processes through which films become associated with the necessary subcultural capital to be framed as 'cult' are different in each of these contexts. These multiple forms of distribution allow for films to become 'cultified' in ways quite distinct from the context of the midnight movie, and the shift to largely private screenings allows for a wider range of practices to come under the banner of cult. I would argue that this shift to the home as an exhibition environment for cult cinema has had implications in three main discursive fields: (1) the relationship between the public and the private, (2) the relationship between wider access and a discourse of mainstreaming, and (3) the ways in which both these relationships are gendered. Taking each of these discursive fields in turn, I will now interrogate how the domestic space specifically impacts the meanings of cult film viewing practices.

Cult in the Privacy of Your Own Home

The first scholarly collection on the topic of cult cinema, J. P. Tellote's *The Cult Film Experience*, was published in 1991 after the height of the midnight movie phenomenon had passed and viewership of cult cinema was largely moving to the home environment. Nevertheless, many of the chapters showed a marked nostalgia for the earlier model of communal viewing, and focused particular attention upon the participatory screenings of films such as *Rocky Horror Picture Show*. Robert E. Wood, for example, celebrated these *RHPS* screenings precisely for countering 'a contemporary tendency – encouraged and accelerated by the video industry – for filmgoing to become less communal, less festive, and in many ways less significant' (Wood 1991: 157). Similarly, in their book on *Midnight Movies*, J. Hoberman and Jonathan Rosenbaum highlighted *RHPS* as 'one of the last gasps of collectivized theatrical moviegoing before video took over and atomized the audience' (Hoberman and Rosenbaum 1983/1991: 20). This relationship between the communal atmosphere of cult cinema screenings and a sense of its broader significance is key. In a 2008 symposium on cult cinema published in *Cineaste*, Jeffrey Andrew Weinstock argued that the 'shift from viewing in the theatre to viewing at home' resulted in the 'surrendering of possibilities for alternative spectator practices' (Weinstock 2008) and when asked about the social function of cult cinema today, I. Q. Hunter responded that cult films 'may have [had a social function] in the early 1970s when screenings showcased the preferences of the counterculture and the sexual underground, but nowadays cult tastes are too private, random and politically unpredictable for cults to have much impact' (Hunter 2008). There is therefore a linking between a specific political agenda tied to the experience of the 1970s counterculture that is then seen to be dispersed when cult film viewing moves to the home. The audience is understood to be atomised within individual private spheres with less potential for collective agency tied to that kind of cult film experience. It is this linking of the private nature of the domestic screening with an assumed lack of social function that underpins much of the criticism of cult cinema within the home.

However, it is important to note that in one of the other chapters in *The Cult Film Experience*, Timothy Corrigan makes a distinction between

B-movies and cult cinema, positioning B-movies as 'the public precursor of the cult' and cult cinema as a more domestic activity given that cult films 'become part of an audience's private space, and in this embracing of public images as private space, they become more like furnishings or material acquisitions' (Corrigan 1991: 26). For Corrigan, therefore, cult film is best understood as a private process with cult films being 'brought home [and] appropriated by viewers who make these images privately and personally meaningful' (26). Rather than positioning cult cinema as a necessarily communal activity tied to the collective film screening, cult is instead defined here by a sense of privacy and personal meaning in the domestic context. 'Home' is therefore more than simply the physical space of the domestic unit but further implies the private internal space of the individual audience member. This relates to what Matt Hills identifies as the paradoxical social functions of cult – 'congregating and individuating' (Hills 2008) – as cult cinema functions both as a marker of being part of a collective 'cult', and also as a marker of individualised personal taste and identity.

Nevertheless, the communal experience of congregation is still the one that is privileged in the majority of discussions of the definition of cult cinema. Mikel Koven, for example, argues that 'To be a cult film, the film must have a particular kind of audience who display a particular kind of behaviour ... You cannot have a cult film on your own' (Koven 2008). For Koven, the defining characteristic of cult cinema is 'public cultural display' and he argues that 'Dressing up in the privacy of your own home, even among friends, or throwing rice at your TV screen, has less inherent alterity than if performed publicly' (Koven 2008). According to this strict definition of cult cinema, it is this public display and its attendant politics of 'alterity' that help define cult cinema, while the equivalent display in the private space of the home is seen to lack that wider political resonance. Yet for Ernest Mathijs, 'Screenings on college campuses or at midnight in urban repertory theaters are now only one part of cult consumption [given that] home screenings, internet viewings, and the sharing of materials through a variety of electronic formats have become widespread' (Mathijs 2008). This more all-embracing approach to the concept of cult cinema suggests that the contexts that once defined the meaning of cult cinema can be treated as contingent rather than necessary conditions. There are numerous forms of cult film experience according to this approach and the originating communal screening of midnight movies is positioned here as only one of many alternatives.

Moreover, this move from the public sphere of the movie theatre into the private space of the home is not always framed as a shift to a less innately 'cult' environment. Comparing his own fandom with that of the *Star Trek* fans known as Trekkers, I. Q. Hunter argues that 'Most cult viewing is considerably less public, organised and socially useful. For many of us it is a private, even hermetic, activity enjoyed at home in front of the video recorder' (Hunter 2016: 30). Meanwhile, according to Steve Chibnall, 'Video transformed films from collective experiences to privatised commodities which may be used (like any others) in the process of individual identity formation and communication' (Chibnall 1997: 88). The individuating social function of cult cinema is therefore especially well-suited to the privacy of the domestic space. The home becomes repositioned as a suitable environment for cult viewing when it is framed as a place of privacy that can help to form an individual subcultural identity. Furthermore, for critic Tim Lucas the loss of the shared experience can actually make for a purer experience of cult cinema: 'the way an audience feels about a film collectively can sway the individual viewer's opinion, so a cult film experience today is far more intimate and undiluted' (Lucas 2008: 46). These associations between cult in the home as being a potentially undiluted experience that is especially well suited to the process of individual identity formation indicate the shifting role of cult cinema within the home, and the central role of the domestic environment in supporting that process of self-individuation. This notion of cult as tied to individual identity formation, however, is complicated by the second discursive context I wish to highlight – the relationship between wider access and a discourse of mainstreaming.

Cult and the Politics of Access

The growth of home video and subsequently DVD, Blu-ray and Internet streaming helped to widen access to cult films that had previously been largely restricted to cinema viewing. For some cult cinema critics, this widening of access was actually central to the development of their own cult fandom, given that the earlier model of the midnight movie had been largely restricted geographically to those who lived close to major urban conurbations. As I. Q. Hunter recounts in the introduction to *Cult Film as a Guide to Life*:

> Cult meant oddball films watched by oddballs at ungodly hours in dingy cinemas; it meant, in England, enthusing about obscure film noirs at the National Film Theatre on London's Southbank and haring off to see a John Waters triple bill under club conditions at the Scala in King's Cross. As a teenager stuck in a provincial extremity of Britain, I could unfortunately do none of these things. (Hunter 2016: xi)

Home video along with television series such as *Mystery Science Theatre 3000* in the US and *Moviedrome* (1988–) in the UK, made cult films available to a wider audience who had been unable to attend midnight screenings at venues such as The Elgin and The Scala. Alongside this rhetoric that celebrates access, however, is an acknowledgement that this wider availability threatens the sense of exclusivity that is often core to the cultist identity formation. According to Hunter, as films have become increasingly easy to access in the home, 'cult movies undoubtedly still exist ... but no real exclusivity clings to them' (Hunter 2016: xii). There is a rhetoric of authenticity that is often attached to the midnight movie experience that lies in contrast with a contemporary cult experience where the ability to purchase those same films on home media is associated with a commodifying of that 'authenticity'. This rhetoric relies on the notion of domestic space as being the location of everyday consumption practices cut off from a wider alternative politics. As Elena Gorfinkel observes,

> The midnight movie, on the wane by the late 1970s, persisted as cult cinema's origin narrative, allowing cult fans to hold on to the idea of cinema as communal place and resistant space of sensual disorientation, rather than as site of quotidian commodity consumption. (Gorfinkel 2008: 36)

Many of the respondents to the 2008 *Cineaste* symposium on cult cinema reflect that attitude. Peter Stanfield, for example, suggests that 'cult may have at one time signified a radical, and perhaps even subversive, form of film consumption' but is now little more than 'a coopted marketing tag used to sell DVDs and anthologies of scholarly studies' (Stanfield 2008: 49). This is tied to a wider rhetoric surrounding the commodification of alternative culture in the late twentieth century where a lost authenticity is contrasted with a contemporary commoditised culture – and in the case of cult, this is very much tied to the shift from the communal space of the midnight movie screening to the private space of home viewing. Meanwhile, Jeffrey Sconce argues that cult cinema 'was very specific to a finite window in the history of cinephilia and exhibition ... [thriving] when film culture itself was growing in the 1970s/'80s and yet access to certain films remained somewhat limited' (Sconce 2008: 48). The subcultural distinction that is seen to be essential to the self-definition as a cult cinema audience member is threatened when access to these films becomes more widely available. Indeed, in his account of the changing meanings of 'cult' as a concept from the 1910s up to the present day, Jamie Sexton argues that much of this recent criticism on cult displays 'a nostalgic harking back to a bygone era, contrasting a previous "authentic" era to a contemporary climate in which cult is merely an artificial construct' (Sexton 2014: 142).

Building on Sexton's work, Matt Hills has subsequently identified a 'mainstreaming' discourse in much of this cult criticism which relies on what Hills describes as 'retro subcultural capital' (Hills 2014: 101). While the sense of subcultural distinction tied to cult cinema is diminished in a contemporary context where such films are more widely available, critics often utilise a strategy of self-narrativising in which they discuss their own personal relationship with earlier key moments in the history of cult cinema's development in order to establish their own subcultural credentials. As Hills argues, technologies such as Internet streaming are positioned as a threat to cult status as they make cult 'instantaneous, "easy", and accessible to all' (Hills 2014: 104), so these evocations of an earlier more 'authentic' era can function to bolster the critics' own subcultural capital in an environment where that sense of distinction is being lost.

Home media, therefore, has functioned to provide access to cult films to cultists who could not attend the original midnight movie screenings, but it has also threatened the sense of exclusivity which was so central to that identity formation in the first place. Director Frank Henenlotter, in an interview in *Incredibly Strange Films*, exemplifies this perspective when he reflects that 'all those obscure films that I would have risked injury and death to see (literally, in some of those theatres) are now available at your local clean video store!' (Henenlotter in Morton 1985: 8). A similar position is also described by Jeffrey Sconce when he notes that 'the moment *Cannibal Holocaust* appeared at the local video store, conveniently filed in the "cult" section, any final remnant of "excess and controversy" passed into history' (Sconce 2008: 48). The association of cult cinema with transgression and excess is therefore threatened when it is 'domesticated' through its appearance on home media and viewed within the relatively 'safe' environment of the home. This is especially the case when the films are no longer associated with illicit video trading as with the 'video nasties' phenomenon in the UK but are instead available to buy (and download) through more formal distribution channels. In sum, cult could no longer be positioned as exclusive to a small group of cultists who see themselves in opposition to the mainstream when these films are made available to a wider audience – and this issue was, of course, heightened with the move to online video streaming. It becomes increasingly challenging to maintain a sense of subcultural distinction tied to being a cult cinema fan when the objects that constitute that distinction become available online to anyone who wishes to seek them out at home. This leads us to the third of the key discursive contexts surrounding cult cinema in the home: gender.

Cult and the Gendered Nature of Subcultural Distinction

The increased accessibility outlined above not only threatens the accumulation of subcultural capital tied to notions of exclusivity and transgression, but this process is shaped by the gendered nature of cult reception more broadly. In her influential essay on the 'masculinity of cult', Joanne Hollows argues that 'many of the practices of cult fandom work ... to naturalise cult as masculine through the ways in which they structurally exclude women' (Hollows 2003: 41). In the era of the midnight movie, this exclusion was partly structured by the physical locations of the cult film screenings – inner city grindhouse cinemas that carried associations with pornography, sleaze and physical danger. Indeed, in a clear illustration of Matt Hills's argument about the role of retro-subcultural capital within recent cult film criticism, I. Q. Hunter has written about cult film screenings at The Scala in London and offers an anecdote from his friend Mo Bottomley who asserts that 'The Scala is the only place where I stroked a cat, was offered a joint and had someone jizz on my shoulder, all within thirty seconds' (Hunter 2013: 27). This kind of account of the illicit excesses associated with cult film screenings evidently plays into what Hollows describes as the self-construction of cult fan as 'manly adventurer' (Hollows 2003: 47), a figure who ventures into the dangerous urban spaces of the downtown movie theatre to be part of an 'authentic' cult film experience.

Yet, as David Church has argued in his account of these historical shifts in *Grindhouse Nostalgia*, 'masculine fantasies of exploitation film consumption are complicated by home video's transition towards the broader demographics and feminine connotations of domestic viewership' (Church 2015: 23). Church identifies a growing nostalgia for the films and viewing contexts of the 1970s grindhouse within contemporary cult film culture and he argues that this retrospective celebration of grindhouses is partly 'an anachronistic defence of the gender-limited access to downmarket urban pleasures that home video has since subverted' (Church 2015: 91). Shifting the viewing context from the grindhouse into the home is therefore clearly problematic for audiences invested in this notion of the 'heroic adventurer' – both in terms of the loss of spatial associations with notions of danger and transgression, but also in terms of the gaining of new associations linked to the space of the home. As Hollows argues, '[n]ot only does television viewing take place in what traditionally has been seen as the feminised sphere of the home, but television has also been strongly associated with the "family viewing" against which youthful audiences have defined themselves' (Hollows 2003: 42). These associations with feminisation and 'family viewing' within the domestic space therefore pose a clear threat to the processes of subcultural distinction underpinning traditional accounts of the cult film experience.

To some extent, however, these associations have started to change in recent years – partly as a result of Hollows's intervention in the field. In the introduction to *Cult Film as a Guide to Life*, for example, I. Q. Hunter provides an overview of the transformations that have taken place within cult fandom and scholarship over the decades. Noting that the American teen comedy *Mean Girls* (2004) appears on many lists of contemporary cult films, Hunter argues that 'cult today is not only chiefly in the domestic sphere (the primal scene of cult may well be sleepovers), but also increasingly reflects the tastes of young women' (Hunter 2016: 19). While Hunter displays some level of nostalgia for the earlier period of cult cinema fandom, he nevertheless acknowledges the shifts that have taken place in recent years to broaden access to cult films and to popularise cult activities beyond the specific (gendered) subcultures that have traditionally constituted the cult film audience – a shift that is clearly tied to the move into the home that I have been describing.

Mystery Science Theater 3000 Lives Again!

The television series *Mystery Science Theater 3000* (*MST3K*) is a particularly resonant case study with which to explore these historical transformations as it originally appeared in 1988 at the moment when cult film practices were moving increasingly into the domestic sphere and was recently relaunched on Netflix in 2017 at a time when the cult film experience is now increasingly moving online. The central premise of the show is that the home audience gets to watch B-movies such as *Manos: The Hands of Fate* (Harold P. Warren, 1966) and *Eegah* (Arch Hall Sr, 1962) in a simulated cinema while seated behind three silhouettes – one human, two robots – who offer a running commentary on the happenings on screen. This format, nicknamed 'Shadowrama' by the show's producers, is therefore designed to replicate some aspects of the communal midnight-movie film screening experience for audiences at home. Taking the three discursive contexts I have outlined above, I will now apply them to the series to investigate how this recreation of the cult film experience for home viewers relates to the broader conceptual frameworks that have underpinned cult film criticism.

Firstly, in terms of the relationship between public and private spheres, *MST3K* is an attempt to recreate many of the core features of a communal public screening in a format that can then be experienced individually in the private space of the home. Central to the communal experience of the midnight movie, for example, was what Hoberman and Rosenbaum call 'counterpoint dialogue' (1983/1991: 176) where the audience shout out comments in response to what they are watching on screen. In *MST3K* we are watching the film alongside three silhouetted figures who similarly shout out sarcastic and mocking observations on the film and this process of 'riffing' helps to simulate the experience of a communal cult screening environment. Indeed, some of the most celebratory criticism on *MST3K* positions the series as an opportunity for viewers in their own private home-viewing environment to be able to experience cinema as a social event. E. Mitchell, for example, argues that *MST3K* 'has reconnected audiences with the social component of the film experience in the face of an increasingly isolating technological age' (Mitchell 2011: 231). This aspect of the series is particularly highlighted in one of the offshoots of the *MST3K* format – *Rifftrax Live!* (2007–) where they perform their riffing in front of a live cinema audience and the viewer at home gets to watch the film alongside this genuine cinema audience. It is important to note, however, that this can only ever be a simulation of the cinematic experience given that the home viewer is still physically separated from that communal viewing environment.

In fact, to turn to the second context I outlined earlier, this ability to access a simulated cult film experience from the privacy of the home environment has clearly inspired many of the familiar discourses of mainstreaming. *MST3K* tends to be positioned within cult criticism as both an inauthentic simulation of a communal screening and as a commercialisation of an activity that had previously been tied to a countercultural politics. In Jeffrey Sconce's seminal article 'Trashing the Academy', for example, he briefly references *MST3K* in order to lament that the 'ironic reading strategies honed by the badfilm community through countless hours of derisive interaction with late-night science fiction are now prepackaged for cable' (1995: 373). Similarly, when Andrew Syder and Dolores Tierney discuss the role of *MST3K* in screening Mexploitation films to US audiences, they comment that 'most cult audiences actively despise the show' (2005: 51). Part of the reason for this resistance to *MST3K* from people who already consider themselves to be part of the cult subculture is the idea that this is a simulated experience rather than an 'authentic' cult film event. There are parallels with DVD 'audience reaction' tracks, such as on the home release of *Planet Terror* (Robert Rodriguez, 2007), where the home viewer gets to watch the film accompanied by the pre-recorded sounds of an actual communal film screening. As Caetlin Benson-Allott has argued, that kind of 'experience can only be simulacral; the spectator has access to a copy of this utopian event ... only because she is not there' (Benson-Allott 2013: 165) and it is this simultaneous tension between presence and absence that defines this form of cult experience.

Furthermore, if we approach *MST3K* through the prism of the 'masculinity of cult', it is clear that this broadening of access to a simulated communal film screening means that this kind of experience is no longer tied to the kinds of midnight screenings in urban centres that might reinforce a sense of the 'manly adventurer' (Hollows 2003) and instead offers potential to reach a broader and more diverse audience viewing at home. Despite that potential, however, it is notable just how male-centric the world of *MST3K* still remains: all of the main 'riffers' in the history of the show have been men and even though there is a 'female' robot named Gypsy who participates in some of the sketches that break up the main screening, she was voiced by a series of three men until Rebecca Hanson took on the role in the most recent relaunched season on Netflix. Nevertheless, there has been an evident shift in emphasis in this redesigned incarnation of *MST3K* regarding gender and this is reflective of the wider broadening of cult fandom in the three decades since the original season started airing. In the earlier incarnation, the cast were almost all men with only the occasional female guest performer, yet the relaunch has introduced Felicia Day in the central role of Kinga Forrester, daughter of one of the mad scientist figures in the original show. What makes this gender switch particularly significant is that Felicia Day is already an established cult figure and one with a particularly notable relationship with online culture. As Elizabeth Ellcessor has observed in her star study of Day, 'She has used gaming media, social networking services, and Internet video to build a subcultural "geek" or "gamer" star text' (Ellcessor 2012: 47). From her position as creator, writer and star of the web series *The Guild* (2017–13) through to her role as Penny in Joss Whedon's musical web series *Dr. Horrible's Sing-Along Blog* (2008), Felicia Day has developed a cult status online that is representative of the ways in which the notion of cult fandom and its associations with a wider geek culture has broadened and transformed with the increasing centrality of social media and internet culture to these processes.

What the relaunched *MST3K* series reflects, therefore, is the changing dynamics of cult fandom within the domestic sphere. The figure of the 'geek' who is invested in cult media is no longer seen to be restricted to the nerdy young men satirised in the *Saturday Night Live* sketch where William Shatner famously told a group of *Star Trek* fans to 'Get a life!' (1986). Geek culture today is increasingly associated with figures like Felicia Day who built her stardom online through social media and subsequently set up the successful 'Geek and Sundry' YouTube channel with Kim Evey and Sheri Bryant. I do not want to overstate these changes – *MST3K* is still primarily a male space that functions to naturalise cult as masculine in various ways – but this reformulated show nevertheless reflects many of the wider shifts within cult film culture in the intervening decades as cult has moved increasingly into the home.

J. Hoberman has proposed that 'The midnight movies of the 1970s were in large measure a nostalgia for the community of the counterculture ... [while in] the age of Netflix, we have nostalgia for the no longer extant movie houses that showed midnight movies' (Hoberman 2008: 45). I would add that the revival of *MST3K* similarly reflects a nostalgia for a home film culture of the late 1980s that has been itself transformed through technological and social changes in the intervening years. Moreover, this is not a teleological history as these different forms of cult film experience continue to co-exist alongside each other. In 2017, to accompany the relaunch of *MST3K* on Netflix, the first live touring show based on the television series appeared across the US. Titled the 'Mystery Science Theater 3000 Live! – Watch Out for Snakes!' tour, the show allowed audiences to experience a simulation of the MST3K format within a movie theatre rather than within the home. The domestic version of cult film viewing embodied by MST3K, therefore, was now no longer positioned purely as a simulation of an earlier more 'authentic' form of cult film experience but was itself now the model for a revived form of collective experience.

Works Cited

Benson-Allott, Caetlin (2013), *Killer Tapes and Shattered Screens: Video Spectatorship from VHS to File Sharing*, Berkeley: University of California Press.

Chibnall, Steve (1997), 'Double Exposures: Observations on *The Flesh and Blood Show*', in Deborah Cartmell, I. Q. Hunter, Heidi Kaye and Imelda Whelehan (eds), *Trash Aesthetics: Popular Culture and its Audience*, London: Pluto Press, pp. 84–102.

Church, David (2015), *Grindhouse Nostalgia: Memory, Home Video and Exploitation Film Fandom*, Edinburgh: Edinburgh University Press.
Corrigan, Timothy (1991), 'Film and the Culture of Cult', in J. P. Telotte (ed.), *The Cult Film Experience: Beyond All Reason*, Austin: University of Texas Press, pp. 26–37.
Ellcessor, Elizabeth (2012), 'Tweeting @feliciaday: Online Social Media, Convergence, and Subcultural Stardom', *Cinema Journal*, 51, no. 2, pp. 46–66.
Gorfinkel, Elena (2008), 'Cult Film or Cinephilia by Any Other Name', *Cineaste*, 34, no. 1, pp. 33–8.
Hall, Arch Sr. (1962), *Eegah*.
Hills, Matt (2008), 'Cult Cinema: A Critical Symposium (Web Edition)', *Cineaste*, 34: 1, <https://www.cineaste.com/winter2008/cult-film-a-critical-symposium/> (last accessed 21 November 2019).
Hills, Matt (2014), 'Cult Cinema and the "Mainstreaming" Discourse of Technological Change: Revisiting Subcultural Capital in Liquid Modernity', *New Review of Film and Television Studies*, 13, no. 1, pp. 100–21.
Hills, Matt (2017), 'A "Cult-like" Following: Nordic Noir, Nordicana and Arrow Films' Bridging of Subcultural/Neocultural Capital', in Jonathan Wroot and Andy Willis (eds), *Cult Media: Re-packaged, Re-released and Restored*, London: Palgrave Macmillan, pp. 49–65.
Hoberman, J. (2008), 'Cult Cinema: A Critical Symposium', *Cineaste*, 34, no. 1, pp. 44–5.
Hoberman, J. and Jonathan Rosenbaum (1983/1991), *Midnight Movies*, New York: Da Capo Press.
Hollows, Joanne (2003), 'The Masculinity of Cult', in Mark Jancovich, Antonio Lázaro-Reboll, Julian Stringer and Andy Willis (eds), *Defining Cult Movies: The Cultural Politics of Oppositional Taste*, Manchester: Manchester University Press, pp. 35–54.
Hooper, Tobe (1974), *Texas Chain Saw Massacre*, USA: Vortex.
Hunter, I. Q. (2008), 'Cult Cinema: A Critical Symposium (Web Edition)', *Cineaste*, 34, no. 1, <https://www.cineaste.com/winter2008/cult-film-a-critical-symposium/> (last accessed 8 April 2018).
Hunter, I. Q. (2013), *British Trash Cinema*, London: Palgrave Macmillan.
Hunter, I. Q. (2016), *Cult Film as a Guide to Life: Fandom, Adaptation, and Identity*, London: Bloomsbury.
Jodorowsky, Alejandro (1970), *El Topo*, Mexico: Producciones Panicas.
Klinger, Barbara (2006), *Beyond the Multiplex: Cinema, New Technologies, and the Home*, Berkeley: University of California Press.
Klinger, Barbara (2010), 'Becoming Cult: *The Big Lebowski*, Replay Culture and Male Fans', *Screen* 51, no. 1, pp. 1–20.
Koven, Mikel (2008), 'Cult Cinema: A Critical Symposium (Web Edition)', *Cineaste*, 34: 1, <https://www.cineaste.com/winter2008/cult-film-a-critical-symposium/> (last accessed 21 November 2019).

Lucas, Tim (2008), 'Cult Cinema: A Critical Symposium', *Cineaste*, 34, no. 1, p. 46.
Mathijs, Ernest (2008), 'Cult Cinema: A Critical Symposium (Web Edition)', Cineaste, 34: 1, <https://www.cineaste.com/winter2008/cult-film-a-critical-symposium/> (last accessed 21 November 2019).
Mitchell, E. (2011), 'From Techno-Isolation to Social Reconciliation', in Robert G. Weiner and Shelley E. Barba (eds), *In the Peanut Gallery with Mystery Science Theater 3000: Essays on Film, Fandom, Technology and the Culture of Riffing*, Jefferson, NC: McFarland, pp. 231–41.
Morton, Jim (1985), *RE/Search No. 10: Incredibly Strange Films*, London: Plexus.
Rodriguez, Robert (2007), *Planet Terror*, USA: Rodriguez International Pictures.
Rosenbaum, Jonathan (2008), 'Cult Cinema: A Critical Symposium (Web Edition)', *Cineaste*, 34, no. 1, <https://www.cineaste.com/winter2008/cult-film-a-critical-symposium/> (last accessed 8 April 2018).
Ryall, Tom (1986), *Alfred Hitchcock and the British Cinema*, Urbana: University of Illinois Press.
Sconce, Jeffrey (1995), '"Trashing" the Academy: Taste, Excess, and an Emerging Politics of Cinematic Style', *Screen* 36, no. 4, pp. 371–93.
Sconce, Jeffrey (2008), 'Cult Cinema: A Critical Symposium', *Cineaste*, 34, no. 1, pp. 48–9.
Sexton, Jamie (2014), 'From Bad to Good and Back to Bad Again? Cult Cinema and Its Unstable Trajectory', in Claire Perkins and Constantine Verevis (eds), *B is for Bad Cinema: Aesthetics, Politics, and Cultural Value*, Albany, NY: State University of New York Press, pp. 129–45.
Shambu, Girish (2014), *The New Cinephilia*, Montréal: Caboose.
Sharman, Jim (1975), *Rocky Horror Picture Show*, UK and USA: Michael White Productions.
Sontag, Susan (1996), 'The Decay of Cinema', *New York Times Magazine*, 25 February 1996, pp. 60–1.
Stanfield, Peter (2008), 'Cult Cinema: A Critical Symposium', *Cineaste*, 34, no. 1, pp. 49–50.
Syder, Andrew and Dolores Tierney (2005), 'Importation/Mexploitation, or, How A Crime-Fighting, Vampire-Slaying Mexican Wrestler Almost Found Himself In An Italian Sword-And-Sandals Epic', in Steven Jay Schneider and Tony Williams (2005), *Horror International*, Detroit: Wayne State University Press, pp. 33–55.
Telotte, J. P. (ed.) (1991), *The Cult Film Experience: Beyond All Reason*, Austin: University of Texas Press.
Warren, Harold P. (1966), *Manos: The Hands of Fate*, USA: Sun City Films.
Waters, John (1972), *Pink Flamingos*, USA: Dreamland.
Weinstock, Jeffrey Andrew (2008), 'Cult Cinema: A Critical Symposium (Web Edition)', *Cineaste*, 34, no. 1, <https://www.cineaste.com/winter2008/cult-film-a-critical-symposium/> (last accessed 4 November 2019).

Wood, Robert E. (1991), 'Don't Dream It: Performance and the *Rocky Horror Picture Show*', in J. P. Telotte (ed.), *The Cult Film Experience: Beyond All Reason*, Austin: University of Texas Press, pp. 156–66.

Wood, Robin ([1986] 2003), *Hollywood from Vietnam to Reagan ... And Beyond*, New York: Columbia University Press.

Wroot, Jonathan and Andy Willis (eds) (2017), *Cult Media: Re-packaged, Re-released and Restored*, London: Palgrave Macmillan.

CHAPTER 13

High-fructose Cinema and the Movie Industrial Complex: Radicalising the Technology of Representation in a Domestic Kind of Way

Bryan Konefsky

There is a crack in everything ... that's how the light gets in. (Leonard Cohen, *Anthem*, 1992)

I have a memory of my mother tucking me into bed on New Year's Eve in 1962. It is a visceral recollection involving all my senses; the soft, tactile feel of the cotton sheets, the fresh scent of the quilt pushed close to my chin and, on hot summer nights, there was the cool, plaster wall that I would press my face into and make contact. My pillow was old and misshapen; however, each night my head would find its way to it's soft, welcoming exhale.

In 1962 I was four years old. That particular night I was allowed to stay up late as a special treat. I imagined that as I grew older I might come to understand what all the fuss was about. However, to this day the meaning and value of the New Year's Eve holiday escapes me. Holidays and vacations are both strange and uncomfortable concepts. In my mind, the idea of a vacation is pointless if one understands the term, as I do, as an expression of withdrawing. Unless we are talking about the hallucinatory promise of sensory deprivation tanks, the idea of leaving oneself behind, even if only for a few hours, is an unimaginable proposition (Lilly and Leary 1988: 102). On that particular evening in 1962, after my mother kissed me and said good night, we re-enacted our daily pantomime of leaving my bedroom door open 'just a crack'. The idea was that this sliver of light might allow the warmth of all things domestic and safe to penetrate my room and stave off fearful imaginings as I lay in my bed, alone in the dark.

The interior geography of our small, two-bedroom house consisted of a long hallway that linked my bedroom to the kitchen, living room, my parents' bedroom and the one bathroom that the three of us shared. This artery not only connected the different rooms, but it also functioned as a mixing board and echo chamber for all the goings-on in the house.

Listening from under my blankets, I tried to make sense of the celebratory clamour that found its way into my delicate psyche that night. It is only now that I have come to understand the interplay between the sounds and shadows that pushed their way through the crack in my bedroom door and were moving about in odd and shadowy ways.

Thinking back on that night, it now seems clear that my memory registered an experience not unlike Plato's description of the allegory of the cave.[1] The crack in my bedroom door – illuminated by the incandescent glow of the hallway light – provided a stage for the shadows and voices that danced their way through the house, down the hallway and into the musings of my youthful subconscious. One might imagine the container for this experience (my childhood bedroom) as a protracted version of a camera obscura. The Latin phrase camera obscura translates to mean a darkened room. In these cinematic terms, one might liken my youthful imaginings to the shadow play performed in Carl Theodor Dreyer's 1932 film, *Vampyr*. For me, what characterised that proto-cinematic New Year's Eve was a twilight populated by extraordinary apparitions and phantasmagoric projections. For me, this childhood, proto-cinematic experience has come to rival some of my most memorable movie-going experiences in the years that followed.

I am thinking about composer John Cage, his life-long study of sound and silence, and his assertion that each reveals something unexpected about the other (Cage 1961: 108). Here, we might consider a parallel relationship between light and darkness and how, in a shuttered experience (twenty-four frames per second), the two are necessarily in cinematic conversation with each other. That is, blackness can only be appreciated within the light that frames it and similarly, light can only be comprehended through a screen punctuated by darkness. However, that evening in 1962, the warm sliver of light that pierced the vast darkness of my bedroom-obscura offered the guarantee of a world still to be discovered and not yet fully formed. To this day that liminality is something that I trust and believe in as a place of sanctuary, knowledge and wisdom.

For me, this sanctuary of in-betweenness is loaded with the visceral promise of touch and contact. This is a promise not unlike the contact my cheek made with the cool, plaster wall from my childhood bedroom. But one must be careful when exposing such experiences to analytical scrutiny; as filmmaker Chris McNamara astutely observed in his 2010 essay film titled *Establishing Shots*, 'to explain it would undo it'. Sidestepping the pitfalls of empiricism, this relationship with my bedroom wall might best be understood through the poetic lens of writer Lisa Gill. In her essay titled 'French', she described her first encounter with Jean Cocteau's 1930 film *Blood of a Poet*:

> When the picture ended, I crawled under the row of seats in front of me and pressed my face into a soda spill. It was sticky and I was interested in this place of contact, the kind of pull between my skin and the floor. Whenever I lifted my face, my skin and the earlier picture's soda made small sucking noises. I pushed my cheek down, and again, for that lift. (Gill 2006: 7–10)

I think it is important to have faith in such fleeting moments of contact. In my case, luminous and shadowy apparitions have monumental implications in terms of rethinking the structure of memory. That is, it might be useful to think about such mnemonic forms in the ephemeral and dynamic ways that Patricia Phillips described in her essay, 'Making Memories' (1997). Thinking about Phillips's essay, I wonder whether it is at all possible to have a false memory if, indeed, memory is always and only about those things we have the capacity to recall. The act of recollection necessarily delineates the parameters of a past accessed only through memory. Here, I am thinking about the phenomenon of forgetting to forget, and I wonder if this condition is an expression of amnesia or simply a different iteration of remembering?

Finding our way back to the proto-cinematic, I would like to explore commonly held cultural (mis)understandings of light and shadow, that are too often evaluated in simple, binary ways. To this end, I offer several different registers of how one might re-examine the light and shadow that haunted the crack in my bedroom door. That is, beyond the gendered horror film tropes of penetration lie a spectrum of nuanced possibilities (Clover 1993). Think about how we might interpret the light radiating from a fire and how different that glow is understood if it exists in the context of a warm and welcoming campfire. In his 2010 film *Cave of Forgotten Dreams*, Werner Herzog reminds us that before there was cinema, there were campfires. Consider the difference between that warm, welcoming campfire and the tragedy of a building set ablaze (the 1911 Triangle Shirtwaist Factory fire in New York City might serve as an example, where 123 female garment workers were killed), and let us never forget the unspeakable horror emanating from a fiery cross at a Ku Klux Klan rally.[2]

More complicated is the notion of darkness, which is often characterised through a negative cultural lens. However, if we approach the concept of black from a painter's perspective – in terms of inclusivity – something different emerges. This abundance of colour might be exemplified through Vincent van Gogh's transcendent 1889 painting

Starry Night. However, in the context of light waves, black is a representation of the opposite, the absence of colour. Or, to come back to the ideas of John Cage, he might simply say why analyse light and darkness along any qualitative spectrum at all? For Cage, I am sure, light and shadow are interesting concepts that exist beyond the burden of judgment. Once again, looping back to the proto-cinematic beginnings of this essay (and not forgetting John Cage), add to the grey scale of images (light and shadow) a sonic component, or the echo chamber-hallway of my youth, and the complexity of interpretations multiply exponentially. Robert Stam (2000), in his essay 'The Amplification of Sound', states that in cinema images make sound their own. And, although sound generated on a Foley stage might easily support this theorem, let us consider the politics of this equation from a different perspective.

Although it is a commonly held belief that we are a 'visual culture', sound permeates our lives in much more insidious ways. We can close our eyes, but it is much more difficult to close our ears (Slouka 1999). If one thinks about it, the sonic landscape of our environment has a unique presence that might supersede visuality. It seems that while watching a movie, if there is a glitch in the image, we accept the faulty projection more readily than when we experience a glitch in the soundscape. Also, understand the gross inaccuracy of my use of language (above) in that we never just 'watch' a movie. The experience always involves image and sound even in the case of a silent film. Additionally, think about how the notion of nostalgia adheres itself so effortlessly to scratches and imperfections in celluloid, something which, I think, is much more complicated to achieve in a soundscape. Last, let us not forget the popularity of software that can provide this 'welcoming', distressed look that has now been popularised through Glitch Aesthetics.

Together, we sit in a movie theatre and wait for the house lights to dim. There is a hush in the audience and a collective sense of anticipation as we pull our imagined childhood blankets close to our chins and contemplate why the overhead lights in such a public space are referred to using the term 'house'. A beam of light pierces the darkness (or is it a crack in a bedroom door?) and we are magically transported to another world.

Today, in a movie theatre, projected light originates from a digital source that passes through a vast analogue (outer) space. This luminescent, analogue journey, a journey that necessarily ends at the screen, complicates the truncated ones and zeroes of the digital world by re-inscribing a sense of in-betweenness into this spectoral (and spectral) galaxy. This is a galaxy where meaning was first invoked through the motion studies executed by Eadweard Muybridge, Étienne-Jules Marey,

Herman Casler and their colleagues in the late 1800s. The politics of their alchemical shadow play, in relation to other technological dalliances was later contextualised in Rebecca Solnit's book *River of Shadows: Eadweard Muybridge and The Technological Wild West* (2003).

That same transitional, proto-cinematic moment was immortalised in a Fleischer Brothers' cartoon from 1939 titled *Customers Wanted*.[3] The cartoon describes the early, rough and tumble days of the Mutoscope (invented by Herman Casler) where moving image peep shows were relegated to arcades and amusement parks. In the seven-minute animation, Popeye The Sailor Man and his competitor Bluto find it difficult to attract paying customers to their respective Mutoscope parlours. The short film concludes with a prophetic nod to 'liveness'. Popeye and Bluto 'duke it out' in a fist fight that, unlike their Mutoscope parlours, attracts a 'standing room only' audience. Apparently, the unmediated space of this fight is much more alluring than the Mutoscope's flip-book style interpretation of reality.

Sitting in the dark, I often gaze up and into the light flowing out from a projection booth. The tango-like movement of smoke and dust captured in that radiant stream make any psychotropic drug experience seem tame and insignificant. This fantastic light show embodies what, for me, is the essence of a cinematic experience. That is, most popular films, with their need to overexplain plot lines and deliver flaccid narrative arcs, leave me weary and unfulfilled. But, there amongst the pirouetting particles and dancing dust devils, lives the promise of real contact. For the moment we will set to the side what happens when the luminescent 'money shot' defiles the silver screen. This dynamic space filled with luscious in-betweenness offers the promise of a world still to be discovered and not yet fully formed.

Perhaps there is a link between my interest in this expanded cinema particle-performance and the cartoon audience who preferred to see a real fist fight rather than that which was recorded at eighteen frames per second. Let us not forget the stubborn resiliency of moving image technology that outlived those early cynics who were fictionalised in *Customers Wanted*. Today, a video feed accompanies most live performances. One could argue that the unfortunate fallout of this resiliency is the prosthetic necessity of the screen to complete what might be termed a meaningful experience. I am certainly not the first to make such a claim if one remembers Dziga Vertov's *Kino-eye* writings from the early part of the 20th century (1984).

To rethink this phenomenon through a slightly different cultural lens, consider cinema as a catalyst that offers a sense of what I call 'everything else'. My sense of everything else is that which exists outside the camera's framing but is simultaneously and necessarily inscribed within that shuttered space. This implied inscription delivers a valuable barometric read of the human condition, and the world in which we exist. In addition to the practicalities of this barometric read, everything else must, for me, always include an element of magic. I am careful to keep my sense of cinematic magic far from the Disneyfication of the human spirit and its Thorazine-like effects. We will leave the image of Mickey Mouse dressed in wizard-drag for RuPaul to deconstruct. That is, RuPaul was famous for stating 'we're born naked, and the rest is drag' (RuPaul 1996: 25). Rather, I am thinking about Maya Deren who suggested that movies are not just faster paintings, that there is something more and possibly uncanny about this medium. To this end, Stanley Cavell referred to cinema as the medium of visible absence (1997: 109). If one remembers Deren's later documentary work in Haiti, this allusion to magic and mysticism makes perfect sense (Deren 1978).

I am suggesting that we think about cinema as having the power to inspire cultural and political change as, once again, I allude to the revolutionary work of Dziga Vertov. To illustrate this point, consider Emma Goldman's words from her autobiography titled *Living My Life* where she states 'the inspiration of the true artist has never been the drawing room. Great art has always gone to the masses, to their hopes and dreams, for the spark that kindled their souls' (Goldman 1931: 464). Or, as Industrial Workers of the World organiser Frank Little stated in Travis Wilkerson's film *Injury to One* (a cinematic study of the American labour movement from the early part of the twentieth century), 'if we cannot speak, how can we discuss. If we cannot discuss, how can we invent?'.

I often wonder why, if cinema is a reflection of the everything-ness of our lives, we allow these extraordinary opportunities, that might otherwise instigate invention, to be neutered within the tyranny of the Movie Industrial Complex. Etched into these theatrical spaces is the empiric hermeticism of corporate ideology that seems to leave no room for the poetics of reference and imagination. Over the years, the failings of popular cinema have led me back to the Platonic sanctuary of my youth. There, I find that, through memory and mnemonic imaginings, I am able to lick my wounds (frame by frame) knowing that the tonic of something more is within reach, and ready to tear down the Capitalist proscenium that separates oneself from one's dreams.

A brief (and incomplete) timeline:

1974 – In a cold, unheated movie house I saw, for the first time, Orson Welles's *Citizen Kane* (1941). In the theatre, I spent more time watching my breath rise and dance before my face than paying attention to what was being deposited on the screen. I came to understand that a cinematic experience is often about much more than just the picture show.

1975 – Media artist Shalom Gorewitz introduced me to video art and the value of generational decay in an analogue, tape-based environment.

1976 – I experienced my first expanded cinema performance. A 16mm film depicting a caged polar bear looped repeatedly as the animal hit its head against a wall. Simultaneously, on stage, a percussionist crashed a cymbal each time the bear made contact with the cement.

1977 – Movie critic George Morris introduced me to the films of Jean-Luc Godard and, in particular, his 1968 film *One Plus One*. This was my first exposure to a movie that contained such refreshingly didactic expressions of radical, political ideology.

1978 – I discovered Anthology Film Archives in New York City and the films of Maya Deren. She was famous for stating that the budget for lipstick in a single Hollywood film matched the entire cost to produce one of her movies.

1985 – I saw Godard's film *Hail Mary* (*Je vous salue, Marie*, 1985). A group of nuns protesting the 'blasphemous' depiction of holy virginity tossed a stink bomb into the movie theatre. I held my nose through much of the film (a reminder of how all our senses construct experience, and an unintentional nod to William Castle's 1960 invention, Smell-O-Vision). When the lights came up, I was the only person left in the theatre. As Mark Thomas McGee (2001: 120) describes, I suspected that I was in the right place at the right time.

1991 – I moved to New Mexico and discovered an art collective called Basement Films where I was introduced to the world of microcinemas.

Those were instructive, malodorous and intoxicating years. By 1991 I felt that my wounds had healed (frame by frame), and with tools in hand to circumvent the shame of (mis)representation, I felt comfortable turning back to face the screen. With fresh eyes, ears and nose, I was prepared to embrace the liminal promise of all things cinematic. In particular, the *undependent* universe of Basement Films was warm and inviting. The 'basement' in Basement Films was a nod to film critic Manny Farber's understanding of works by artists such as Andy Warhol, George Kuchar, Jack Smith and John Waters, which he termed Underground Film (Farber 1998: 12–24). However, for me, the 'basement' in Basement Films had a domestic inflection that brought me back to the bedroom-obscura of my youth. Standing in Basement Films' subterranean studio and screening room (with the door open just a crack) I knew that I had found my way home.

The microcinema movement of the 1990s paralleled my experience of Punk Rock clubs in the late 1970s, both of which were informed (for me) by my proto-cinematic childhood home (Daily 2009). One form supported alternative music, the other supported alternative cinematic practices, and both welcomed and embraced creativity not unlike the way your favourite aunt might press you close to her bosom when she visited (Kashmere and Forsberg 2013: 10–15). In both communities the amateur eclipsed the professional if one understands the term amateur as having something to do with passion, and the term professional as having something to do with the tedium of careerism. Microcinemas and Punk Rock clubs encouraged participation and championed a dynamic sense of community. In fact, many of these clubs and cinematic spaces also functioned as 'crash pads' and temporary homes for the communities they served (perhaps one might explore the intersection between the safe-house aspect of these venues and how they might be interpreted as their own camera obscuras). Through Basement Films I was proud to be amongst fellow misfits and moving image odd-balls, whose collective (and tribal) interest in cinema-different crossed the proscenium (or mosh pit) in a DIY environment that can only be described as *mi familia* (my family).

In many ways Basement Films (and so many other microcinemas) did not need the trappings of a movie theatre to stage their events or host touring, *undependent* filmmakers. There was a sense of urgency in this like-minded global cinematic movement in terms of a sense of survival and tribalism. We were not interested in emulating traditional Cineplex experiences or mimicking popular distribution models. Rather, the microcinema movement was invested in bringing a cinematic experience home, both literally and figuratively. Unique venues and passionate audiences required a different sense of engagement. At most screenings the artist was present to interact with attendees both during and after a show. There were no professional divisions that separated artist and audience, as we were all 'in it' together, supporting each other as an extended family. At these events one would often see tapes, zines, DVDs and other media being exchanged as a gesture of trust and sharing. We re-imagined and reinvented the idea of venue, repurposing (as screening rooms) coffee shops, used car lots, warehouses, churches, bookshops, funeral homes, rooftops and everything in between. Today, this kind of activity might be termed a 'pop-up event'. Our goal was to always support media artists who might not otherwise find an audience in a world dominated by the vulgarities perpetrated through the corporatised cineplex system.

In terms of reimagining the idea of venue, the Basement Films event that resonates most for me took place in 1995. Sarah Lewison, Julie Konop,

Florence Dore and Gina Todus had just completed a cross country, bio-diesel road trip and documentary film project titled *Fat of the Land*. We projected their visionary look at the future of fossil fuel on the side of their white, F-250 Ford van. The van was parked on a stretch of Route 66 that runs through Albuquerque, New Mexico. On the sidewalk facing the van, we set up lawn chairs and a barbecue grill, making the whole experience feel more like a displaced, backyard family gathering.

Marc Moscato was inspired by Basement Films and set up his own particular version of a microcinema in Eugene, Oregon. His venue was called My House and was in operation from 1997 to 2003. I visited Eugene in 2002 and discovered that My House was literally in the basement of Marc's home. He whitewashed the walls and set up a screen between the furnace and the hot water heater. It was a tight but cosy space that accommodated no more than fifteen people including the visiting film artist. The ceiling was low, and you would often hear people bumping their heads against the rafters. Performance artist Jerry Jacuzio once said that pain is an important component of any religious experience. Indeed, the low hanging rafters in My House microcinema were certainly an expression of such a spiritual encounter.

Since the earliest days of moviemaking, alternative screening spaces, unique film clubs and film societies have had a strong presence in the history of the moving image arts. Microcinemas mark an important contribution to this historic trajectory of searching, between the frames, for the 'something more' that is so often embedded in, but difficult to extract, especially from a more sanitised cinematic experience. In fact, as this historic trajectory advances, we are now seeing the emergence of a second wave of microcinemas as well as a new phenomenon called artist-run film labs. As Kodak and other companies move their operations in different (digital) directions, more and more artist collectives are either occupying these abandoned labs or creating their own film developing labs, reinvigorating the use of celluloid amongst a new generation of media artists. LaborBerlin is an example of such an artist run lab. This vibrant organisation, located in Germany, is largely responsible for European artists' renewed interest in celluloid.[4]

At the dawn of this search for something more, it is important to remember the Kolb Brothers who were pioneering contributors to this notion of radicalising the technology of representation (in a domestic kind of way). Emery and Ellsworth Kolb built a home and screening room on the edge of the Grand Canyon in 1902 (see Kuester 2010: 10–30). Today, their Arizona home still stands at the head of the canyon's famous Bright

Angel trail. The Kolb brothers were early explorers of the Grand Canyon and in 1911 they made a 16mm film about their adventures titled *Grand Canyon Film Show*. Every day, from 1915 to 1976 the brothers screened their silent, forty-four-minute movie (with live narration) in the parlour of their home at the top of the canyon. This may be an example of the only theatre in the entire history of cinema that ever only screened a single movie. And, one could argue that the (endless) film loop, which has become a popular experimental form in recent years, was first prototyped through the seemingly endless screenings of the Kolb Brothers' *Grand Canyon Film Show*.

Pausing on the idea of a film loop, there is a popular expression – sometimes credited to Albert Einstein – which states that performing the same task over and over, and expecting different results is an expression of insanity. However, in the mediated world of cinema, such repetition can actually deliver varied results. Although the film itself never changes (we will save scratches and digital artefacts for another discussion), time and experience gather in ways that shift and change meaning(s). Similarly, different iterations of looping exist in the synapses of my memory. On many occasions I have revisited and 'looped' my way through the memory of my childhood bedroom. My sense of those memories is never the same.

This essay marks the first time I have considered the concept of home in proto-cinematic terms, or as an oversized camera obscura. To this end, like a hoarder whose domestic space is littered with the mnemonic memory of the past, I can never be sure how time and experience are gathering (and looping) around me. Perhaps I am simply part of the clutter, like a reel of film that has lost its way through the projector, I am now in the way and gathering, in a chaotic mess, around something else. Perhaps there is still hope if one believes that cinema is in a constant state of becoming. Maybe if I click my heels together three times my youthful imaginings might continue to conjure the promise and magic of a world that is still to be discovered and not yet fully formed.

Notes

1 See Stephen Watt's introduction to Plato's *Republic*, 1996: xiv–xvi.
2 See for instance Staff reporter, 'Factory Firetraps', p. 1.
3 Fleischer Brothers, *Customers Wanted*, <https://www.youtube.com/watch?v=JWeJPrxSQAA> (last accessed 21 November 2019).
4 Laborberlin is an independent nonprofit film collective, Berlin, Germany. See <http://www.laborberlin-film.org/> (last accessed 9 November 2018).

Works Cited

Cage, John (1961), *Silence: Lectures and Writings*, Middletown: Wesleyan University Press.
Cavell, Stanley (1997), 'Psychoanalysis and Cinema', in *Contesting Tears: The Hollywood Melodrama of the Unknown Woman*, Chicago: University of Chicago Press.
Clover, Carol (1993), *Men, Women, and Chain Saws: Gender in the Modern Horror Film*, Princeton, NJ: Princeton University Press.
Daily, Chris (2009), *Everybody's Scene: The Story of Connecticut's Anthrax Club*, Pennsylvania: Butter Goose Press.
Deren, Maya (1978), 'Cinematography: The Creative Use of Reality', in P. Adams Sitney (ed.), *The Avant-Garde Film: A Reader of Theory and Criticism*, New York: Anthology Film Archives, pp. 60–73.
Farber, Manny (1998), *Negative Space: Manny Farber On the Movies*, New York: Da Capo Press.
Gill, Lisa (2006), *Dirt Cabaret*, Albuquerque: Destructable Heart Press.
Goldman, Emma (1931), *Living My Life*, New York: Alfred A. Knopf.
Kashmere, Brett and Forsberg, Walter (2013), *INCITE Journal of Experimental Media* #4: Exhibition Guide, Pennsylvania: INCITE Journal of Experimental Media.
Kuester, Lanny (2010), *Secrets Of The Grand Canyon: A Spiritual Journey*, Indiana: Xlibris.
Lilly, John C. and Timothy Leary (1988), *The Scientist: A Metaphysical Autobiography*, Berkeley: Ronin Publishing.
McGee, Mark Thomas (2001), *Beyond Ballyhoo: Motion Picture Promotion and Gimmicks*, Jefferson, NC: McFarland & Co.
Phillips, Patricia (1997), 'Making Memories', in *Sculpture: Memory, Testimony, and the Body in Contemporary Sculpture*, 16, no. 3, pp. 22–7, Washington, DC: International Sculpture Center.
RuPaul (1996), *Lettin It All Hang Out: An Autobiography*, New York: Hyperion.
Slouka, Mark (1999), 'Listening for Silence', *Harpers Magazine*, April, 63–8.
Solnit, Rebecca (2003), *River of Shadows: Eadweard Muybridge and the Technological Wild West*, London and New York: Penguin Books.
Staff reporter (1911), 'Factory Firetraps Found by Hundreds', *The New York Times*, 14 October.
Stam, Robert (2000), 'The Amplification of Sound', in *Film Theory*, Hoboken, NJ: Wiley-Blackwell, pp. 212–23.
Vertov, Dziga (1984), *Kino-eye: The Writings of Dziga Vertov*, ed. Annette Michelson, Berkeley: University of California Press, pp. 40–2.
Watt, Stephen (1996), 'Introduction: The Theory of Forms (Books 5–7)', *Plato: Republic,* London: Wordsworth Editions.

Index

1080 Brussels, 165
23 Commerce Quay, 165
23, quai du Commerce see *23 Commerce Quay*

À bout de souffle, 175
A House in Jerusalem, 188
À propos de Nice, 159
A Quiet Passion, 7, 57, 58, 64, 65, 66, 67
A Woman is a Woman see *Une femme est une femme*
Adieu Philippine, 185
Adventures of Ozzie and Harriet, The, 29, 30
Akerman, Chantal, 10, 110, 119, 156, 163, 165, 166, 168, 169
All That Heaven Allows, 6, 33, 34
Almendros, Néstor, 130
Amityville Horror, The, 110, 113, 114
Amžinai kartu see *Together Forever*
Andersen, Thom, 155, 159
Anger, Kenneth, 164
Antonelli, Alessandro, 197
Antonioni, Michelangelo, 130
Apartment, The, 3
Architecture as Autobiography, 159
Architectures of Memory, 11. 189, 191, 192, 193, 194, 195, 197, 198, 200, 201, 203, 204, 206
Assayas, Olivier, 9, 119, 128
Autumn Ball, 144

Baby Face, 3
Bad Day at Black Rock, 38, 44, 55
Badlands, 129
Bale, Christian, 130

Balfour, Jodi, 127
Barbicania, 4, 10, 156, 157, 159, 163, 168
Bartas, Sarunas, 142, 148
Bêka, Ila, 4, 10, 156, 157, 159, 160, 161, 168
Belly of an Architect, The, 159
Berlin Jerusalem, 189
Big Eyes, 56, 69
Bigger Than Life, 37
Blaževicius, Andrius, 143, 148, 149
Blood of a Poet, 228
Borgate, 159
Brakhage, Stan, 156, 164
Breathless see *À bout de souffle*
Bright Star, 58
Brontë, Charlotte, 62, 63, 64
Brontës of Haworth, The, 62
Brutalität in Stein see *Brutality in Stone*
Brutality in Stone, 158
Bryant, Sheri, 222
Bryars Gavin, 106, 112, 116
Buñuel, Luis, 120

Campion, Jane, 119, 128
Camus, Albert, 139, 140, 150
Cannibal Holocaust, 217
Carol, 7, 8, 72, 73, 75, 76, 77, 78, 79, 80, 81, 82, 83, 84, 85
Casler, Herman, 229
Cassavetes, John, 127
Cave of Forgotten Dreams, 228
Chabrol, Claude, 173
Checkmate see *Le Coup du berger*
Chelovek s kinoapparatom see *Man with a Movie Camera*
Christmas in Connecticut, 6, 19, 23

INDEX

Cilveki Tur **see** *People Out There*
Citations, 192
Citizen Kane, 231
Citron, Michelle, 164
Cléo de 5 à 7, 10, 173, 174, 179, 181, 184
Cléo from 5 to 7 **see** *Cléo de 5 à 7*
Clooney, Rosemary, 26
Coco before Chanel, 56, 57
Cocteau, Jean, 228
Cohen, Leonard, 12, 226
Collins, Max Allan, 127
Corbett, Glenn, 51
Corridor, The, 142
Crash, 92
Crime of Passion, 37
Crimson Kimono, The, 38, 51, 53
Cronenberg, David, 119, 126
Crosby, Bing, 23, 24, 26
Customers Wanted, 230

Daguerréotypes, 179
Dangerous Game, 127
Davies, Terence, 64, 65, 66, 67, 69
Day, Felicia, 221, 222
Days of Heaven, 124, 130
Denis, Claire, 8, 89, 90, 91, 92, 94, 95, 96, 98, 100, 101, 128
Dešimt priežasčių **see** *Ten Reasons*
Desperate Hours, The, 37
Destination Tokyo, 49
Dickinson, Emily, 59, 64, 65, 66, 67, 68, 69
Disengagement, 189
Distant Voices, Still Lives, 107
Doniol-Valcroze, Jacques, 173
Donna Reed Show, The, 30
Donnie Brasco, 127
Dr. Horrible's Sing-Along Blog, 221
Dreyer, Carl Theodor, 227
Drive, 92

Eadie, William, 131
El Topo, 12, 210, 212
Emigholz, Heinz, 159
Englert, Alice, 128
Erin Brockovich, 58
Evey, Kim, 222
Exorcist, The, 114

Fat of the Land, 234
Father Knows Best, 29, 30

Ferrara, Abel, 127
Ferris Bueller's Day Off, 34
Fiennes, Ralph, 60
Ford, John, 9, 118, 119, 125, 126, 127, 207
Free Zone, 189, 198, 200
Frost, Mark, 9, 129
Fry, Christopher, 62

Gardiner, Reginald, 20
Gitai, Amos, 11, 188, 189, 192, 193, 194, 195, 196, 197, 198, 199, 200, 201, 202, 203, 204, 205, 206, 207
Go For Broke!, 38, 46, 49, 50, 51
Godard, Jean-Luc, 10, 92, 93, 96, 101, 118, 171, 173, 175, 177, 179, 232
Goldbergs, The, 32
Grand Canyon Film Show, 235
Greenaway, Peter, 159
Greenstreet, Sydney, 20
Guadalcanal Diary, 49
Guild, The, 221

Hail Mary, 232
Hardcore, 127
Haunting, The, 110, 113
Henenlotter, Frank, 217
Herzog, Werner, 228
Hidden Figures, 56, 69
Highsmith, Patricia, 72
Hinchliffe, Dickon, 94
Hingle, Pat, 41
History of Violence, A, 126
Hitchcock, Alfred, 51, 111, 131
Hobbit, The, 107
Hodgson Burnett, Frances, 119
Holiday Inn, 23, 26
Horse, Michael, 129
House, 188
House, The **see** *Namai*
House of Mirth, The, 66
How Green Was My Valley, 126
Hunter, Jeffrey, 39
Husbands, 127

I am the Pretty Thing that Lives in the House, 110, 111, 112, 113, 114
I Love Lucy, 32
Injury to One, 231
Invisible Woman, The, 7, 57, 58, 59, 68

Irma Vep, 128
Iron Lady, The, 56, 69

Jackie, 56, 69
Jacuzio, Jerry, 234
Japanese War Bride, 52
Je vous salue, Marie see *Hail Mary*
Jeanne Dielman, 165
Jefferson, Thomas, 17, 18
Jodorowsky, Alejandro, 12, 210
Johnson, Van, 50
Jones, Felicity, 60

Kar-wai, Wong, 128
Karapetian, Aik, 143, 146
Kaye, Danny, 26
Keiller, Patrick, 155
Khrushchev, Nikita, 136
Kiemas, 142
Kippur, 189
Kluge, Alexander, 158
Knight of Cups, 130
Kolb brothers, 234, 235
Koolhaas Houselife, 159
Koridorius see *Corridor, The*
Král, Petr, 123, 124, 125, 132
Kuchar, George, 164, 232
Kursietis, Juris, 143, 144

La Belle Vie, 185
La Môme/La Vie en Rose, 56
Le Corbusier, 136
Le Coup du berger, 173
Leave it to Beaver, 29, 30
Léger, Fernand, 160
Lemercier, Valérie, 90
Lemoine, Louise, 4, 10, 156, 1567, 159, 160, 161, 168
Lightning Over Water, 120
Lincoln, Abraham, 24
Lindon, Vincent, 95
Little Mermaid, The, 107
Lluvia, 92
Locke, 92
London, 155
Lord of the Rings, The 107
Lord, Jack, 27
Los Angeles Plays Itself, 155
Lubezki, Emmanuel, 130
Lullaby to My Father, 189, 192, 199, 201

Lusty Men, The, 120
Lužytė, Lina, 144
Lynch, David, 9, 119, 129, 131

MacLachlan, Kyle, 129
Malick, Terence, 119, 124, 129, 130, 131
Malle, Louis, 171
Man with a Movie Camera, 155, 162
Marey, Étienne-Jules, 229
Marie Antoinette, 68
Marshall-Green Logan, 127
Mean Girls, 219
Mekas, Jonas, 156, 164
Menken, Maria, 156, 164
Mitchell, Cameron, 42
Modris, 143, 144, 145, 146
Morder, Joseph, 164
Morgan, Dennis, 20
Moss, Elisabeth, 128
Moviedrome, 216
Muybridge, Eadweard, 229
Mystery Science Theatre 3000, 12, 211, 216, 219, 220, 221, 222

Namai, 142
Navasaitis, Valdas, 142, 148
Newell, Mike, 127
News from Home/News from House, 188, 192
Night on Earth, 92
No Down Payment, 7, 37, 38, 40, 45, 49, 51, 53, 54
No Home Movie, 10, 156, 163, 164, 165, 166, 167, 168
No Sex Last Night, 92
North, Sheree, 40
Notorious Bettie Page, The, 58, 68

Ohno, Kaoru, 122
Ollier, Claude, 122, 127
One Plus One, 232
Ophüls, Max, 127
Others, The, 9, 109, 144
Õunpuu, Veiko, 144
Owens, Patricia, 39

Pall, Gloria, 51
Paranormal Activity, 9
People Out There, 143, 144, 145
Personal Shopper, 128, 129

Pink Flamingos, 212
Planet Terror, 221
Plus tards, tu comprendras, 189
Poltergeist, 109
Psycho, 111

Quadro, 159
Quarry, 127
Queen of Katwe, 56, 69

Ramsay, Lynne, 119, 131
Randall, Tony, 40
Ratcatcher, 131
Ray, Nicholas, 120
Rebecca, 2
Reckless Moment, The, 127
Reconversão see *Reconversion*
Reconversion, 159
Renoir, Jean, 128
Resnais, Alain, 155, 159
Reynolds, Marjorie, 23
Risky Business, 34
Rite, The, 114
Rivette, Jacques, 171, 173
Rocky Horror Picture Show, The, 12, 212, 213
Rohmer, Eric, 171
Roosevelt, Franklin D., 19
Roses à credit, 189
Rozier, Jacques, 185
RuPaul, 231
Rush, Barbara, 41
Ryan, Robert, 44

Safety Last!, 3
Saga of Anatahan, The, 119, 121, 122, 129, 131
Saint, The, 148, 149, 150
Sakall, S. Z., 20
Sartre, Jean-Paul, 139, 140, 143
Saturday Night Live, 222
Sayonara, 52
Schamoni, Peter, 158
Schrader, Paul, 127
Schreiber, Lotte, 159
Scorsese, Martin, 127
Searchers, The, 2, 9, 118, 125, 126, 127, 129, 130
Sharman, Jim, 12, 212
Shatner, William, 222

Shigeta, James, 51
Shining, The, 8, 113
Smith, Jack, 232
Star Trek, 215, 222
Stewart, James, 131
Stewart, Kristen, 128
Struycken, Carel, 129
Sügisball see *Autumn Ball*
Summer Hours, 128

Take a Giant Step, 53
Taxi Driver, 127
Ten, 92
Ten Reasons, 143, 144, 145, 148
Texas Chain Saw Massacre, The, 211
There's Always Tomorrow, 33
Thin Red Line, The, 129
To the Wonder, 130
To Walk Invisible, 7, 57, 58, 59, 62, 64, 65, 68
Together Forever, 144
Top of the Lake, Song to Song, 130
Top of the Lake: China Girl, 119, 128
Toute la mémoire du monde, 155, 159
Traces, 192, 194
Tracy, Spencer, 44
Truffaut, François, 171, 173
Twin Peaks: The Return, 119, 129

Une femme est une femme, 10, 173, 174, 175, 177
Une Visite, 173

van Gogh, Vincent, 228
Varda, Agnès, 10, 171, 173, 179, 180, 182, 184
Vendredi soir, 8, 90, 91, 92, 93, 95, 97, 99, 101, 103
Vera-Ellen, 26
Vertigo, 131
Vertov, Dziga, 155, 162, 230, 231
Vigo, Jean, 159
von Sternberg, Joseph, 119, 121, 122, 123, 124, 127

Wainwright, Sally, 62, 63, 64, 66, 69
Wall Street, 3
Warhol, Andy, 232
Waters, John, 232
Wayne, John, 125, 126

We Need to Talk About Kevin, 131
Weekend, 92, 96, 101
Welles, Orson, 231
Wenders, Wim, 119, 120, 128
Wendy and Lucy, 92
Wexler, Haskell, 130
Whedon, Joss, 221
White Christmas, 6, 23, 26, 27
Wilkerson, Travis, 231
Williamsburg: The Story of a Patriot, 27, 28, 29
Wizard of Oz, The, 2, 107

Woodward, Joanne, 42
Woolf, Virginia, 89, 90
Worden, Hank, 129
Wright, Frank Lloyd, 22

Yaitanes, Greg, 127
Yang, Edward, 128
Yard, The **see** *Kiemas*
You Were Never Really Here, 131

Zabriskie Point, 130
Zabriskie, Grace, 129

EU representative:
Easy Access System Europe
Mustamäe tee 50, 10621 Tallinn, Estonia
Gpsr.requests@easproject.com